# Julian Woolford

Julian trained as a director at the Bristol Old Vic Theatre School, and his first play *The Oedipus Complex* was premiered at Bristol New Vic.

In collaboration with composer Richard John, he has written musicals based on *The Railway Children* and *The Wind in the Willows* for Sevenoaks Playhouse. *The Railway Children* has since had many productions worldwide. Their original musical about airport security staff, *Terminal Four Play*, is part of Theatre 503's Urban Scrawl project, is available as a podcast, and played at the Latitude Festival.

For BBC Radio 3 he has written *Broadway Hall of Fame: Cole Porter* and *Broadway Hall of Fame: Leonard Bernstein* (Palace Theatre, London, and broadcast live). His musical *Oh Carol!* won the Covent Garden Festival Search for a New Musical and he co-wrote *Let Him Have Justice*, produced at the Cochrane Theatre, London.

Julian was commissioned by the Estate of Lionel Bart to completely rewrite Bart's infamous flop *Twang!!* Other works include *Liberace Live from Heaven* (Leicester Square Theatre, London, Edinburgh Festival and New Zealand tour), *BlueBirds* (three productions off-West End) and *The Snow Queen* (Theatre North).

As a director, he has directed major national tours of classic musicals including *Oklahoma!*, *Fiddler on the Roof* and *South Pacific*, and has directed in the West End, off-Broadway and worldwide.

Julian lectures on the MA in Musical Theatre at Goldsmiths College, University of London, in writing and producing. This is the only university course in musical-theatre writing in the UK, and he works extensively as a dramaturg in musical theatre. He is a member of Mercury Musical Developments and the Society of Authors. You can find out more about Julian's work at www.julianwoolford.net, and follow him on Twitter: @Julian_Woolford

# *How Musicals Work*

## *and How to Write Your Own*

## Julian Woolford

NICK HERN BOOKS
London
www.nickhernbooks.co.uk

# A Nick Hern Book

*How Musicals Work*
first published in Great Britain in 2012
as a paperback original by Nick Hern Books Limited,
The Glasshouse, 49a Goldhawk Road, London W12 8QP

Reprinted 2013

Cover designed by Ned Hoste, 2H

Typeset by Nick Hern Books, London
Printed and bound in Great Britain by
T.J. International, Padstow, Cornwall

A CIP catalogue record for this book
is available from the British Library

ISBN 978 1 84842 175 2

MIX
Paper from
responsible sources
FSC
www.fsc.org
FSC® C013056

*For Richard John,*
*without whom my work is half-complete*

*and*

*Stephen Barlow,*
*without whom my life is half-complete*

# *Contents*

*There are some wonderful female creators of musicals, among them Betty Comden, Dorothy Fields, Mary Rodgers, Jeanine Tesori and Lynn Ahrens, but for reasons of clarity, I have used the male gender throughout to mean a person of either sex. This is simply because the alternatives are too clumsy.*

# 1
# *Beginnings*

# Beginnings

Musicals are like children. They are conceived out of an act of excitement, the pregnancy is long, frustrating and rewarding, birth can be very painful, raising them is an act of collaboration with many people, and, if you are very lucky, they will support you in your old age.

Writing a musical, like a pregnancy, will take your care and attention, it will often be demanding, it will fill you with love and it might even put a strain on your other relationships. It will tie you to the people you created it with for ever. But once you have created a musical, it will always be part of your life, and you should always be proud of it.

This book is, therefore, a prenatal guide for musicals. It will help you generate ideas to conceive your show, make sure that the skeleton is all in place and healthy, help you fill out the flesh and bones of the characters and help you finally see it born onstage in a living, breathing performance. It also has a section on how to put it to work and make it earn its living.

As the title suggests, this book also examines how musicals work. It looks at the storytelling and structure of some well-known musicals, and shows how the best musicals draw on ancient myths and tap into the human psyche to engage the audience. You cannot create great art until you understand how that art has been created in the past, even if you then work in your own idiosyncratic manner.

Like the creation of all arts, it is easy to write a bad musical. Some bad musicals even get produced and some of those shows even become hits. A bad painting can be walked past, bad novels can be put down, but bad theatre must be endured (at least for its running time!).

Shoddy work, ill-considered decisions and a lack of craft will generally mean that the work will not take its rank among those shows that are often revived. A true classic, like Sondheim's *Into the Woods*, or Rodgers and Hammerstein's *Oklahoma!*, will have a long and successful life. This book looks at how successful musicals work, gives an indication as to why some musicals fail and considers the ways in which writers can ensure that their musical will be as good as possible. It can help you understand how the musical you want to write can have truth and depth, and how it might be more likely that people will want to produce and perform your musical for a long time to come.

Writing a musical is 10 per cent inspiration and 90 per cent perspiration. It is a lot of hard work. This book is full of the techniques that I use to write, developed through working as a professional writer of musicals and plays, from my work as a theatre director, from working as a dramaturg for Mercury Musical Developments, and from teaching the creation of musical theatre for the University of London.

### Exercises

Throughout this book you will find shaded boxes like this one. Each box contains an exercise that is designed to stimulate ideas and to make you really think about the musical you are writing. Do whichever of them interest you, but at least read them and consider the point of each of them. You might find it helpful to buy a copy of a libretto for a musical that you like, as some of the exercises involve analysing existing musicals. If you do them all, you will have enough ideas to last you a lifetime.

Before starting you should think about the type of musical you want to write and about what your distinctive, original voice will be. I often read musicals that are derivative of other works. It is no good setting out to write like Sondheim, Lloyd Webber or Jason Robert Brown: those three have already mastered those styles. You need to think about who *you* want to be as a writer.

The techniques can be taught, but the combining of the techniques with your own unique talents is something that only you can do. Some of the biggest hits of recent years like *Matilda*, *Avenue Q*, *Spring Awakening* and *In the Heights* have come from writers who understand the art form, but have combined it with a distinctive voice. It is time to find yours.

## What is a Musical?

For the purposes of this book, I define a musical as a theatrical presentation where the content of the story is communicated through speech, music and movement in an integrated fashion to create a unified whole. The written work is formed of three elements, the *book*, the *music* and the *lyrics*. The book is sometimes known as the script, and is the unsung sections of the work; the lyrics are the words that are sung. The book also refers to the character development and the dramatic structure of the work; together, the book and lyrics are called the *libretto*, which is Italian for *little book*. The music and lyrics together are referred to as the *score*.

The following diagram shows how the different terms relate to each other and overlap:

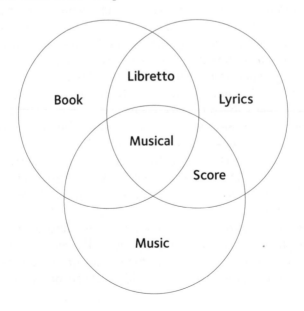

You will note that there is no word for the book and music together. Music that comes under spoken scenes is referred to as 'underscore', as it comes 'under' the dialogue at a level at which the audience can still hear and understand what is being said.

## Why Write a Musical?

The fact that you are reading this book probably means that you are interested in writing a musical, but have you taken a second to ask yourself, 'Why?'

For some, there is a love of the art form. The best musical performances feature 'triple-threat' performers who can sing, dance and act to a highly professional level, who can remain convincingly in character when combining all their skills and who can perform work that is thought-provoking, exciting, moving and stimulating. Along with opera, it is the most theatrical art form, and can deliver some stories better than any other. It is removed from real life yet capable of acting as a prism to it, transporting an audience to see sights and hear sounds they never imagined.

For some, the attraction is financial. The musical is the most commercial form of theatre. Broadway box-office income tops $1 billion every year, and this means that something in the region of $45 million of royalties is split between the writers of the twenty or so Broadway musicals playing at any time. That is before you take into account the national tours, the West End transfers and other overseas productions. If a writer of a musical mega-hit ever offers to buy you a drink, then let him because he can afford it. And if he ever offers to buy you a house, he can probably afford that too.

For some, the attraction is fame. Rodgers and Hammerstein, Andrew Lloyd Webber and George Gershwin are well-known names and this kind of recognition lights some people's fires.

For me, the attraction is creative. I write musicals because I love the form. I love being able to tell a story in a truly theatrical fashion, and to be able to elevate the emotional content through song and dance. Musicals are often criticised for being unrealistic, that people do not suddenly burst into song and dance in real life. I live real life every day, and for me the attraction of the musical is its theatricality. I don't want to go to the theatre to see the ordinary everyday; I want to go for an elevated, emotional experience where a performer is able to connect with an audience using all the skills they possess.

And, for me, writing musicals is simply the best fun I ever have.

## Collaborators

There is a good chance that you are going to write a musical with a collaborator. A few successful writers manage book, music and lyrics all by themselves; Lionel Bart for *Oliver!* and Sandy Wilson for *The Boyfriend* have done so, but these are the exceptions rather than the rules. Most musicals are written by more than one person, and choosing your collaborators is one of the most important decisions you will make.

Depending on which parts of the musical you want to write, you will need to find a collaborator or collaborators to undertake the remaining work. You need to define how you see yourself:

*Bookwriter:* Writes only the book, but none of the sung components (e.g. Arthur Laurents for *West Side Story* and *Gypsy*).

*Librettist:* Writes the libretto, i.e. the book and lyrics (e.g. Oscar Hammerstein II for *Oklahoma!* and *Carousel*).

*Lyricist:* Writes only the lyrics (e.g. Stephen Sondheim for *West Side Story* or Oscar Hammerstein II for *The Sound of Music*).

*Composer:* Writes only the music (e.g. Leonard Bernstein for *West Side Story* or Richard Rodgers for *Oklahoma!*).

*Composer-Lyricist or Songwriter:* Writes both music and lyrics (e.g. Stephen Sondheim for *Follies* or *A Little Night Music*).

Think about your talents, what you are good at and which parts of the musical you want to write. Having defined your role, by deciding which part of the process you want to be responsible for, you should easily be able to define the talents you need in your collaborators.

You may already have a potential collaborator in mind, and you must begin a collaboration for the right reasons, not the wrong ones. The right reasons are that you like and respect their work, they like and respect your work, and that you think you are temperamentally suited to one another. A good collaboration is like a good marriage; a bad one, like a bad marriage, is a disaster. A good one is based on mutual trust and respect; a bad one can send you into emotional meltdown. If you are working with a friend, ensure that you like and respect their work. You don't want to wreck a good friendship writing a bad show!

If you know you want a collaborator but don't have an individual in mind, then finding one can be a tricky task. Some organisations, like Mercury Musical Developments, offer the opportunity to advertise for one, and theatres that produce new writing may know of other writers looking for collaborators.

A good collaborator will let you have the space to do your best work, kindly point out when you haven't, and can do better, give you the space to fail, and support you when you are wrestling with a tricky problem. You should do the same for them.

You might end up with more than one collaborator. It is not uncommon for musicals to have three writers, one each for book, music and lyrics. Three-way relationships can sometimes be difficult, and you should treat each partner equally.

Having found someone you think you want to write with, then try the collaboration out on a very small project. Suggest to your collaborator(s) that you try out your relationship by writing a song, or a very short musical. As part of the course that I teach at the University of London, the students have to write a fifteen-minute musical, using a cast of no more than four actors and accompanied by nothing more than a piano. I usually give them a broad theme to write around, and these pieces are then performed in very limited productions for an audience of fellow students. A project like this can be an excellent way to assess your relationship with your collaborators. Alternatively, if both you and your collaborator(s) have written songs or scenes previously, then listen to or read each other's work, and then spend ten minutes talking about things you liked about it, and things you didn't like, or weren't sure about.

## Sharing Work

Share some of your previous work with your collaborators and then talk about the three things you thought were best about the work and the three things you thought were least successful. By doing this you can begin to establish a relationship where you can be honest and constructively critical.

Collaborator relationships vary as much as the people in them. Some writing teams have incredibly close personal relationships, some see each other only at meetings. Gilbert and Sullivan had a famously strained working relationship in which Gilbert would frequently write the entire libretto without consulting Sullivan, who would then compose the music without consulting Gilbert. I know of a Broadway writing team who never see each other except at the office. When questioned about this, they say that they are worried about what would happen if they spent time together socially! Similarly, there are partnerships that have close emotional or blood ties, such as the Gershwin brothers. The personal relationships you have with your collaborators are entirely up to you.

The relationship may impact on the methodology you use to write. You might go for the Gilbert and Sullivan approach and complete a whole libretto before a note of music is written. Richard Rodgers famously wrote the music before the lyrics when working with Lorenz Hart, but when working with Oscar Hammerstein II, the lyrics were written first. Kander and Ebb used to write music and lyrics simultaneously in the same place. You need to negotiate this with your partners, and it may never truly become fixed.

I have written a number of musicals with composer Richard John. I prefer to write the book first, then the lyrics, and then he writes the music, but we have many long discussions about the work before any words are written. We may change our methods for a particular number. When we wrote *The Railway Children* we literally locked ourselves in a room together until we had completed one particular song we were having problems with.

However you decide to work with your collaborators, you must never stop talking to them. Later on, other collaborators will join your team as the show goes into production: directors, choreographers, designers, etc. Musical theatre is one of the most intensely collaborative art forms. Talk about every moment of the show, talk about the musical style, talk about the physical look you imagine, talk about the story, talk about the characters. For this reason, I suggest that everyone in your writing team reads all of this book, not just the sections they think are relevant to them. I directed a workshop for a writing partnership where the composer took great pride in telling me that he never read the script – he just sat down with the lyrics provided and set them to music, not reading the scenes between.

He's a talented, capable composer.

He's never had a hit.

## Ideas on Paper

This exercise takes a bit of setting up but it is worth it. It is one my favourite exercises when working with groups of people and is especially useful if you are working with three or more potential collaborators. In a room with a hard floor, roll out paper (like plain wallpaper or wrapping paper) the length of the room. At one end write, in big letters, '*The type of musical I want to write is...*' and at the other end write '*The type of musical I don't want to write is...*' In silence and all working simultaneously, each person takes a different-coloured pen and writes their response to these statements, commenting on each other's responses as they go. No one is allowed to delete their own or anyone else's work, but they are allowed to comment on it by writing on the paper. Spend at least thirty minutes in silence, creating thoughts, adding and commenting, and then decide to stop and begin a discussion. You will talk for hours and will gain a very clear insight into your potential collaborators.

## COPSE

COPSE is a term I use to describe the process of writing a musical. In the enthusiasm of the early ideas, of projects born out of excitement, it is possible to conceive a show and then very tempting to dive straight into writing beautiful songs and scenes that you can be proud of and play to your friends. That's when you should think of COPSE.

COPSE stands for:

1. **Co**ncept
2. **P**lot
3. **S**tructure
4. **E**xecution

Never start one stage until you have completed the last.

*Concept:* The best musicals are built on good, strong concepts. You should be able to write your concept in one sentence, such as 'A Rock Adaptation of Jane Austen's *Pride and Prejudice*' or 'An Opera Based on the Life of George W. Bush'. Then move on to:

*Plot:* This is the narrative that you want to tell. There is a difference between story and plot, which is covered in Chapter 4, along with many of the basics for this stage of the process. If you are taking a plot from a pre-existing source then you will already have a good idea of the story. If it is a true-life story you will have the facts. But regardless of the source material, I usually write a version of the story that is approximately 1,000 words as a good starting point. By reducing the plot of, say, *Pride and Prejudice* or the life of George W. Bush to this length, you will necessarily begin to focus on the aspects of the subject that most excite you. Once you have your plot synopsis, move on to:

*Structure:* Having got a good grip on your plot, you need to think about how to structure it as a musical. How do you translate the story you are passionate about into a piece of musical theatre? By the time you have finished the work on structure you will probably have a document of at least 2,000 words, maybe as many as 10,000, that will provide the backbone for your musical. This is all about making sure you have created a good, strong skeleton for your show so that it can be fleshed out when you come to:

*Execution:* This is the final stage of writing a musical. This is when the book, music and lyrics are written and by the time you have finished this, your show will be ready to rehearse.

It is important to work through these stages in order, and not to move on to the next stage until you are happy that you have successfully completed each step.

Some projects come out of a clear idea about a story; some projects originate as commissions where a subject, even a concept, is suggested. Some writers want to write a musical but do not have a clear concept that they want to write about. If you are in this final group, you have all the collaborators you need, but are not sure what you want to write about, here are a few exercises to help you on your way. If you decide to work up any of these concepts and are concerned about potential copyright issues, make sure you have read Chapter 3.

## Ten Treatments

Take a well-known story and create ten different treatments for it, by varying the place it is set, the musical style or the time it is set in. For *Little Red Riding Hood*, you might end of with:

1. A classic fairytale approach.
2. Set on a space station.
3. Set in the inner city, the wolf is a drug baron.
4. Set in the 1920s among a group of gangsters.
5. A rock 'n' roll setting about a teenage werewolf.
6. Set in a political system; the other politicians are wolves.
7. Set on a farm in the Midwest.
8. Set during the Russian Revolution.
9. A puppet show.
10. Set in a Victorian music hall.

Don't worry that any of these ideas may have been used before: keep generating them and building on them. Try it with other well-known tales.

## Mash-Up

Modern music has popularised the idea of a 'mash-up': taking two songs and 'mashing' them together. Use this musical idea to create concepts. Use TV shows, fairytales, song titles, film plots or anything else you can think of. Take two of them and mash them together, so you might end up with:

- Fairytale characters on a desert island.
- Dickens characters on a talent show.

## Before and After

Is there an interesting idea in the *before* or *after* of well-loved tales or classic novels?

- What happened *after* Elizabeth Bennet and Mr Darcy married?
- What happened *before* Oliver Twist was left at the orphanage?
- What happened *after* the Little Mermaid got everything she wanted?

I can't tell you whether your musical is going to be the next smash hit. No one can. And if they tell you they can, they are lying.

I can't tell you whether the subject you choose will make you happy writing about it. Only you can know that.

I can only teach you the techniques I use, and that others use, to create a musical. You can learn these techniques, master them and adapt them to make them your own.

But the hard work, the late nights and, most of all, the talent, you have to supply yourself.

Above all, you should write the show that you truly believe in. It should be a story that you can see and hear as a musical.

Don't try and explain it to anyone except your co-authors at this stage. Many musicals, reduced to cocktail chatter, sound pretty uninspiring ('It's about a milkman in Russia just before the Revolution,' or, 'It's about a girl who has trouble speaking the King's English'). The best way to truly explain a musical is to write it. And write it *only* if you truly believe in it.

# 2
# Forms of
# Musical

# Forms of Musical

## A Potted History of the Musical

Humans need stories. All societies have them and the ability to communicate a narrative is one of the defining characteristics of a human being. Ever since the Greeks got together in groups to act out a narrative, music has played a fundamental role in theatre. The earliest Greek theatre had a singing (and, sometimes, dancing) chorus, as did the theatre of the ancient Romans, who attached *sabilla*, a kind of metal clip, to their stage footwear in order to make their footsteps more audible and thereby created the first tap shoes. The mystery plays and travelling players of the Middle Ages all interpolated music and dance, and by the Renaissance these earlier forms of theatre had developed into *Commedia dell'Arte*, which went on to develop into comedies and opera buffa, an Italian form of comic opera.

In England, Elizabethan and Jacobean plays often included music and dance, and Shakespeare's comedies nearly all end in a dance or song. During this time, court masques – elaborate presentations of singing, dancing, elaborate costume, and special scenic effects – became very popular among European royalty and aristocracy, and Shakespeare frequently included masque-like scenes in his plays, such as the Act Four sequence of *The Tempest*.

In Britain during the 1600s, the masques began to develop into a form of English opera, which survives most successfully in the work of Henry Purcell. After the death of Charles II, opera began to fall out of favour in Britain, but the eighteenth century saw hugely successful ballad operas, most notably *The Beggar's Opera*, which held the record for the longest-running show when in 1782 it ran for sixty-two consecutive performances (about three months). Its author, John Gay, wrote new lyrics to popular tunes of the day, and became the first musical writer to ensure that his audience hummed the songs on the way *into* the theatre, as well as on the way out.

Whilst Colonial America didn't have any significant theatre until 1752, after Independence, New York began to develop as a centre for the performing arts in the newly United States, as European operas, operetta, ballad operas and music halls began to find an audience amongst the European immigrants who wanted to be reminded of home.

The show generally credited as being the first 'musical comedy' is *The Black Crook* of 1866. This show largely came about through a series of catastrophes: the theatre Nibblo's Garden was committed to producing *The Black Crook*, a reworking of the Faust legend (by Charles M. Barras) when a Parisian ballet troupe was stranded in New York with nowhere to perform as the theatre they were booked in to had burned down. The manager of Nibblo's invited the ballet troupe to perform excerpts of their show during performances of the Faust play and the resulting mishmash became an unexpected smash hit, the first show to run more than a year in New York. Not surprisingly, the writer of *The Black Crook* claimed that the production had made a travesty of his script, but found that the pain was much easier to bear when he received a cheque for $1,500. In 1954, Broadway saw the opening of *The Girl in Pink Tights*, a musical about the creation of *The Black Crook*. It ran for only 115 performances.

This mash-up of songs, dances, sketches and a bare minimum of plot set the style for what became known as musical comedy. These shows were loosely held together by well-worn stories, which were simply an excuse for the routines. Musical comedies of this type were particularly popular during the 1920s and '30s. Any real drama was ignored, and, although the scores were often strong, the shows of this period have proven un-revivable since modern audiences expect a much more integrated show.

Ironically, around the same time that *The Black Crook* was wowing New York, a new theatrical genre was growing in popularity: naturalism. Most notably exemplified in the plays of Émile Zola, Henrik Ibsen and Anton Chekhov, naturalism aimed for the recreation of reality onstage, devoid of artifice. Whilst naturalism quickly took deep root in the theatre (and is still strong today), it radically diminished the importance of music, spectacle and theatricality onstage. These things survived in opera, operetta and the newly born musical theatre, but this divergence between naturalistic theatre and the more theatrical musical forms has led to a snobbery, most notably in the UK, that the musical is somehow a lesser, more populist, less serious form of theatre. In many ways the musical is the oldest form of theatre, and when I meet people who say, 'I hate musicals,' I immediately think, 'No, you don't. You hate theatre.'

Easily the most notable musical in the entire history of the genre is the granddaddy of the modern book musical, Jerome Kern and Oscar Hammerstein II's *Show Boat* (1927).

Kern and Hammerstein's achievement with *Show Boat* was remarkable for its time: they created a panoramic story with ten leading characters, of which eight are still in play at the end of the story. Most importantly, they tackled the important social theme of racism and they drew on different musical styles for the different couples in a way that no one imagined before them. Magnolia and Gaylord sing the music of European operetta, Julie sings the music of popular song, Queenie and Joe sing the music of the African-Americans, Cap'n Andy sings ballyhoos, and Ellie and Frank sing the music of vaudeville.

In their themes, their structure, their characterisation and their storytelling, Kern and Hammerstein created the first modern Broadway musical and a template for all of those that have followed. From *Oklahoma!* to *My Fair Lady* to *Jesus Christ Superstar* to *The Producers* to *Avenue Q* to *The Book of Mormon*, all modern musicals have their roots in *Show Boat*.

Although it was a smash hit, *Show Boat* proved surprisingly uninfluential at the time, and Hammerstein followed it with a string of flops. In 1943, he joined forces with Richard Rodgers to create a show with even greater integrity and proved to have an instant revolutionary influence: *Oklahoma!*

---

### Show Boat

If you have never seen *Show Boat* in any form, then watch the 1936 film version on DVD. It stars Allan Jones, Irene Dunne and Paul Robeson. (Don't bother with the 1951 version starring Howard Keel unless you are very keen!)

---

There are many forms of musical theatre, and one of the most fundamental decisions you have to take is about the form of your work. At one end of the scale is the musical play, which might have only a few songs and where the drama is predominantly spoken; and at the other end of the scale is opera, which is normally fully sung and with an orchestral score that requires no amplification for the singers.

Categorising types of theatre is a tricky business. The terms are like slippery fish which wriggle away just as you think you have grasped them. It is important, though, to understand the different sub-genres because you need to be able to understand them in order to create structure and content. All art has a generic context and is judged against the generic orthodoxy: you can only create a truly great work of art if you understand how it develops work that has preceded it.

It is often said that 'content determines form'. Put another way, this is about determining the best type of musical for the story you want to tell. It makes sense that *The Phantom of the Opera* is written in a form that is very close to opera; that *The Producers*, which is about a 1960s classic Broadway musical, should be written in that form; or that the form of *Sunday in the Park with George* is a musical and theatrical metaphor for the 'pointillist' work of its subject, Georges Seurat, in which the audience have to 'join the dots' to see the whole picture.

Here are the broadly defining characteristics of the different styles of musical, starting with the form that has the least music and moving through to the forms with the most music. You can write any one of these, but will probably want to think about which of them best suits your story or concept.

## The Play with Songs

Many plays use songs in their storytelling. Sometimes this is an editorial decision by a director to add context or atmosphere, in which case the songs are not part of the writer's concept of the work, such as when Trevor Nunn decided to add gospel songs to *A Streetcar Named Desire*, which might have caused Tennessee Williams to raise an eyebrow. Some playwrights include songs as part of the play, and write lyrics as part of their script. The most notable exponents of this are William Shakespeare and Bertolt Brecht, who used songs in many of their plays in very different ways.

Brecht's *Mother Courage and Her Children* contains twelve songs, designed as a theatrical technique to shatter any notion of naturalism. These had music by Kurt Weill in the original production, but the play is not what most people would class as a musical. Sometimes directors cut some of the songs, and it is very common for directors to invite current composers to set the texts to new music for new productions. This is very different to another Brecht/Weill piece, *The Threepenny Opera*, in which Weill's score is an integral part of the work.

Many of Shakespeare's plays include at least one song (such as 'With hey, ho, the wind and the rain' in *Twelfth Night*), reflecting the fact that music was important in both Elizabethan theatre and life. *As You Like It* contains lyrics for six songs, but again, it is not a musical. In Shakespeare's plays the songs can be, and sometimes are, cut in production without damaging the story, although possibly reducing the theatricality of the audience experience.

Most importantly, in a play with songs the drama is carried in the spoken, not the sung text.

## Physical Theatre

This is a catch-all term that is used to describe a wide range of works that exist in a largely non-commercial milieu, but still use dance, text and sometimes song to create a theatrical experience that often does not fit into any simple category. In 2010, the Cornish physical theatre company Kneehigh took their physical-theatre piece based on Noël Coward's *Brief Encounter* to Broadway, the commercial home of the musical. This was a reinterpretation of the play with interpolated songs of the same period which used movement to explore the emotions of the leading characters.

The notion of physical theatre is very contextual, and the commercial success of *Brief Encounter* was surprising to many. Kneehigh's next project was a physical reinterpretation of Michel Legrand's musical *The Umbrellas of Cherbourg*, produced as a West End musical. Whilst *Brief Encounter* was quirkily endearing in the commercial context, *The Umbrellas of Cherbourg* was not able to trade on such charm for a second time and was a short-running failure.

Physical theatre tends to rely less on songs and more on the physical interpretation of moments, although music (often instrumental) may be very important.

## The Book Musical

The book musical is still the most predominant sub-genre of musical and is often what comes to mind when the term 'musical' is used. The chances are that, if you want to write a musical, this is probably what you think you want to write. This is where the book, music and lyrics have been written specifically to tell a linear story. It will have songs, probably some kind of dancing, and some spoken scenes. The book musical is able to carry a vast range of subject matter and styles. It is this style of musical that we will look at most closely in this book, as it combines sung and non-sung text and music.

The story may be comic, such as *Me and My Girl* or *The Producers*, in which case it is usually known as 'musical comedy', or dramatic, such as *My Fair Lady* or *Carousel*, in which case it is known as a 'musical play'.

Most of the classic Broadway and West End musicals fall into this category, including such diverse titles as *Show Boat*, *Oklahoma!*, *The King and I*, *Oliver!*, *Annie*, *Half a Sixpence*, *Avenue Q*, *The Lion King*, *Hairspray*, *Wicked* and *The Book of Mormon*.

## The Chamber Musical

A small-scale book musical that does not include an ensemble, normally takes place in only one or two locations and includes little dance is sometimes known as a chamber musical. It is no different from a book musical except in terms of scale. Some examples of this are *Thrill Me* and *I Do! I Do!*

## The Concept Musical

The concept musical is similar to a book musical, but is one where the concept or theme of the show is more important than the linear story but it is all told through bespoke book, music and lyrics.

This term is applicable to George Furth and Stephen Sondheim's *Company*, which tells the story in a non-linear fashion; to *Cats*, in which the entire musical is largely a revue of character songs set within a loose framing device and in which the production concept is to take the audience into the world of the cats; and to *Hair*, which does away with plot almost entirely.

If you want to write a concept musical, you need to ensure that the concept you have is robust and interesting enough to allow you to eschew the audience's desire for story – and you also need to be very careful about how you introduce your audience to your concept.

## The Meta-Musical

A meta-musical is a book musical wherein the characters are conscious that they are performing in a musical. This is not the same as the 'backstage musical' which is a book musical where the plot concerns putting on a musical (such as *Kiss Me Kate*). Characters in a meta-musical generally believe that being in a musical is perfectly normal, or are commenting on their status. Examples of this genre are *[title of show]* which is about a group of friends writing a musical, or *Urinetown: The Musical*.

## The Dance Musical

A dance musical is one where much of the storytelling is accomplished through dance, as much as through spoken or sung text, such as *West Side Story* or *A Chorus Line*. I would argue that *West Side Story* is a dance book musical and that *A Chorus Line* is a dance concept musical, because *West Side Story* tells a linear story with some of the story told through dance, and *A Chorus Line* is a concept musical with a very high proportion of dance. Most musicals include dance or movement, but in many musicals you can remove the dance element without damaging the storytelling, whereas in a dance musical you cannot.

Dance musicals can be hugely exciting and if it is appropriate to include a strong dance element in your story, I would encourage you to do so, as you can show a character in physical action.

## The Jukebox Musical

A jukebox musical is one that uses a pre-existing song catalogue, often by one person or a pop group, as the score for a book musical. Jukebox musicals fall into two types: the first is a straightforward book musical telling a fictional story, such as *Mamma Mia!*; the second is a biographical-style musical of the original artists' lives, such as *Jersey Boys* or the long-running West End hit *Buddy*.

The obvious advantage of the jukebox musical is that it is hugely attractive to producers because it automatically has a score of known songs, which will appeal to fans of that pop group or singer.

The disadvantage of the jukebox musical is that you will invariably be dealing with pop songs that may not have any true dramatic content, because pop music works in very unspecific terms. For a musical to engage the audience, and meet their expectations, it is usual for the songs to develop character and action, and so the songs must be very carefully chosen or you could end up with a deeply unengaging show. This may explain why many jukebox musicals, including

*Lennon, Good Vibrations, All Shook Up* and *Desperately Seeking Susan* have proven unsuccessful.

If you are interested in creating a jukebox musical you will need to get permission from the owners of the copyright to the songs early in the process. You may wish to write a musical using the songs from one band, or by a range of bands, but the important factor is who wrote the songs, not who performed them. Some bands, such as ABBA, only performed material written by their members. Other bands, such as Take That and The Spice Girls, performed songs by a wide range of writers. You might also be interested in taking songs from a certain period from a range of writers. *BlueBirds*, a play with songs that I wrote as a commission, uses songs from the Second World War, all by different writers.

## The Through-Sung Musical

The through-sung musical, also sometimes called the through-composed musical, is one in which all, or nearly all of the material is sung, and the music is continuous or nearly continuous, using recitative, or moving from song to song, such as Tim Rice and Andrew Lloyd Webber's *Jesus Christ Superstar*. It has been a hugely successful commercial form, particularly in the European musicals that opened during the 1980s, including *The Phantom of the Opera* and *Les Misérables*. Americans sometimes refer to this form, somewhat disparagingly, as 'European poperetta', but it is different from opera and operetta in two major regards: it uses music in the popular, not classical tradition and it uses amplification.

The advantage of this over the book musical is that it does not include those occasionally awkward moments of elision between the spoken and sung text. Andrew Lloyd Webber maintains that this was a huge attraction for him in his early work, as he always found that those moments when the orchestra struck up emphasised the un-naturalistic style of the musical, and that by eliminating the spoken text altogether he could create a musical language that, to him, remained consistent.

The disadvantage of the through-sung musical is one of time. One minute of spoken dialogue contains considerably more words than one minute of sung text. Therefore, if you have a complex plot, it can be difficult, or time-consuming, to convey everything you need to in sung form. In the case of a musical like *Jesus Christ Superstar*, the plot is already well known and is very simple. In more complex plots like, for example, *Aspects of Love*, it takes a deftness of touch to cover the material successfully. In a musical such as *Les Misérables*, singing all the complexities of such an epic text was clearly impossible and so the writers chose a 'pageant' style in which slightly drawn characters are given a song in which to establish characterisation, and the plotting of Victor Hugo's novel is savagely simplified.

Some musicals, such as Sondheim's *Sweeney Todd*, are pretty much 'through-composed' in that the music is almost continuous. This means that the moment of lifting into song is never a jolt, but there are spoken scenes for some of the exposition. The entire piece is about 80 per cent sung and the music only stops at very carefully executed moments, giving added power to the moments of silence.

# Revue

A revue is a collection of songs, dances and sketches which do not form a narrative but may have a collective theme. An example of this might be *The Shakespeare Revue*, a collection of songs, sketches and comedy pieces with a Shakespearean theme. The link might be that they are all written by the same person, such as *Side By Side By Sondheim* or *Jacques Brel is Alive and Well and Living in Paris*, and if they have no sketches are often known as 'musical revue'. Sometimes a performer may create a biographical revue from materials taken from shows in which they have appeared, such as Chita Rivera's *A Dancer's Life*. Some works that are often thought of as musicals, such as *Hair*, have a structure that is closer to a revue.

## Music Theatre

Like physical theatre, music theatre is a catch-all term that is often used to describe work that includes song, music and text, and sometimes dance, to create a non-commercial theatrical experience that often does not fit into another category. Sometimes it is close to modern opera; sometimes it is closer to the more popular music style of a musical.

This term is normally used to describe works that include the elements of a musical, but where the audience experience will be different from a commercial musical, and the companies want to manage the audience expectations accordingly. It is often more experimental than commercial musical theatre and, in the UK, is usually produced by companies with public funding. You will find work of this type at the ROH2 (at the Royal Opera House) and the annual Grimeborn Festival which takes place on the London fringe.

## Operetta

Operetta is a light form of opera, often romantic, comedic or satiric, performed without amplification, but containing spoken scenes, such as Gilbert and Sullivan's celebrated work *The Mikado*. Today, operetta tends to be a historical form, and its heyday was from the 1880s to the 1920s, although musicals such as *The Phantom of the Opera* and *Love Never Dies* nod heavily towards operetta in both their romantic and comic passages. Songs such as 'All I Ask of You' and 'Once Upon Another Time' pastiche romantic operetta and the theatre managers' number 'Notes' is very similar to a comic operetta style. New operetta is rare, but its influence is still felt in a good deal of modern musical-theatre writing.

## Opera

The grandest form of musical theatre is opera, which at its finest is the pinnacle of the classical traditions of the performing arts: classical singing, classical dancing (ballet) and acting. The defining characteristics of opera, compared to other forms of musical theatre, is that it is generally performed acoustically (without amplification), is commonly through-sung without dialogue, and that the music is in a classical rather than popular style. This means that the construction of the musical material does not follow popular musical song forms, but is rooted in the structures of classical music. Compared to new musicals, new operas tend to be fairly rare. Most major opera companies commission very few new works and some opera companies never perform world premieres.

Opera companies that do perform new works generally commission them from established composers, who may not be established opera composers but may have built a reputation through their orchestral, concert or vocal works. The composer normally chooses their librettist and between them they settle on a subject. It is very rare that a company would produce a new opera that it has not commissioned.

In recent years, certain opera companies have commissioned operas from artists from other strands of music, such as *Monkey* by Damon Albarn and *Prima Donna* by Rufus Wainwright, and some opera companies have new-writing schemes where composers and librettists can learn about the art of creating opera.

If you want to write an opera, it is worth getting in touch with opera companies near you to see if they have any of these schemes. You are likely to be expected to already have created some classical music. There are some small opera companies who develop new work, and it is also worth searching them out if you are interested in creating opera. Opera demands large resources and I would advise you to have a strong idea about who might produce your work, and to have sounded them out, before you begin writing.

---

### Try Something New

Try and experience as many different forms of musical as possible. Go to see opera, jukebox musicals, concept musicals, operetta, physical theatre, etc. By experiencing these you will make yourself more aware of the choices of form available to you. Which are your favourite genres? Which are you least attracted to?

---

New musical writers constantly blur the lines between these definitions of genre. *Follies*, for example, is a book musical until about two-thirds of the way through, when it suddenly becomes a concept musical. Bernstein's *Candide* and Gershwin's *Porgy and Bess* have had commercial productions as musicals and also been presented in opera houses by opera companies. Are they operas or musicals? For Sondheim, whose *Sweeney Todd*, *A Little Night Music* and *Pacific Overtures* have all played on Broadway and in opera houses, the distinction is unimportant but largely about context. He said:

> I really think that when something plays Broadway it's a musical, and when it plays in an opera house it's opera. That's it. It's the terrain, the countryside, the expectations of the audience that make it one thing or another.

This book is largely concerned with the book musical, as it is the most useful model to examine because it involves the integration of music, lyric and script, but everything I have written in this book is relevant to creating an opera, a musical play, a concept musical or piece of physical theatre.

# 3
# *Source*
# *Material*

# Source Material

If you start young and have a long career, you might reasonably expect to write twenty musicals in your lifetime. In 2010 Andrew Lloyd Webber was sixty-two years old and had written about fifteen to date, and Sondheim was eighty and had written about twenty. Richard Rodgers wrote forty in his lifetime and Oscar Hammerstein wrote thirty-nine, and they both wrote some films as well. Bear in mind, too, that Rodgers and Hammerstein wrote shows at the beginning of their careers when there were sometimes more than 300 Broadway shows opening in a year. In one year, 1926, Rodgers and his first collaborator Lorenz Hart opened *The Fifth Avenue Follies*, *The Girlfriend*, *The Garrick Gaieties* (*Second Edition*), *Lilo Lady*, *Peggy-Ann* and *Betsy*. All of these were Broadway openings except *Lido Lady*, which opened in London. Today it would be remarkable for any writer to open more than one musical in either London or New York per year.

My point is that the number of musicals you are likely to write is quite small. Today it takes quite a long time for a musical to be produced from the moment that you have finished writing it. It is very rare for a musical to be produced in less than a year, and a large-scale West End or Broadway musical might be in the planning stages for two or three years or longer.

The process of getting a musical produced in the twenty-first century is generally a long one and, even with a commissioned show, the journey from first idea to opening night is rarely less than three years. You should therefore choose the subjects for your musical very carefully. You want to be sure that this subject is going to sustain your interest for the writing process and for the production period. Like having a child, you should really want it.

Most musicals are based on a previously existing work in some other form. The truly 'original' stage musical is a very rare beast. *Hair*, *A Chorus Line* and *Anyone Can Whistle* are the exceptions rather than the rules. For every truly original musical you will find numerous adaptations from other sources, whether they be from novels (*Oliver!* or *The Phantom of the Opera*), short stories (*Guys and Dolls* or *South Pacific*), plays (*Carousel* or *My Fair Lady*), a poem or group of poems (*The Wild Party* or *Cats*), films (*Ghost* or *Sunset Boulevard*) a TV series (*Avenue Q* is a spoof of the children's TV series *Sesame Street*), or a real-life story (*Gypsy* or *Evita*).

Inspiration for a musical can come from many sources, and from almost anywhere. Stephen Sondheim has based two of his musicals on pictures. Seurat's painting *A Sunday Afternoon on the Island of La Grande Jatte* is so integral to *Sunday in the Park with George* that the picture itself is practically a character in the show. The other, a photograph of Gloria Swanson in the rubble of a Broadway theatre, formed the initial inspiration for *Follies*, but is never seen, nor mentioned in the show. Sondheim's other inspirations have ranged wildly, from an obscure Italian film (Ettore Scola's *Passione d'Amore*, which was, in turn, based on Iginio Ugo Tarchetti's novel *Fosca*) for *Passion*; to Bruno Bettelheim's academic analysis of folk tales for *Into the Woods*; to a British play, which was in turn based on a folk legend, for *Sweeney Todd*; and, perhaps most surprisingly, the political events that led to the opening up of Japan to Western trade for *Pacific Overtures*.

You must find your own inspirations and find the stories that you want to tell. You must be able to understand what it is in any story that you want to make 'sing'.

## Adaptations

The great musicals that have been created by adapting from other sources such as plays, short stories, novels, films, etc. have always added value to the source material. They have not just added songs, they have transformed the work into a new greater artwork in the art of the adaptation.

*Oklahoma!* adds value to *Green Grow the Lilacs* in the unlocking of the romantic subtext. *Cabaret* adds value to *I Am a Camera* in the opening up of the cabaret scenes to comment on the action. *Cats* adds value to *Old Possum's Book of Practical Cats* in the creation of a magical stage language in which the poems are illuminated.

When the process of turning a work into a musical does not add value, or is not able to add value, then the process becomes redundant. *9 to 5, Napoleon, Carrie, Breakfast at Tiffany's*: the list of flops is a list of projects where the adaptation was not able to add sufficient value to make the project viable goes on and on. It is not the only reason for a flop, but it is often a major factor.

The most important thing to bear in mind when adapting is that you are creating a *new* work of art. Each art form has strengths and weaknesses and you need to understand how you are going to transform the source material by turning it into a musical. You do not need to follow every detail of the original slavishly. Feel free to cut characters, change the time frame, alter the story, and make any other changes you wish, so long as you are true to the spirit of the original.

Sometimes practitioners talk about the 'needs' of the musical to describe the aspects of stories that work well as musicals, and you need to understand something of these needs to make the right choices in your source material.

If you want to see how adaptation has worked in practice, it is worth looking at the genesis of the work *Cabaret*. The source material for the work is two short novels by Christopher Isherwood: *Goodbye to Berlin* and *Mr Norris Changes Trains*, which were based on his own experiences in Berlin in the 1930s. These were adapted by John Van Druten into a successful play, *I Am a Camera*, which is the source material for the stage version of *Cabaret*, which then went through one final transformation as it became the multi-award-winning film musical. The interesting thing about each of these works is that at every stage the creators completely understood the strengths of the art form into which they were adapting their source material: Isherwood understood how to take his own experiences and tell them as stories. Van Druten understood how to turn this material into a play: he builds up the character of Sally Bowles, and the whole play is set in one shared apartment. Joe Masteroff, John Kander, Fred Ebb and director Harold Prince understood how to take this play and make it a stage musical: they re-imagined the story into multiple settings, took the audience into the cabaret where Sally works and introduced the character of the EmCee, the host of the club and the only person who speaks directly to the audience. Finally, Bob Fosse took the stage musical and understood exactly how to turn it into a film, cutting many of the songs, adding new ones and creating a film where all the musical performances are completely natural within their context.

---

### One Story, Four Works

Read Christopher Isherwood's two Berlin novels, then read (or see if you can) John Van Druten's *I Am a Camera*, then read (or see) the stage version of *Cabaret*, listening to the songs on the original Broadway or London cast recording as you come to them in the script. Finally, watch Fosse's film of *Cabaret*. Each time, see how many major changes you can notice between the works. (It is worth noting that, such is the influence of Fosse's film version, many current stage versions of the show incorporate changes made for the film, so reading the original Broadway libretto is advised.)

---

Every writer or writing team has their own style and finds their own solutions to the knotty problems of adapting a text. Rodgers and Hammerstein, at the height of their fame, were approached to musicalise George Bernard Shaw's *Pygmalion*, but couldn't find a way to 'open it up' and use the kind of large-scale chorus required in a Broadway musical at that time. They turned it down. Lerner and Loewe later found the perfect set of solutions when they moved a tea-party scene to Ascot, showed the Embassy Ball, and enlarged the character of Alfred Doolittle to provide two rip-roaring chorus numbers: 'With a Little Bit of Luck' and 'Get Me to the Church on Time'.

When we adapted E. Nesbit's *The Railway Children*, composer Richard John and I faced two major issues. The first was that the novel is very domestic: there are a few minor characters in the village to which the family move but most of the story takes place with about eight characters. The second was that the novel, like many books written for children, was really a set of short stories, each one a self-contained adventure, and each short enough to be read at bedtime. There was a 'framing device' of Father's disappearance, which causes the move to the country and the adventures to begin, but there was no overarching narrative.

We solved these two problems in a number of ways. Firstly, we 'built up' the characters in the village into more rounded human beings. Secondly, we chose very carefully which of the 'short-story' adventures to include and which to omit. One of them, 'Perks' Birthday', which is a charming chapter in the novel, was only cut late in the writing process. Thirdly, we took a long hard look at the character of Roberta and decided that the central theme of the musical, but not the novel, was her rite of passage from childhood to adulthood. This is most obvious in Act Two when Roberta accompanies Mother to London to help secure Father's release from prison, and in the romanticising of her relationship with Jim. Both of these elements are an original invention and not included in the novel. The rite-of-passage theme was also built into the architecture of the musical in the songs written for Roberta. In the first act, her part is written as one of the children and she joins in with songs, such as 'Together' and 'Fancy Talk', as a child. In Act Two, as she learns and grows, her music becomes more mature and she sings solos, similar in musical language to those the adult characters have sung, culminating in the long solo sequence 'Nearly Autumn'. Audiences don't sit and analyse the writing in this way, but you can see them 'feel' it as the emotional pitch heightens towards the inevitable 'Daddy, Oh My Daddy' that ends the show. You need to find elements of the story that you are adapting that will be strengthened by musicalising them. If you are not transforming the story, adding new dimensions by making it a musical, then why bother?

When the legendary librettist Oscar Hammerstein II mentored the young Stephen Sondheim in the writing of musicals, he designed a course for Sondheim on adaptation and the construction of a musical. He set Sondheim an assignment: to write a musical based on each of the following:

1. A play he admired.
2. A play he thought was flawed.
3. An existing novel or short story not previously dramatised.
4. An original story of his own.

Each of these types contains its own challenges for the adapter and Hammerstein knew that each would teach Sondheim a good deal. For the first of these, the young Sondheim chose *Beggar on Horseback* by George S. Kaufman and Marc Connelly, which was later performed at Williams College where he was a student. For the second, he chose *High Tor* by Maxwell Anderson; the third, *Mary Poppins* (the Disney film had not been released at this time); and the fourth, an original show, *Climb High*, from which a number of songs have been recorded. Only the first was produced, and that has never had a professional production. *Climb High* was abandoned, and the other two remain unproduced as the rights-holders refused permission. How I would love to see what Sondheim's *Mary Poppins* might have been.

---

### The Hammerstein Challenge

Oscar Hammerstein's programme for Stephen Sondheim is a wonderful challenge. It is certainly worth thinking about what stories you would choose for this exercise, even if you don't go ahead and write four complete shows.

---

## Third-Party Rights

Sondheim's experience with the rights-holders of *Mary Poppins* and *High Tor* is certainly not unique. Once you have decided on your subject, you need to make sure that you can acquire any necessary third-party rights. Third-party rights are sometimes called underlying rights and they refer to the copyright of the source material. (You are the 'first party', your producer is the 'second party' and the holder of the rights to the source material is the 'third party'.)

If you wish to adapt an existing work you *must* acquire any necessary rights. Most countries in the world are signed up to the Berne Convention, which means that copyright is covered by similar law across the world. The Convention decrees that written works remain the copyright of the writer until fifty years after the death of the last surviving author. Countries may not decrease the term in their own territories, but they may extend it; in Europe, it is now seventy years from death. As a general rule, films remain in copyright until fifty years after the first screening.

The good news is that if you write a musical, you own the copyright and, if it generates income through performances or music sales, etc., you and your estate continue to receive income until fifty or seventy years after your death.

The bad news is that works remain 'in copyright' for a long time after they are originally created, especially if the author is quite young when they write the piece and then have a long life. The history of the musical is littered with projects that have never seen the light of day because the owners of the copyright of the source material have not granted permission for it to be turned into a musical.

It is not only novice writers who find this. Sondheim came up against exactly the same problem later in his career, even after he had won a number of Tony Awards. When looking for a romantic subject for a musical after their two 'anti-romantic' shows, *Company* and *Follies*, Sondheim and Harold Prince tried to secure the rights to Jean Anouilh's *Ring Round the Moon*, only to be refused. They turned instead to Ingmar Bergman's film *Smiles on a Summer Night* for the inspiration for *A Little Night Music*.

Works where all the authors have been dead for more than fifty years (in Canada and some other territories) or seventy years (in Europe, the USA and Australia) are said to be 'in the public domain'. So the works of Shakespeare, Molière, Dickens and a host of other authors can be adapted without permission or payment. The Bible has proved to be a rich source of material for musicals (*Godspell, Children of Eden, Jesus Christ Superstar, Joseph,* etc.) – there are no third-party rights with God!

Whatever you do, do not begin any serious work on a musical until you have secured the necessary rights. Follow these steps:

1. Check when the authors of the source material died. You need to find the latest date if there is more than one author. You can normally find this information online. If this is more than the copyright term for the country you live and work in (or are going to produce your musical in), you can probably assume that the work is now out of copyright, but you should also check the term of copyright for your country. If it is out of copyright, you can proceed without permission or payment.

2. If the work appears to be in copyright then contact the publisher, agent, estate or organisation responsible for the rights. In the case of a play or story, this will usually be included somewhere in the first few pages of the publication. Many publishers have a permissions office, to which your approach should be made. In the case of a film, this will normally be the film studio that released the film, and they are certainly the best people to start with. If you know who the publisher or film studio is, then it is often easy to contact them through their websites, and you should include the following details in your email:

   • The name of the work you want to adapt (known as the 'property').
   • The author(s) of the property.
   • The date of publication or release.
   • Your name and contact information.
   • An outline of your project: how you would treat the story and what kind of musical language you might use.
   • A *brief* biography of you and your writing partner(s). Don't worry if you feel that you don't have much in the way of biography, so long as you are honest. If they like the concept, they will probably be interested.

You may get a response that tells you that you need to contact another agent or office, but eventually, you will get to the person who can either grant or deny the permission for you to go ahead. Whether the author is dead or alive, the procedure is basically the same: they will either grant you, or deny you, the right to turn the work into a musical. If they grant you the right then, normally, some kind of agreement is made whereby they stand to take a percentage of the writer's royalty from the work, once it is commercially exploited, i.e. once the work is being performed.

If they deny you the right, there is little you can do about it. They own the rights and if they don't want you to turn their work into a musical, then that is their wish. If you continue, the chances of getting a producer on board are very slight.

Rights get withheld for many reasons. There are many dramatic rights to a book, as many possibilities as there are art forms; so in any book there will be film rights, stage play rights, musical rights, radio rights, operatic rights, etc. Often, if a property is bought for development by a film studio they will buy the whole set of rights for all art forms, in order to prevent a stage play or musical appearing and harming the earning potential of the film they plan to make. In the case of the Broadway musical *Wicked*, Universal Pictures bought the dramatic rights to Gregory Maguire's novel, tried unsuccessfully to develop a screenplay and then used their rights to develop the musical instead. It will be no surprise when the film version of *Wicked* finally gets made.

When I first began teaching at the University of London, two of the students had written a musical based on *They Shoot Horses, Don't They?*, a novel by Horace McCoy and a famous film starring Jane Fonda, little knowing that the stage rights were already held by a playwright and that the *Cabaret* authors John Kander and Fred Ebb had been denied permission to musicalise the work. I only came into the process after they had already written the show. These students had only discovered quite late in proceedings that their work could be seen in a private performance at the college in order for it to be assessed, but could never have public performances. If, as we saw earlier, you can only expect to write twenty or so musicals in a long career, you really don't want to be writing shows that will be denied performances because you haven't secured the underlying rights at the start. That way madness lies.

When dealing with film studios, the situation can get a little more complex. As film studios get bought and sold, and sometimes rights to works get bought and sold, it can be hard to establish who currently owns those rights. They are also very protective of their rights, especially if a successful film has been made, or may be made, of the property. Since the turn of the millennium, prompted largely by the success of Disney's theatrical operation, many film studios have established theatre-production businesses to exploit the titles they own, and these companies become one of the producers of the musical, as is the case with *Priscilla, Queen of the Desert* and *Legally Blonde*. The sad news for novice writers is that these companies tend to choose writers with a proven track record when developing a property. Still, it is always worth a try and an email to the film company costs nothing. Simply go to their website and see if there is a 'contact us' form or email address. The worst that can happen is that they say no (or sometimes, just say nothing), in which case you are no worse off than you were before. There is always a chance they will like your idea, or be honest enough to tell you that they don't own the stage rights and to let you know who to contact.

This all sounds potentially depressing, but there is a lot of good news. Living authors are, on the whole, flattered by an approach and will often be encouraging. Once the author has died and the control passes to his estate, permission will often be decided by someone who is not a creator of the work, but recognises the financial value in having the work exploited. It is true that estates can sometimes be trickier to deal with than living writers, as more than one person may control the rights, and all of them have to agree before permission can be granted. It is also true that the more of a track record you have as a writer, the more likely you are to have a favourable response to an approach. Remember, also, that a writer may have sold the rights many years earlier and may no longer control them himself.

# Permissions to Use Songs in a Jukebox Musical

If you want to write a jukebox musical, you will need to seek permission for the use of the songs and you may need to do this before you start.

Make a list of the songs, the writers and the publishers of the music. You can normally find this information on CD recordings of the material or on the internet. If the songs are all by the same writer(s) you will need to seek permission from the writer(s) and I would strongly advise you to do so before you go too far into the writing process.

In the UK, songs that are performed in theatres in concert can be licensed without permission through an organisation called the Performing Rights Society (PRS), but they cannot license music that is used dramatically. PRS for Music define performance as being dramatic if the story is told through any dramatic action, whether acted, danced or mimed, and/or through the use of costume, scenery or other visual effects. In the USA, there are more Performing Rights Organisations (PROs), the situation is more complex and you should contact the publishers of the individual songs. Eventually you will probably need to employ a lawyer.

My experience of PRS is that they are incredibly helpful, and if you have specific questions about licensing music for your musical, they are usually ready to help identify publishers if you cannot find them yourself.

Therefore, if you are writing a script which will include copyrighted songs and action that is acted, danced or mimed, you will need to license the songs. Technically, you don't need to do this until your musical is being produced, but the smaller the number of writers whose work you wish to use, then the earlier I would advise you start seeking permission.

There are three broad rules as to whether you are likely to get permission:

1. The fewer songs by a single writer in your selection of songs, the more likely you are to get permission. Many writers are happy to have one song included in a musical, but not to supply a whole score unless they are involved in the project.

2. The older the song, the greater your chances of getting permission. If songs are not making much money for the writers they tend to be more willing to license them for use.

3. If your song has been included in another musical, especially a successful one, your chance of getting permission is greatly reduced.

If you are using songs from many writers and can be flexible about the songs that you want to use, then you can afford to wait to clear the licensing until you have production dates (and some publishers will only want to know when you do have a definite production), but my clear advice is that if you are looking to create a jukebox show from one specific band or writer, then seek permission before you begin. Shows like *Mamma Mia!*, *We Will Rock You*, *Movin' Out* and *Lennon* only got permission because the writers or rights-holders (ABBA, Queen, Billy Joel and the estate of John Lennon respectively) were involved from the start of the process.

You should email the music publishing company with an outline of your project, a plot summary, any firm production plans you have and a short biography of yourself and any collaborators you have. After that, it is a case of sitting back and waiting for a response. If you have a production planned, this is really a job for your producer, who may have to do a fair amount of chasing and cajoling to tie up a deal. You can expect to pay the writers of the songs a percentage of the writers' royalty for the show.

## Adapting from a Story or Novel

When adapting from a story or novel, you are likely to need to edit the work. Without editing, most novels have far too much incident and far too many characters to be successfully translated to the musical stage. In the case of *Les Misérables*, I have always felt that I've been watching a kind of exam-notes version of Victor Hugo's story rather than a work that truly reflects the depth of characterisation and incident that the novel has (I know there are many people who disagree with me). Lionel Bart's *Oliver!* similarly reduces the complexity of the original story into something much more simple in order to succeed.

With a novel you are likely to need to identify the heart of the story. Does the novel's structure lend itself to musicalisation? There is a lot more about the structure of musicals in the next few chapters.

All musical adapters will necessarily make choices about what to include and what to remove. Every adapter will make their own choices and this will affect how the final musical will work with an audience. You only need to imagine the differences between the Disney film *Mary Poppins*, the Disney/Cameron Mackintosh stage musical *Mary Poppins* and what Sondheim's *Mary Poppins* might have been, to realise this.

Bear in mind that, generally, songs take more time to tell the same information than spoken text does, because songs tend to have fewer words per minute than speech. If you take a long novel, with a lot of incident and character, you will need to cut heavily, as the adapters of *Les Misérables* needed to. With that in mind, short stories can be a very effective source of material. Michel Legrand and Didier van Cauwelaert's *Amour* (which did not find favour in New York, but has been a hit in other countries) was adapted from a very short story by Marcel Aymé, *Le Passe-Muraille*. The story is about fourteen pages long; the musical's running time was one hour forty minutes with no interval.

Short stories also formed the basis of *South Pacific* and *Guys and Dolls*; in each case two short stories from each collection, by James Michener and Damon Runyon respectively, were melded together to create the book of the musicals. *Fiddler on the Roof* was also based on a collection of short stories. The advantages of taking a collection of short stories is that it is generally easy to omit whole stories, whilst not damaging the central plotting of the drama. It is important, however, to have a clear idea about what the central theme of your musical is, and this can be shaped by the stories you choose. For *South Pacific*, Rodgers, Hammerstein and Joshua Logan chose two stories that had multiracial relationships as their theme and created a musical about the destructive nature of racism. For *Fiddler on the Roof*, the creators chose stories from Sholem Aleichem's *Tevye the Milkman*, where the theme of the generation gap was amplified through the collapse of traditional values in a Jewish shtetl.

Whether you choose a long novel or a short story, the nature of the task is identical. You have to be prepared to be bold with the detail of the work you choose to adapt, whilst remaining true to the spirit. Ask yourself, 'Am I staying true to the spirit of the original?' If the answer is negative, then why are you adapting this source material?

---

### Short Story

Find a short story of no more than 3,000 words and write an outline for it as a musical. Where do the songs come? What do you have to edit? What might you need to add?

---

## Adapting from Plays

Musicals tend to be plot-driven. During the twentieth century, this became decreasingly the case in non-musical drama where plays have become more character-driven. For Shakespeare and his contemporaries, and for the dramatists of the Restoration, plot was the most important dramaturgical element. Watch one of the plays from these periods and you follow a story as it unfolds and as the characters are experiencing the unfolding of the plot in the present tense.

With the birth of naturalism, dramatists began to eschew plot for the sake of character development. By the mid-twentieth century (and in some cases quite a good deal earlier), drama often became about the playing out of the effects of events that had happened some considerable time earlier, or situations that characters found themselves in that could not be satisfactorily resolved. Plays have tended towards the psychological. So the characters of Ibsen's *Ghosts* deal with the sins of the parents being visited on the children, and the characters in Edward Albee's *Who's Afraid of Virginia Woolf?* deal with the mistakes made in the central characters' marriage. In many plays from the latter half of the twentieth century, including the works of Arthur Miller, Harold Pinter, John Osborne and David Storey, what plot there is, is just enough to hold the characters together for them to be in action. In the hands of master writers, like those listed above, the characters and their behaviour are fascinating. In the hands of lesser writers, one can feel the audience lurch into boredom.

But where, in a play, the actions and behaviour slowly illuminate the psychological truth of the characters, in a musical characters must sing – and when they sing, they tend to sing truthfully about their emotions. Characters in plays often lie about their motivations and feelings; characters in musicals can speak untruthfully, but they usually sing truthfully, especially in solos. Give a character a solo and they'll be telling the truth. This is also true in Shakespeare: a character giving a soliloquy alone onstage always tells the truth. There is an unspoken pact between writer, character and audience that when only one character is in front of the audience the character speaks (or sings) honestly.

Musicals also tend to need a forward thrust in the narrative. This is probably why musicals based on Shakespeare are more common than those based on Pinter. Whereas Shakespeare's plays take place in many locations, plays of the twentieth century, again since the rise of naturalism, often take place in a single location or a small number of locations. The musical that takes place in a single location is a fairly rare beast, although it is becoming more common. One reason to change location is to vary the number or type of people that can be onstage, allowing for chorus or ensemble scenes. I have already mentioned how Lerner and Loewe opened up *Pygmalion* into *My Fair Lady*, and it is impossible to see how they might have introduced the cockneys and racegoers without changing location. The works of Andrew Lloyd Webber and productions of Cameron Macintosh have become famous for their multiple and lavishly realised locations, including spectacular stage effects, such as falling chandeliers and rising helicopters that have become as famous as any performer in the show.

## Adapting from Films

If musicals seem to thrive on stories that have a strong narrative thrust, multiple locations and a clear sense of storytelling, rather than internal character revelation, then it is no surprise that many successful musicals have been based on films which have the same attributes. One can surmise that if Shakespeare were working today he would probably be turning out scripts in Hollywood.

Films have a number of advantages as sources for musicals. Firstly, is running time. Most films run between 90 and 120 minutes, which allows time for the musical numbers (a standard-length musical being 120 to 170 minutes).

Secondly, when a novel or other property is adapted into a film, there is usually a focus on a strong narrative approach. Film is more about watching people *do* things than a modern play, which is often about listening to people *say* things, and this focus on action is a strength in a musical.

Movies are also often about characters learning something about themselves, and these moments of self-knowledge lend themselves excellently to musical moments, especially solos.

The multiple locations in a film facilitate the opening up of the story, allowing opportunities for chorus scenes and spectacular staging. Many musicals that are adapted from books are often influenced by film versions of those tales. *The Phantom of the Opera* owes much to the 1925 movie version, and *Oliver!* owes much to David Lean's film *Oliver Twist* for its editorial choices. Remember that anything invented for the screenplay that did not appear in the original story is the copyright of the screenwriter, not the novelist.

There has been considerable commentary recently about the number of musicals being adapted from films, but this is actually nothing new. *My Fair Lady* specifically credited the screenplay of *Pygmalion* as a source, and *Sweet Charity, 42nd Street, Little Shop of Horrors* and *Nine* were all based on films. The major difference today is that movie studios are working as stage producers to exploit their back catalogues. Just remember that for every success like *Hairspray, The Producers* or *Beauty and the Beast* there is a flop like *Tarzan, Cry Baby* or *Young Frankenstein*.

And never, never, never begin to work on an adaptation of a film until you have the underlying rights.

## Adapting from Real Life

If you want to avoid all the tedious legal business of securing underlying rights, you can turn to other sources for your story. One popular source is to adapt from real life.

Whilst everything a person creates during their life is subject to copyright, there is no copyright in the actual life story. If the person is still alive you can write what you like about them, but musical theatre is subject to the same laws of libel as anything else. Once a person is dead, they cannot be libelled, but remember that the other people who shared that person's life in whatever way, if alive, can be libelled.

In a dictionary, 'libel' is defined as:

1   a. defamation by written or printed words, pictures, or
    in any form other than by spoken words or gestures.
    b. the act or crime of publishing it.
2.  anything that is defamatory or that maliciously or
    damagingly misrepresents.

In the UK (and there are international variations to this), broadly speaking, you can write what you like about someone so long as it is either true, or not damaging to their reputation. If they consider it to be untrue, or damaging to them, they may choose to sue you, at which point you have to prove it is true or withdraw it (and sometimes settle damages to them). That's a situation you want to avoid, but sometimes it can be worth the risk.

When I was working with a large group of writers on the devised musical *Let Him Have Justice*, which told the story of the life, death and legacy of Derek Bentley, who had been wrongly hanged for the murder of a policeman, we had to make a judgement about the character of Christopher Craig, who had actually committed the crime. Ironically, Craig was the only person in our telling of the tale who was still alive. All the family members of Bentley, Craig and the policeman had since died, but Craig had not hanged because he was too young. He had served time in prison and was a rehabilitated member of society.

Obviously, we could not leave him out of the story, as he was the perpetrator of the very crime at the heart of the plot. We were careful to present as factual a version of the story as possible. We were also aware that Craig had recently made a statement to the effect that he would make no further comments on the case for the rest of his life. We surmised that he was unlikely to cause any problems, and that if he did make any objections we would take his point of view on board and try to present him in a fashion that he could not object to. Although the show was widely covered in the press, we heard nothing from him.

If you are taking a real-life story from an autobiography or biography, you need to be careful. These works are subject to the same copyright laws as any other work. The facts of the matter cannot be copyright, but the interpretations can be. The key here is to use as many sources as possible and ensure that you do not include information that you find in only one source. The internet is a good source of material (although prone to inaccuracy), as major lives tend to be well documented on a number of websites. No one can stop you using the facts, but any invention by another author is subject to copyright. If you are in doubt, it is worth contacting the publisher of the biography for clarification.

I categorise 'true-life story' musicals into two types: firstly, there are the *biographical musicals* that attempt to tell the story of a whole life, or the major part of a life, in a musical. Secondly, there are those musicals that use *real-life* events as a source, but tell a defined story. *Evita* is an example of a biographical musical; *The King and I* and *The Sound of Music* are examples of a real-life story.

In my work as a professional reader for Mercury Musical Developments and as a dramaturg specialising in musical theatre, I often receive scripts by post. Often I have no idea what the subject matter of the musical will be, but my heart sinks when I see a title followed by the words '*a musical based on the life of...*'

F. Scott Fitzgerald wrote, 'There are no second acts in American lives,' but actually the biggest issue with the biographical musical is that nobody lives their life in a handy two-act structure. Real people's lives are messy, unstructured, but contain fascinating stories. Often when I talk to the writers of these biographical musicals and I ask them why they have chosen the story of this person's life, they reply that it is a fascinating story.

Fascinating it may be, and a fascinating life story may be a great subject for a wonderful biography, but is it a good story for a musical? The fact is that there have been many more unsuccessful biographical musicals that have reached the West End or Broadway than successful ones. James Dean (*Dude*), Coco Chanel (*Coco*), Manuel Benítez (*Matador*), the Hilton sisters (*Side Show*) and Marilyn Monroe (in two different musicals, one in New York and one in London, both called *Marilyn*) have seen their fascinating lives reduced to musical song cycles with little dramatic merit.

On the other hand, the musicals of the lives of New York's Mayor La Guardia (*Fiorello!*), Peter Allen (*The Boy from Oz*), Gypsy Rose Lee (*Gypsy*), Eva Perón (*Evita*) and P.T. Barnum (*Barnum*) have been huge successes. But consider this:

*Fiorello!* was only a hit in New York, where La Guardia is a folk hero; the London production lasted less than three months and it is practically unrevivable today. I should know: I directed the first UK production since the original London cast, for Guildford School of Acting in 2008. It is a real curiosity with some great songs but a book that is no longer relevant.

*The Boy from Oz* was a massive hit in New York, due almost entirely to Hugh Jackman's magnificent Tony Award-winning performance as Peter Allen. The producers wisely closed the show when Jackman's contract expired and it has never been seen in Britain, although Jackman toured Australia in a specially staged arena version in 2006.

*Gypsy*, *Barnum* and *Evita* are therefore oddities, in that they are enduring biographical musicals and, although they are fundamentally different, I believe that they have succeeded for the same reason. In all three cases, the writers had a very strong concept about how to tell their tale, and were prepared to reshape the historical facts to serve their own ends.

In *Gypsy*, Arthur Laurents, Stephen Sondheim and Jule Styne focused on the mother of their biographical subject, pushing the character of Louise to the edges of the story for most of the first act and ending the story as their ostensible subject finds fame. In this, they wrote less a biography of Gypsy Rose Lee, and more a classic tragedy about an archetypal stage mother.

In *Barnum*, writers Mark Bramble, Cy Coleman and Michael Stewart used the physical staging of a circus to tell the story of their hero, using circus routines to act as metaphors for the events in their hero's life, effectively turning his biography into a night in the big top.

In *Evita*, Tim Rice and Andrew Lloyd Webber had the equally strong, but different, idea that the story of Eva Perón could be portrayed as the dynamic rise and fall of a supremely ambitious woman, within a musical structure, providing a massive bravura role for the leading lady. Lloyd Webber has written, 'Clearly it provided an extraordinary framework in which to set a big "aria", and he goes on to note that it was the contrast between the private moments of solo and duet writing, compared with the epic choral writing, that was a huge attraction to him.

You might be able to find other successful biographical musicals that I have overlooked, and I am sure that there will be successful biographical shows in the future, but I am also certain that, if they are truly successful, they will have a very strong central idea about the life of their protagonist.

If you decide to tackle an entire life story, my advice to you is to ensure that you have a very strong concept about the theme of the show, and what your 'take' on the life story is. Just because someone had a fascinating life does not mean that you will be able to fashion a fascinating musical. How are you going to create the drama?

This brings us to the *real-life* stories. I define a real-life story as being different to a biographical musical, in that it is self-contained, with a clear beginning, middle and ending, which is based on historical events. Real-life musicals do not attempt to tell the whole, or major part, of a life.

There have been many successful real-life musicals, among them *The Sound of Music*, *The King and I*, *1776* and *Annie Get Your Gun*. Most of these stories became musicals after they had already been dramatised for another medium, usually non-musical biographical films. The advantage here is that the story has already been structured and the question of the central theme answered. And remember that if you are basing your musical on a film, or other treatment, you may need to acquire the underlying rights to those works. Rodgers and Hammerstein acquired the rights to Maria von Trapp's autobiography before they began work on *The Sound of Music*.

There are also shows like *They're Playing Our Song* and *Dreamgirls*, which deal with heavily fictionalised real-life situations (in these cases, the relationship between Marvin Hamlisch and Carole Bayer Sager, and the rise of the pop group The Supremes). *Dreamgirls*, for example, is very loosely based on the story of The Supremes, but most of the book is invention and what is not is based on well-known fact. The writers were also at pains to point out that their story is a fiction, giving the group and all the characters invented names.

All stories that are based on real-life tales are fictionalised to some extent. Rodgers and Hammerstein based *The King and I* on Margaret Hamilton's book about the life of Anna Leonowens, and on the film adaptation of it. So much of the King's barbarity in the musical is invented (and in the non-musical film) that the people of Thailand (modern-day Siam) view the piece as an offensive American fiction, based only on the fact that a Welsh woman came to teach at the King's court. The real King Mongkut was a forward-thinking, modernising monarch and if he was as barbarous as the musical's book makes out, how did Anna Leonowens come to be invited to teach at the court in the first place?

As a writer, you should take these stories, and fashion from them the tale that you want to tell. Ask yourself, 'What is the theme at the core of this story?' In *Let Him Have Justice*, it only became possible to musicalise the story successfully when we established that Derek Bentley's wrongful execution caused such public outrage that there was suddenly a popular movement for the abolition of the death penalty. The dynamic between the private tragedy and the public context became the key that allowed us to move forward with the musical. You need to 'find the key' for your story.

> ## Today's News, Tomorrow's Musical
>
> Open today's newspaper and find three stories that you think might have potential as a real-life musical. Don't necessarily think of this in terms of a two-act musical, it could just be a ten or twenty-minute piece. Imagine the parts of the story that are not written about in the newspaper: for example, if it is the story of a divorce, what has led to this? How have the characters behaved? Why do you believe these stories will 'sing'? Which of these is the strongest?

## The Original Story

An original story is one that is not based on any previous source material. You might decide that you want to go it completely alone and invent a story from scratch for your musical. This is, after all, what many playwrights do all the time, but it is surprisingly rare in musical theatre. And an advantage is that as you will own the story, you do not need to clear any copyright to begin work. They are, however, notoriously difficult to write.

Rodgers and Hammerstein created two original musicals, *Allegro* and *Me and Juliet*, both of which flopped. Sondheim has written only one absolutely original, not-based-on-anything piece, *Anyone Can Whistle*, and Andrew Lloyd Webber has had varying success with his original pieces: *Starlight Express*, *Tell Me on a Sunday* and *The Beautiful Game* – although it should be noted that in all of the musicals mentioned above, most critical opprobrium has been reserved for the book, even when, in the case of *Starlight Express*, the show became a long-running success. Recently, one totally original musical stormed Broadway, pushing the boundaries of subject matter and garnering a Pulitzer Prize for drama along the way. That musical is *Next to Normal*, and its musicalisation of a family living with bipolar disorder has shown that nothing is off-limits, and that an original story can succeed as a musical.

Original musicals tend to have some inspiration from a source, but often it is no more than a concept. *The Beautiful Game* was inspired by the football teams that played during the Irish troubles of the 1970s; *Allegro* was inspired by Hammerstein's experience of his father's and brother's lives as doctors. Richard John and I wrote a short piece for London's Theatre503, when they asked us to write something inspired by the Heathrow Terminal Four London Underground station for their Urban Scrawl project. The result was our only truly original piece to date: *Terminal Four Play*.

If you are going to write an original musical, you need to make sure that it is, first and foremost, a good story. You could actually write it as a story, of whatever length, and then treat it as a musical later. Alternatively, you might start with a synopsis and then work from that. If this is your chosen route, I would strongly suggest that you work on a very thorough synopsis and use the exercises in this book to create a strong storyline, interesting characters and a suitable dramatic language.

The disadvantage of the original story is twofold. Firstly, there is the complexity. As I pointed out earlier, writing a musical is an incredibly complex undertaking and I find it is made considerably easier by fashioning it from another source. Secondly, there is a commercial question. If your musical has a completely original story, then you are going to a producer without the one thing that might interest him: namely a story that he is already aware of, or familiar with.

There is a reason why so many movies have been adapted into stage musicals: audiences know the titles, the stories and can delight in the way in which they have been musicalised. It is self-evidently a different piece of work, but when they are spending their money, it is much easier to get them to part with it for something they are familiar with. If you do manage to crack the completely original musical, it can be the most satisfying creation. As Richard Rodgers wrote about *Allegro*:

> An original concept gives you the feeling of special pride, and you don't have to worry about a playwright approving or disapproving of what you've done to his creation. It's all yours, and if you can pull it off, the mere fact that it's difficult to do makes the success all the more rewarding.

# A Thought

One further question is always worth pondering about adaptations, especially from novels or plays: is there a good reason why the original author did not write their story in a musical form in the first place? For example, Oscar Wilde and the musical-comedy partnership Gilbert and Sullivan all lived at roughly the same time (Wilde and Sullivan died the same year), and yet there have been many attempts at musicals based on stories by Wilde. My own feeling is that had Wilde wished to write a musical (which at that time would have been an opera or operetta) there would have been any number of collaborators lining up to work with him, but he chose plays, short stories and poetry as his forms. Musical adaptation of Wilde's best works, such as *The Importance of Being Earnest* and *The Picture of Dorian Gray* have crashed and burned.

Consider Charles Dickens, who lived a little earlier, but could have also written for the theatre he loved. Whilst *Oliver!* has proven a durable success, who now remembers *Mr Quilp*, the musical version of *The Old Curiosity Shop*, or the thirteen-performance Broadway flop, *Copperfield*? Indeed, the success of *Oliver!* led to a rash of copycat Dickens adaptations, and without it we might have been spared the endless *Great Expectations* and *A Tale of Two Cities* debacles. You have to ask yourself what it is you are going to bring to this piece that Dickens or Wilde, or any original author, did not. That is not to say do not attempt such adaptations: just ask what is your unique take. Sometimes they can work. For example, I worked on a workshop of a musical version of *A Tale of Two Cities* set during the 1989 Romanian revolution called *The Last Ceausescu*, and there is an interesting film of *Great Expectations* set in modern New York.

Tim Rice and Andrew Lloyd Webber took possibly the world's best-known story and had a very strong attitude to it. Their concept was to treat Jesus Christ as a modern-day rock star. It was as simple as it was brilliant, and in doing so, they chose a concept that meant that it was completely logical for this piece to be a musical. The result, *Jesus Christ Superstar*, is a modern classic.

It doesn't have to be a shift in time frame or musical style; it might be in setting, or in theme, or in focusing on a minor character in the book (I have always thought there is an interesting drama in the story of Miss Havisham from *Great Expectations*). Whatever you do, adopt a strong attitude to the source material, so that you can fashion something uniquely yours from someone else's work.

---

### Change One Aspect

Take a novel or story that is out of copyright. Change one major aspect of the work (time frame, lead character, location, etc.) in order to conceive a treatment for a musical. Might that change make your story more suitable for a musical or less?

---

# 4
# *Foundations*

# *Foundations*

Never forget that any musical is drama. Some musicals are certainly better drama than others, just as some plays are better drama than others. But the basics of theatre apply just as much to musicals as they do to plays.

A musical is a very specific style of play, but it is a play all the same. That makes every member of your writing team a playwright. Alan Ayckbourn refers to playwriting as a 'Crafty Art', and that pretty much captures it.* To write a musical, you need to understand both the craft and art of playwriting, and then you need to be able to write the songs and musical material to enhance the playwriting, not to distract or diminish it.

If one describes a musical as a play with songs, that does not mean that the songs are just frivolous additions. The best musicals tell their stories as only a musical can. This is because the writers who create them understand the form, know how to work within it and use its strengths to their advantage. This is how they know how to create a musical that adds value to the source material. A great musical would be a lesser piece in any other form.

This chapter is about the basics of playwriting with specific reference to writing a musical, and it will help you think about story and plot. The traditional approach to writing a musical is that the bookwriter will write a play, without songs, and present it to the composer and lyricist, to add the songs. This is often a surprise to songwriters who are keen to get writing, but there is a good reason why this is the best way to write: because the musical is a play.

---

\* There are many good books on playwriting. I find David Edgar's *How Plays Work* and Alan Ayckbourn's *The Crafty Art of Playmaking* particularly useful. These, and others, are listed in the Bibliography.

## Aristotle's Elements

Back near the birth of drama, around 330 BC, the Greek philosopher Aristotle wrote a document called *Poetics*, which has formed the foundation for pretty much all literary criticism ever since. Although he was writing specifically about tragedy, his work on the elements of drama is still the touchstone for playwrights today.

Aristotle identified six elements of tragedy (or drama), which he arranged in order of importance. They were:

- Plot
- Character
- Thought
- Speech
- Melody
- Spectacle

### *Plot*

Aristotle identified this as the 'structure of incidents'. These incidents must be logical, even if they come about by surprise and are then explained to be logical. Plot should also include a change in fortune for the protagonist.

### *Character*

He stated that the lead character should be identified as 'good'. By stating that the protagonist should be good, Aristotle meant that even if he does bad things, the audience must be able to understand why the protagonist has behaved in this way.

Aristotle wrote that characters should be appropriate and consistent. By 'appropriate', he meant that if a character is supposed to be wise, he is unlikely to be young (the Greeks put great emphasis on the wisdom of age). By 'consistent', he meant that if a character has a function or job, such as being a soldier or nurse, they must behave accordingly, so these examples are unlikely to be scared of blood. Aristotle also wrote that it is better if a character does not change their opinion too much, in order not to confuse the audience. He wrote that if characters need to be inconsistent, then this should be explained as a character trait; they need to be 'consistently inconsistent'.

## Thought

Today, 'thought' is more commonly called 'philosophy' or 'ideas'. Aristotle believed that ideas were important to the success of a play.

## Speech

As in dialogue, but also including lyrics, Aristotle believed that nearly all plot, character and philosophy onstage is communicated by speech.

## Melody

This refers to the sounds of a play. When Aristotle wrote *Poetics*, the Greek chorus, who always sang their lines, were an essential element of performance. In the twentieth century, the role of music and song in drama has diminished, but it is alive and well in the musical, where it is a vital element.

## Spectacle

This refers to the visual images onstage. Aristotle says this is the least important element because it is 'least connected with the work of the poet [playwright]'. Spectacle does not have to be about special effects: it can just as easily be about actors pulling a few props out of a trunk and beginning to tell a story. That, too, is spectacle.

---

### Aristotle's Elements

Choose a musical and a non-musical play that you know well. Make a list of Aristotle's six elements and consider the importance of each element in both the play and the musical.

---

When thinking about the modern musical it is easy to see how important these six elements still are, although it is equally easy to see how, in some musicals, spectacle has moved high up the list of importance and thought has moved down. Since the naturalists at the end of the nineteenth century, playwrights have debated whether character or plot is the most important in modern drama. Many playwrights who don't write musicals believe in the primacy of character over plot, but I think one of the distinguishing features of musical theatre is that it is best when plot-driven. Perhaps this is because character can be more easily communicated through song than through dialogue, and so the non-musical scenes tend to focus on the plot. The musical is one form in which the Shakespearean device of the soliloquy (solo) is still accepted, and perhaps that is why musicals still value plot so highly.

Think about the drama of your story. Drama is created by a character wanting to do something (which David Edgar calls a 'project'), and an obstacle is in their way (which he calls a 'contradiction' or a 'reversal'). Put simply, true drama can almost always be expressed in a sentence that uses the word *'wants'* followed soon by the word *'but'*. So *Cinderella* becomes: 'Cinderella *wants* to go to the ball, *but* her sisters won't let her.' *Company* becomes: 'Bobby *wants* to be loved, *but* cannot commit to one person.' *Nine* becomes: 'Guido *wants* to make a movie, *but* his personal life is driving him insane.' *Hello, Dolly!* becomes: 'Dolly *wants* to marry again, *but* she has to let go of the past.' Can you capture your story in a sentence like this? If not, do you have enough drama to power your tale?

---

### 'Wants' and 'Buts'

Reduce some musicals you know well to a sentence using 'wants' and 'but', like the ones above. Now see if you can do it with the story you plan to turn into a musical.

---

---

**Mini-Musical**

This exercise is especially useful if you are working with new collaborators. A YouTube clip can be ten minutes long. Write a sentence using a 'project' and 'reversal', like the ones above (e.g. Fred wants to love Nellie, but is married to Anna). Then expand it into a musical scene of less than ten minutes. How does the drama resolve? Video or audio record your piece and post it on YouTube if you want to. You will get an excellent sense of accomplishment, the chance to try out your working relationship and your writing style, and have something to show your friends.

---

## Story and Plot

In playwriting, there is a distinction between *Story* and *Plot*:

- *Story* is the events that happen in chronological order.
- *Plot* is the selection of the events that the playwright uses, and this implies causality (that one event causes the next).

E.M. Forster described it like this: 'The King died and the Queen died is *story*; the King died and the Queen died of grief is *plot*.'

Playwrights select the parts of the story that they wish to use, and by doing so they use their artistic judgement to decide what it is that they want to draw from the story and say about it. Different playwrights make different choices. The late-nineteenth-century naturalistic playwrights generally selected a few short periods of time to show onstage, in which events from the past (previous events in the *story*) would have an impact on the present (current events in the *story*). Different writers selected different aspects of the story, depending on their own interests and preoccupations.

Take, for example, the play *Mrs Warren's Profession* by George Bernard Shaw. This is a late-nineteenth-century naturalistic play which takes place in four acts. Acts One and Two have their stage time on the same day, which is a Tuesday.

Act Three is the next morning, and Act Four is the early afternoon of the following Saturday. In the course of these four acts, Mrs Warren's daughter, Vivie, discovers that her mother has made her substantial wealth through operating a chain of brothels across Europe. She is accepting of this as the only way her mother could improve her circumstances, but when she finds out that the brothels are still running, despite the fact that her mother has more than adequate wealth, she resolves never to see her again. This is a simple story, which I have outlined in two sentences, but Shaw's choices determine that this is a polemical play, with substantial argument about the choices available to women in a patriarchal capitalist society at the end of the nineteenth century. Notice also how the relatively short time frame of the *plot* (five days) belies the long time frame of the *story* (thirty years). Mrs Warren gives lengthy monologues about her past when she explains her choices, but the audience only hears about it.

This is typical of drama of this period. Late-nineteenth-century writers tended to write about their own preoccupations. Shaw was preoccupied by a false morality that denied a sordid reality whilst allowing it to continue. But every playwright finds an outlet for his own preoccupations; every writer makes a story about something different; each writer draws a different plot from the same story. David Edgar describes this as the *currency* of the play, but many American writers describe it as the *take* on the material. It all comes down to the same thing: what is your play about?

We can imagine what different playwrights might make of the same story of Mrs Warren. Shaw's currency is disillusion (in this case, Vivie's disillusion with her mother). Ibsen's currency is often exposure, so his version of this story might revolve around the exposure of the shame of Mrs Warren's profession, something Shaw underplays. Chekhov's currency is often regret at lost opportunities, so his version of the story might be about how Mrs Warren regrets the situation she has put herself in, and didn't take opportunities in her past. All these three writers write plots that involve considerable backstory, so in all three of these cases, the audience is likely to be presented with a play in which the plot takes place over a short time frame, but the story over a long one. Brecht, on the other hand, does not deal in the past; his currency is the choices made by individuals at any given moment, and he asks the audience to understand these choices, but not necessarily to agree with them. Brecht's version of this story, then, would begin with the young Miss Vavasour (later Mrs Warren) discovering the difficulties of her position, and then setting out to change them, beginning with going into prostitution herself and then starting her chain of brothels. The story and the plot would use the same time frame and Brecht would choose the moments in which Mrs Warren would have to make key decisions, to dramatise. Shakespeare's currency is like Brecht's. He would probably deal in Mrs Warren's ambition as a tragic flaw, and would use multiple stories to draw parallels with Mrs Warren's choices.

One question I always return to when writing and mentoring writers, is: 'What is this show about?' By that I mean, what are your preoccupations that attract you to this story? What is your currency? When Richard and I were writing our musical adaptation of *The Wind in the Willows*, we kept coming back to 'What is the musical about?' It seemed to be an incredibly gentle pastoral with no real subject, but as I read it and re-read it, it became clear to me that what I wanted to write about was family, and how a group of disparate people, in this case animals of different species, could come together in mutual support to make a family of their own.

### Currency

What is the currency of your piece? Along with your collaborators, each write down in one sentence what you think your musical is about. Don't show each other until you have written your own sentence. Then show each other and debate. You could be there all night!

Don't worry if you haven't made that decision yet. We will return to it, and sometimes you don't discover it until later in the process.

## The 'Needs' of the Musical

Lehman Engel (1910–82) was a composer and musical director during the 'Golden Age' of the Broadway musical. He also wrote some of the first books to consider the process of writing a musical and he founded the BMI Lehman Engel Musical Theater Workshop. Engel considered that there were six 'needs' of a musical and, whilst he was writing at the beginning of the 1970s and some of these ideas may now seem a little outdated, I think it is always worth considering how your choice of story measures against these needs. We might easily think of them as Engel's Elements of the Musical, in the way that we think of Aristotle's Elements of Drama. Engel said that a musical needed:

- Feeling
- Subplot
- Romance
- Lyrics and Particularisation
- Music
- Comedy

*Feeling*

A musical needs a story with a strong emotional content, rather than an intellectualised one. Music appeals to the emotional side of our characters, and so a story with a slight emotional content is likely to be difficult to 'make sing'. Engel believed that feeling was at the heart of all great art.

*Subplot*

A musical needs a secondary story that runs parallel to the main plot, and also illuminates it. These are found in the musicals of Broadway's 'Golden Age' and are most notable in the early works of Rodgers and Hammerstein where, for example, the subplot of *Oklahoma!*, Ado Annie's love triangle with Will Parker and Ali Hakim, is a lightweight mirror to the more serious main love triangle of Curly, Laurey and Jud.

Similarly, the relationship between *Carousel*'s Carrie and Enoch reflects the relationship between Julie and Billy. In recent years the subplot has often been considered dated, and many musicals are now written without subplots, such as *Evita* and *Jesus Christ Superstar*.

### Romance

A musical doesn't only need romance of the 'boy meets girl' type, but also of the generic type. Closely related to 'feeling', romance might be a liaison, a setting or a style. One might argue that the Midsummer 'Jellicle Ball' that lasts all night in *Cats* is deeply romantic, where the musical contains no 'romantic entanglements'. Engel emphasises this by choosing the example of *Hair* (the romance of self-discovery) and *1776* (the romance of high ideals).

### Lyrics and Particularisation

A musical needs lyrics with specificity to the dramatic situation, focusing on appropriateness to character. Musical-theatre lyrics work because they are specific to the situation, and the more specific they are, the more successful they will be in dramatic terms. Does your story allow for specific character songs? Of course it does, unless you have very dull characters. One of the joys of musical theatre is that songs that one might hear out of context – on the radio, or in concert – take on a different patina of meaning when sung in their original contexts.

### Music

That a musical needs music might seem obvious, but Engel's question was: is there a *need* for the music? He believed that the music should be as specific to the character as the lyrics should be. Engel believed that the music should play a vital role in the storytelling and he also put great emphasis on the individuality of the composer's style.

*Comedy*

However dark the story, without the light there is no dark. It is as simple as that. I believe this is true of all theatre. Shakespeare's greatest tragedies have comic characters and moments.

The chances are that the story you choose will have at least some of these elements, or you would not have been attracted to it in the first place. Sometimes, the 'needs' may be emphasised in the way you treat the story. For example, *Sweeney Todd's* 'Johanna' song near the top of Act Two is a deeply romantic moment because of the way that Sondheim has treated it, emphasising the deep sense of calm that Sweeney achieves through his murders. Together with Hugh Wheeler, Sondheim doesn't shy away from the comic possibilities of the tale, not only in the overtly comic character of Mrs Lovett, but also in the treatment of the shaving contest, of Pirelli, and in other small moments such as when Sweeney has to let a potential victim escape. In this darkest of tales, Sondheim reaches the pinnacle of his comic-songwriting career in 'A Little Priest'. Other writers might have made different choices, but Sondheim is aware that black humour can increase the tension of the thriller.

Aristotle and Engel agreed that drama is at its best when there is an element of time compression. Aristotle believed that all plots should take place in no more than twenty-four hours, and Engel wrote that musicals tend to work best when they have short onstage time spans. *West Side Story* takes place in three days, *Oklahoma!* takes place in one day, except for the final scene which is three weeks later, and *The Rocky Horror Show*, *On the Town* and *Hello, Dolly!* all take place in twenty-four hours. Some epic musicals, from *Show Boat* to *The Color Purple*, take place over very long time spans, but Lehman Engel points out that a good general rule is that the shorter the time span, the better. I think that one reason for this is that the greater the time compression, the greater the emotional stakes appear to be, so the easier it is for characters to sing.

## Diegetic and Non-Diegetic Songs

When considering the role of music and lyrics in a musical, as Engel did, a writer has to be aware of whether the musical will have moments that are diegetic or non-diegetic.

*Diegetic* means 'of performance' and refers to moments in a musical or play where the characters are self-consciously performing, such as Sally Bowles' performances in the Kit Kat Klub of *Cabaret*, or Maria von Trapp teaching the children to sing with 'Do-Re-Mi' in *The Sound of Music*. If a character is not aware that they are performing, such as when the nuns sing 'How Do You Solve a Problem Like Maria?', then this is referred to as *non-diegetic*. Obviously, if a story contains opportunities for diegetic songs, then adapting it as a musical has some logic. Many musicals mix diegetic and non-diegetic songs. In *Carousel*, for example, 'If I Loved You' and 'Soliloquy' are non-diegetic, but 'You'll Never Walk Alone' and 'That Was a Real Nice Clambake' are diegetic because the characters are aware that they are singing them. It is rare to find a musical that is entirely non-diegetic, although *Sunset Boulevard* is one (if the characters are not aware that they are singing at the New Year's scene). It is equally rare to find a musical where all the songs are diegetic, although this is exactly the decision that Bob Fosse made when adapting *Cabaret* for the movie version. The stage musical mixed diegetic and non-diegetic songs, the film has only diegetic songs.

---

### Diegetic and Non-Diegetic Songs

Take a musical you know well. In which of the songs are the characters aware that they are singing? These are the diegetic numbers. In which of them are they not aware that they are singing? These are the non-diegetic numbers. Make a list of each. Sometimes you will find that it is very difficult to tell which is which.

---

## Produceability

I believe that a musical only really exists when it is performed for an audience. A musical is such a live and collaborative art form that reading it, playing the music or listening to the score can never capture the experience of watching it in performance. I am not interested in writing musicals or plays that are never going to be performed. I have always chosen subjects that I believe an audience will be interested in seeing. I like to think about what I call the 'produceability' of a musical before I write it.

Musicals are expensive to produce. Even a small musical in a London 'fringe' theatre is likely to leave little change from £20,000 ($32,000) and these figures aren't going to go down any time soon. The most expensive musical in the history of Broadway, at the time of writing, *Spider-Man: Turn Off the Dark*, checked in at a budget of more than $70 million. That's five times the GDP of the world's smallest nation!*

As a writer you are in the business of persuading a producer to risk this money and a lot of time and energy to earn a return on this money. A producer is only likely to do so if he believes that he can persuade investors to put their money into the production. Investors are only going to do this if they believe a sufficient audience can be persuaded to part with the price of admission to repay the investment. A writer forgets this at their peril.

This is not to say that you should write only what you think a producer will produce. If you do, you will probably write a musical similar to one that a producer has already brought to the stage, and that way lies derivative dross. Many of the most successful musicals, from *Show Boat* to *Spring Awakening*, have been innovative, but it is worth considering the factors that a producer will consider before you start to write. Too many musicals are written without the writer thinking about the producer's role.

I believe that the elements of produceability are:

* Subject Matter
* Originality and Quality
* Scale and Cast Size

---

* Tuvalu, since you ask.

- Casting
- Good Times
- Audience Profile

## Subject Matter

The subject matter must engage and excite the producer, and this will be because he believes an audience will also be engaged and excited by it. This is a purely subjective decision. If you can interest the producer, you can interest an audience.

## Originality and Quality

Despite their commercial reputation, producers will always be attracted to quality and originality. Producing theatre is a risky business, but regardless of his financial success, a producer will always be willing to stand by a show he can be proud of. Hal Prince may have produced *Pacific Overtures* and lost all the investment, but he is still proud to have produced something so original.

## Scale and Cast Size

You need to think about the scale of your musical before you begin writing. Many novice writers set out with ambitious plans to write the next Broadway hit, and write on a large scale that makes production very difficult. Bear in mind that the unknown writer who has his first musical produced on Broadway or the West End is very rare. If you are writing your first show, maybe it is best to limit yourself to four or five performers and three or four musicians. If you write a good musical at that scale, producers will be happy to consider your larger projects.

## Casting

Any producer is going to look at the cast list and think about the lead parts and the featured roles. A producer will consider casting as a way of attracting an audience. What roles does your show offer? Some subjects automatically offer possibilities: biographical musicals, for example, offer a meaty lead role. Sometimes it is cameo or supporting roles that offer opportunities for casting. After its first cast, *Wicked* has generally cast 'star names' as Madame Morrible and the Wizard rather than the two lead roles.

## Good Times

It may sound trite, but people like to have a good time, and producers, for all you may hear, are only human. Think about your show – what are the aspects of your work that are going to give the audience that rush that comes from truly great musical theatre? It might not be a musical comedy, but is it going to be a good night out? Whether you have ballet sequences, comic characters or amazing power ballads, ask yourself this: 'Are the audience in for a good time?'

## Audience Profile

Think about who your audience are going to be. Who is going to want to buy a ticket for your show? What age group is it likely to appeal to? What are their tastes likely to be? But write about what you are passionate about. If you share your passion, you may well ignite it in others.

As a general rule, people go to the theatre most between the ages of thirty-five and sixty-five. Research shows that up until the age of approximately thirty-five, people spend any disposable income on items such as a house, a car, the cost of children, etc. At around this age, they have often acquired most of these physical items and begin to spend their excess income on buying 'experiences'. This is why the markets for certain types of holidays are heavily dominated by the over-thirty-fives, and it may also go to explain why jukebox musicals using songs popular in the youth of the over-thirty-fives have also succeeded. After the age of sixty-five, theatregoing tails off as people become less mobile, and sometimes have less disposable income. It is a sad truth, but getting large numbers of young people to go to the theatre has always proven difficult, but don't underestimate the over-thirty-fives. Bear in mind, too, that some shows simply find their own audience in other age groups: *Wicked* and *Legally Blonde* are two shows that rely heavily on younger audience members.

---

### Produceability

If you are writing your first show, or if you have not yet had a show produced, try and conceive a show that is strong on produceability. Limit yourself to a cast of four and only a piano as accompaniment. Make sure the story has interesting subject matter, has audience appeal and will be a good night out. Most importantly, aim for originality and quality in your conception. See what stories you come up with. Whatever the story is, if you decide to write it, you will stand a better chance of getting the show produced.

---

## Comedy

In the section above, I mentioned 'Good Times', and it may be that you want to write a very fun piece, a musical comedy.

How do you write 'funny'? How do you make your script amusing to an audience? This is a particularly relevant question when writing a musical, because the history of the modern musical is traced back to the history of musical comedy. It wasn't until the era of Rodgers and Hammerstein that the more serious 'musical play' became popular. Even today, many musicals are musical comedies. Every Tony Award for Best Musical from 2001 to 2005 was won by a musical comedy: *The Producers, Thoroughly Modern Millie, Hairspray, Avenue Q* and *Spamalot*.

Aristotle's elements are just as relevant, but comedy has its own extra foundations. Comedy isn't something you can 'tack on to' a script. In order to be funny, your show must be built on a comic premise. This is an intrinsically funny idea, which is based, as most comedy is, on the 'gap' between comic reality and reality. So, the comic premise of *The Producers* is that two theatre producers have a great idea to produce the worst show ever on Broadway. That's something no theatre producer would ever do, yet because Mel Brooks finds a logical reason for them to do so (greed), it becomes a comedy mine full of comic diamonds. The comic premise of *Avenue Q* is that it is a *Sesame Street*-style show that deals with adult themes. The comedy comes from the incongruity of seeing the type of characters remembered from childhood TV in adult situations.

Comic premises occur when characters come into conflict with their expectations. This might be due to:

- A situation
- Another person
- Something within themselves

*Situational Premises*

Comic premises due to a situation, or situational comedy, arise in two scenarios:

1. The Ordinary Hero in a Crazy World/Situation
2. The Crazy Hero in an Ordinary World/Situation

In the first of these, the ordinary world of the hero is a realistic world, and in the second of these the ordinary world of the hero is a non-realistic world. The comedy is in the gap between them.

An example of the ordinary hero in the crazy world would be the relatively sane Leo Bloom plunged into the crazy world of Max Bialystock's producing scheme (*The Producers*), or Seymour Krelborn the mild-mannered florist tending to a bloodsucking plant that is bringing him fame, fortune and love (*Little Shop of Horrors*).

Examples of the crazy hero in the ordinary world might be the film *Elf*, in which a man who has lived as one of Santa's elves comes to New York, or the Disney movie *Enchanted* in which the heroine of a Disney movie comes to New York (New York is often an ordinary world in these scenarios).

Not surprisingly, many television 'sitcoms' (situation comedies) are based on one of these two scenarios, among them *Mork and Mindy, Third Rock from the Sun* (which are both based on the scenario of aliens on Earth), *The Fresh Prince of Bel Air* and *Fawlty Towers*.

## Character Premises

Comic premises that exist due to another character arise when there are gaps between a character's expectation and the behaviour of the other character. The classic example of this is Neil Simon's *The Odd Couple*, in which chaotic Oscar invites the neurotically tidy Felix to come and stay. Oscar expects that Felix will also be untidy, but he is not. Mel Brooks finds comedy in the gap between Leo Bloom's expectations of his life as a Broadway producer, and the crazy reality of a Max Bialystock production. Sometimes both characters have a gap between their expectation and the reality, such as Danny DeVito and Arnold Schwarzenegger as spectacularly different *Twins*. This kind of 'buddy movie' comedy is best exercised when you can throw your characters into situations they cannot easily get out of.

Finally, there is an internal comic premise for a character. This is when a character carries the comic premise within himself. This might be externalised, as it is in *Tootsie* or *Big*, in which there is a physical transformation from man to woman or from child to adult. It might also be a trait that causes him difficulties that can be explored comically, such as Hugh Grant's character in *Four Weddings and a Funeral*, who cannot commit to marriage.

When I wrote a new book for Lionel Bart's *Twang!!*, the brief was that it had to be a musical comedy about Robin Hood. I knew that I wanted to have a twin-hero story, so I built the show on two separate comic premises. The first was that everybody around him viewed Robin Hood as a hero, but that he had lost all his heroic ability and was not able to admit it; he had lost his 'twang'. This was an internal comic premise for Robin Hood. The second comic premise was about a young man, Much the Miller's Son, who hates musicals, but when he is forced to join Robin Hood's gang, he finds out that they live in a musical comedy that he cannot escape from. This was a situational comic premise of an ordinary hero in a crazy world. The two together gave me ample scope for comedy throughout the show.

In all of the scenarios mentioned above, there is disappointment and heartache for the protagonist in the gap between their expectations and the reality. I am afraid that humans are remarkably heartless beings, we laugh at other people's pain. In *Avenue Q* there is a wonderful song about this: 'Schadenfreude'. There is a theory that we laugh as a release because we experience pain vicariously through comedy. This does not mean that the more you put your character in pain, the funnier it will be. You must keep logic and truth in the situation and in the character's behaviour, or the audience will cease to believe. But comic premises invariably involve making life difficult for your character. If you want to write comedy, prepare to unleash your vicious side!

---

### Ten Comic Scenarios

Invent ten comic scenarios using situational premises, character premises or internal premises. This sounds a lot, but it is important to generate as many comic ideas as possible and then use the best ones.

Here's one to start you off:

- A native American Indian finds himself in modern Manhattan.

---

## The Elements of the Musical

By combining Aristotle and Engel's Elements with the Elements of Produceability, we might consider that we have a set of eighteen 'Elements for the Musical'. You need to be able to identify that there are possibilities for each of the elements in your story. Only subplot is now arguably unnecessary but still desirable.

The chart below lists all the elements, starting with the most important in the top left box, and moving down to the least important in the bottom-right box. We might think of the table below as the Periodic Table for Musical Theatre:

*Most Important*

| Aristotle | Plot | Character | Thought | Speech | Melody | Spectacle |
|---|---|---|---|---|---|---|
| Engel | Feeling | Subplot | Romance | Lyrics and Particularisation | Music | Comedy |
| Produce-ability | Subject Matter | Originality and Quality | Scale and Cast Size | Casting | Good Times | Audience Profile |

*Least Important*

We can use this collection of elements to analyse musicals.

## *Case Study:* Little Shop of Horrors *by Howard Ashman and Alan Menken*

### *Aristotle*

| Plot | B-movie story about a flesh-eating plant from outer space. Plot has reversal of fortune for the better. |
|---|---|
| Character | Seymour and Audrey are very sympathetic. Seymour is good although he does bad too. |
| Thought | Philosophy of the show is a morality tale warning against temptation and greed. |
| Speech | B-movie speech patterns are amusing. Plant talks in a 'jive' style. |
| Melody | Many sounds, including noise from the plant. Many musical opportunities. |
| Spectacle | The plant grows to an enormous size, realised through puppetry. |

### *Engel*

| Feeling | Seymour and Audrey's relationship is central, but there is a strong emotional attachment to the plant too. |
|---|---|
| Subplot | There is little subplot, except in the relationship between Orin the dentist and Audrey, which is violent. |
| Romance | Seymour and Audrey's relationship goes from work colleagues to lovers, but is doomed. |

| Lyrics and Particularisation | The florist's shop setting gives opportunities: Audrey dreams of 'Somewhere That's Green'. Girl-group doo-wop and Motown-style lyrics are also used. |
|---|---|
| Music | Draws heavily on doo-wop and early Motown. Pop styles from the period of the original movie. |
| Comedy | Heavily comic. The central premise of the man-eating plant nurtured by the good-natured florist is comic. |

## Produceability

| Subject Matter | The Faust tale given a horticultural, musical-comedy treatment. |
|---|---|
| Originality and Quality | Book, music and lyrics all witty and appropriate. Quite original, some similarities to *Rocky Horror*, but more family-orientated. |
| Scale and Cast Size | Cast size of ten, small rock band. Single set with one other setting required. Puppetry potentially expensive. |
| Casting | Two strong lead parts suitable for star names. Mushnik is suitable for an older character actor. The voice of the plant is also a potential casting opportunity. |
| Good Times | The pop music, the girl group, the plant and the plot are all great fun. |
| Audience Profile | Likely to appeal to all ages. Especially of interest to B-movie and Motown fans. |

Now let's look at a very different kind of musical.

## Case Study: The Phantom of the Opera *by Andrew Lloyd Webber and Charles Hart*

### Aristotle

| Plot | Adaptation of a romantic horror novel, with close parallels to the fairytale *Beauty and the Beast*. |
|---|---|
| Character | Christine is sympathetic. Raoul is a classical, but bland romantic hero. The Phantom is an interesting anti-hero who murders but keeps Christine's sympathy. |
| Thought | Philosophy of the show is an appeal for understanding for those scarred by life. |

| Speech | Very little dialogue, and what there is is perfunctory. The language of the sung libretto is very romantic. |
|---|---|
| Melody | Styles of opera are pastiched in four different sections. The show uses the style of romantic operetta. |
| Spectacle | Many opportunities in the opera sections, the chandelier crashing and the journey to the Phantom's lair. |

## Engel

| Feeling | Lushly romantic and operatic, with some comedy. |
|---|---|
| Subplot | Little subplot, the love triangle is central to the entire work. |
| Romance | The musical is proudly romantic and no opportunity for romance is missed or underplayed. |
| Lyrics and Particularisation | The lyrics parody opera libretti and are lushly romantic, with much romantic imagery throughout. |
| Music | Music is witty pastiches in the opera sections, romantic ballads and some early 1980s pop. |
| Comedy | Comedy is found away from the central love triangle, in the theatre managers and opera-diva characters. |

## Produceability

| Subject Matter | Well-known title from film and literature. |
|---|---|
| Originality and Quality | Book, music and lyrics draw heavily on opera influences. |
| Scale and Cast Size | Large-scale cast and production. |
| Casting | One major 'star name' role. Two other lead parts suitable for star names. Featured comedy parts for strong performers. |
| Good Times | Very romantic, lavish spectacle and melodies. |
| Audience Profile | Likely to appeal to romantics and lovers of spectacle. |

**The Periodic Table**

Measure your planned musical against the Periodic Table for Musical Theatre, like the chart above. Reproduce a blank chart, giving yourself space in each of the boxes to write brief notes about the strengths and weaknesses of your story in relation to each of the elements. Don't worry if you can't fill all of it in yet. Some of these answers will only become apparent as you write.

By now you should have a solid conception of the show you want to write. You should have the concept and a strong idea of the story. You should be sure what its strengths are, measured against the elements of the Periodic Table.

Before the bookwriter begins work on the first full draft of the book, the synopsis should be carefully considered in depth by the whole writing team. If this is a commission, it is not uncommon for the producer (or commissioning company) to be involved at this stage too.

Every moment of the synopsis should be discussed. Explore every possibility and keep notes of the good ideas. It was out of a meeting like this that Rodgers and Hammerstein came up with the idea that 'Soliloquy' should begin with Billy Bigelow wondering what his son will be like, and then realising halfway through that the child might just as easily be a girl.

Think about the possibilities for the songs that you are planning. What is the most effective way of treating any moment? If you are planning a full-company production number, how are the ensemble going to be featured in the scene beforehand? What is the stage business of any number? Where and how are you going to use reprises? I have a rule at these sessions: that every idea is valid, however crazy. Note them down, talk them through, and then make the assessment. Out of the craziness, brilliance may flow.

It is not uncommon for some songs to be written once the synopsis has been hammered out, but it is always better to have a draft of the play in front of you when beginning to write. This will generally be a first draft of the book in which the bookwriter will give the work structure. He will also give it many other things, such as the characters and their voices and the theatrical language. At heart, though, it will be the structure that will be most important. This vital element should not be only the work of the bookwriter; composer and lyricist should come together with him to discuss the storytelling and theatrical language. Writing a musical is, above all, collaborative.

Before you start, you must communicate with your collaborators to hammer out a shape and style for the show. You must make sure that your ideas about the piece you want to write are all unified. Only then can you write a great show.

---

### Concept and Story

For your project, complete the concept and story stages. Make sure that you capture the concept of your musical in one sentence. Write a treatment for the story that is between 500 and 1,000 words long. At this stage, write it as a story, don't worry too much about editing it, but focus on the aspects of it that interest you most. Begin to trade in the currency of your work.

---

# 5
# *Structure*

# *Structure*

At the heart of every great musical is a great book. As mentioned earlier, the book is not only the spoken scenes, but refers to the playwriting basics of the work: the structure, the theatrical language and the storytelling. The music and lyrics may be great, but the success or failure of the musical relies on the book. More musicals have been sunk by a bad book than by any other cause. Listen to some cast recordings of famous flops, including the scores to Jerry Herman's *Mack and Mabel*, Sondheim's *Anyone Can Whistle* or Lloyd Webber's *The Beautiful Game*, and you will hear some wonderful songs. But wonderful songs alone do not make a musical; that is about being able to give the audience a theatrical experience with a narrative, in which the songs, the story and the action together engage the audience.

The book is what holds the musical together, and at the heart of the book is the structure.

Structure is to the musical what the skeleton is to the body. It is what will give your work form, and will allow your musical to sing and dance in all its glory. It will stop your musical falling flat, lying like a shapeless lump, gasping for breath.

Getting the structure right is a craft, and if you succeed, you will have the strongest foundation for your musical you can possibly have.

There are many ways of looking at structure for a musical, and many writers have their own idiosyncratic methods. I find that using some of the finest techniques of story analysis developed during the twentieth century has been indispensable in my work. Many of these techniques and theories were developed for, and by, screenwriters, but I have found them incredibly relevant for musical theatre.

I first used this structural model when I led a group of students through the process of creating *Let Him Have Justice*. This musical was based on the true-life story of Derek Bentley, a nineteen-year-old with a mental age of eleven who was hanged for a murder committed by his friend Christopher Craig, aged sixteen, who was, himself, too young to be hanged. The case caused outrage and led, in part, to the abolition of capital punishment in the UK. This piece began as a college project and ended up with a West End run, reviews in the British national press and a cast recording recorded at the legendary Abbey Road Studios. What was remarkable about *Let Him Have Justice* was that, despite the undeniable emotional power of the source material, the audience became engaged in the story at an almost primitive, or instinctive level. People leaving the theatre at the end of the show looked like they had been to a funeral. I first realised that something special was happening with this show when I needed to go behind the scenes, during a duet in the dress rehearsal of the original drama-school project, and found the entire cast sobbing quietly whilst their classmates performed. When the group first chose the story of Bentley for their project I was extremely sceptical, concerned that the piece could easily become mawkish, sentimental and horrifically tasteless. Whilst the piece had an interesting score, with some strong numbers, I put the overall success of the work down to the structural work we did.

Anyone writing a musical hopes to write a show with universal appeal, a show that everybody can relate to. Some stories appear in different forms in many cultures. I have a book of versions of *Cinderella* from around the world that has twenty-four different versions of this tale. In some, a cow or a fish takes the Fairy Godmother's role. How does one write a musical that has the universal appeal of a tale like *Cinderella*?

You may have heard that there are three, four, seven or eight basic plots, and may wonder how they relate to musical theatre. I believe that there are hundreds of plots, but I use work developed by the great story analysts Joseph Campbell and Christopher Vogler in their books *The Hero With a Thousand Faces* and *The Writer's Journey* to help me analyse my own work and to help me structure.

Campbell developed the term the 'monomyth' when analysing stories. With his disciples (of whom Vogler is one), he theorised that all myths contain structural similarities. These similarities are fundamental to the endurance of the myths. Vogler's work, in particular, had a dramatic effect in Hollywood in the 1980s, when he issued a memo outlining twelve major structural stages in stories in films. This was a simplification of Campbell's work, which outlines seventeen such moments, but not all moments appear in all stories.

Academic study around the monomyth is a considerable field and, like a good story, everyone takes the monomyth and makes it their own. I am going to provide the simplest explanation of the theory, in the way I use it to facilitate writing a musical. You should think of the monomyth as a little like the game of chess: it takes an afternoon to master the basics and a lifetime to master the complexities.

Before I outline the twelve stages, there are two things that you should bear in mind:

1. The monomyth is a tool for analysis, not a recipe. You cannot simply move from step to step to step, and come out at the other end with a perfectly structured story. In fact, you should not even think about this until after you have decided upon and written your story as outlined earlier. What it does allow you to do is analyse your story to decide if certain stages are carrying enough weight or if the characters' journeys are strong enough at this point.

2. Depending on your story, some stages will have greater importance than others. For nearly every stage I can cite an example where it either does not appear at all or does not appear 'onstage'. I will point out some of these as we go through.

## Character Archetypes

Regardless of their characteristics, characters have functions within a story. The monomyth identifies similarities between certain types of characters, called archetypes. Remember that not all stories will have all of these archetypes, but most of your major characters will fulfil one of the archetype models.

There are differences between an archetype and a stereotype. Briefly these are:

| Archetype | Stereotype |
|---|---|
| • A typical example of a certain person or thing. | • A widely held but fixed and/or oversimplified image or idea of a particular type of person or thing. |
| • An original which has been imitated. | |
| • In Jungian theory, a primitive mental image inherited from the earliest human ancestors, and supposed to be present in the collective unconscious. | • A person or thing that conforms to such an image. |
| • A recurrent symbol or motif in literature, art, or mythology. | |

Stereotype deals in cliché, whereas archetype deals with the essence of a character. Of course, an archetype can be portrayed as a stereotype – the figure of a 'mentor' is an archetype, but to portray the role as an old man living in a cave has become a stereotype. Stereotypes can also apply to groups of people in society and can be offensive, such as the clichéd stereotype of the camp homosexual.

Your characters will conform to archetypes, as they will fulfil certain roles within the story, but you should avoid stereotypes. If you think your character might be heading towards stereotype you should stop and rethink.

These are the major archetypes:

*The Hero:* Before you can begin analysing the story, you must decide who is your Hero. This is the word that we are going to use for the protagonist. This does not mean that your Hero does things that are necessarily heroic, but it does mean that he is the person that the story is *going to happen to*. Cinderella is the Hero of *Cinderella* – it is her story – but Sweeney Todd is the Hero of *Sweeney Todd*, even though he is a murderer, because it is his story. Remember Aristotle's comments that the Hero doesn't need to be 'good': he needs to be the protagonist – it is his story.

A story can have more than one Hero, but it is rare for it to have more than three. A story with two Heroes is not uncommon; *Chicago*, for example, has two Heroes in Roxie and Velma. You should also be aware that all major characters should be Heroes of their own stories, even if they act as villains (antagonists) or Mentors (teachers) in the tale you are telling, as both Roxie and Velma do at different times.

*The Shadow* is what most people think of as the villain or antagonist – but it is a little more complex than that. The Shadow generally shares many qualities with the Hero, but because the Shadow is attempting to fulfil his own journey as Hero of his own story, the qualities often appear in a negative form. The Ugly Sisters, for example, are very like Cinderella in that they are eligible females of the correct age, but they function as antagonists, or Shadows, to Cinderella.

The re-imagining of well-known stories casting the Shadow as the Hero of their own tale has become very popular recently. The novelist Gregory Maguire has built most of his career on this simple premise, penning novels imagining the story of *Snow White* from the Wicked Queen's point of view, *Cinderella* from the Ugly Sisters' point of view and, of course, *Wicked, The Wizard of Oz* from the Wicked Witch's point of view.

Always remember that your Shadow must be the Hero of his own story. They should completely believe that what they are aiming to achieve is good, even if their world view is flawed. Darth Vader believes that he brings stability to the universe, not that he is inherently evil.

*The Mentor* is a teacher. This character is often, but not
always, older, but he always carries truth and
knowledge that the Hero needs. Sometimes he bears
gifts, totems, or magic that facilitates a development
in the Hero's journey. Mentors come in a myriad of
shapes and sizes, from fairy godmothers to genies to
wise old men in caves. Sometimes they are not even
human (for instance, *Star Wars'* Yoda or *Pocahontas'*
speaking tree, Grandmother Willow). Characters
sometimes fulfil a Mentor role for a period and then
revert to another role, and you can have a Shadow
Mentor, a character who appears to be a teacher, but
who is actually trying to persuade the Hero to act in a
particular way to fulfil the Shadow Mentor's agenda.
In this scenario, it is common for the Hero to reject
the Mentor at some point and treat them as a
straightforward Shadow. Films like *Wall Street* and
*The Devil's Advocate* are good examples of this.
Alternatively, think of the way in which Sweeney Todd
mentors Anthony in the second act of that musical.

*The Shapeshifter* is usually the 'romantic interest'. In
straightforward psychological terms it is the 'anima'
in response to the Hero's 'animus', the halves of each
other that make each other whole. This reflects the
way in which the opposite sexes often have trouble
understanding each other. Shapeshifters often behave
in elusive ways and, surprisingly often, betray the
Hero before discovering the error of their ways and
repenting. They often give off contradictory signals,
attracting the Hero at first then repelling them later,
only to attract them again. If you want to grasp the
notion of the Shapeshifter, think of the James Bond
films. In practically every Bond tale there is an
alluring woman (because our Hero is male) who
seduces Bond, betrays him and repents, either dying
in the process or joining him in a romantic setting as
the final credits roll. Think how the great lovers of
literature initially find each other unfathomable:
*Much Ado About Nothing*'s Beatrice and Benedick, to

*Pride and Prejudice*'s Elizabeth Bennet and Mr Darcy to *Gone With the Wind*'s Scarlett O'Hara and Rhett Butler. In musical theatre you might like to think of *Guys and Dolls*' Sky Masterson and Sarah Brown, or the relationships that Bobby has with his three girlfriends in *Company*.

Shapeshifters often literally shift their physical shape during a story. We are all familiar with the moments in great stories where the leading lady arrives for an event looking surprisingly, unspeakably beautiful, such as Eliza Doolittle's entrance dressed for the ball in *My Fair Lady*. In this musical, Eliza and Henry Higgins act as Shapeshifters to each other.

I consider the Hero, the Shadow, the Mentor and the Shapeshifter to be the major character archetypes. There are three others, which I consider minor archetypes:

*The Herald:* These are characters that bring information, such as the character that delivers the invitations in *Cinderella*. They are peripheral characters that commonly occur in the earlier stages of the story.

*The Threshold Guardian:* These characters guard places and people and restrict access to them. Typically, they test the Hero in order to let them pass to the next stage of their journey. A good example is the Gatekeeper in *The Wizard of Oz*.

*The Trickster:* These characters provide comic relief and are often sidekicks. Think of the Disney sidekick characters like the parrot Iago in *Aladdin* and the mischievous racoon Meeko in *Pocahontas*. Sometimes Tricksters are also Heroes, such as Brer Rabbit. Similarly you might like to think of Cosmo Brown in *Singin' in the Rain* or *South Pacific*'s Luther Billis.

These archetypes make up your cast of characters. This does not make them interesting in themselves; it just gives you a way of analysing their functions.

> **Archetypes**
>
> Take three stories you know well. They can be films, fairytales or novels. Make a list of the five or six lead characters and examine which functional archetype (Mentor, Shapeshifter, etc.) each character fulfils.

## The Stages of the Monomyth

With your cast in mind, let's look at the stages of the monomyth. The monomyth is also referred to as 'The Hero's Journey' because it describes a story as a type of journey that the Hero undertakes. Sometimes, as in *The Wizard of Oz*, this involves a physical journey. Sometimes, in a work like *The Music Man*, the story all takes place in one physical place but the journey is an emotional one, a journey of the heart.

I find it easiest to use the monomyth in a twelve-stage format. Different story analysts use different numbers of stages but I have always found this the simplest version that satisfactorily covers all the major stages. To look at the twelve stages of the monomyth, I am going to consider three major examples: the generic tales of *Cinderella* and *Aladdin*, but sometimes with reference to the Disney version, and *Star Wars*. In a book about musical theatre, it might seem strange to be analysing *Star Wars* (the original film, sometimes known as *Episode IV: A New Hope*), but George Lucas specifically credits the monomyth as an influence in its creation. More specifically, it has particularly strong archetypes that are very clear types: Princess Leia is a classic Shapeshifter – she appears to be a Princess in distress, but later (in the saga) turns out not to be that at all, but to be Luke Skywalker's sister. Obi-Wan Kenobi is a classic Mentor, a mysterious man who is full of wisdom and magic and lives in a cave. Whilst Luke Skywalker looks every bit the Hero, Darth Vader is even dressed as a Shadow. In all the seminars and lectures I have ever done, I have found the use of *Star Wars* incredibly useful to students so have included it here. Maybe one day a student will write a *Star Wars* musical and blame me!

Consider the major casts:

|  | Hero | Shadow | Mentor | Shape-shifter | Herald |
|---|---|---|---|---|---|
| Aladdin | Aladdin | Abanazar/Jafar | Genie | Princess Jasmine | |
| Cinderella | Cinderella | Ugly Sisters | Fairy Godmother | Prince | Invitation Bringer |
| Star Wars | Luke Skywalker | Darth Vader | Obi-Wan Kenobi | Prince Leia | R2-D2 |

## The Twelve Stages

*Stage 1: The Ordinary World*

All stories begin at a place of stability. The Hero lives in a place of stability, where every day is much the same as the last. Often the Hero yearns for more excitement, or to change their life in some way. The key element here is that the situation is ongoing, stable, and that there seems no immediate way of changing it.

---

Aladdin is a poor young man living in a big Arabian city. There appears to be no way to change the circumstances of his poverty.

---

Cinderella is a rich young girl, forced to work as a scullery maid for her Ugly Sisters (and, in some versions, her unpleasant Stepmother). Again, there appears to be no way to change her circumstances.

---

Luke Skywalker is a young man, in presumably stable economic circumstances, a farm boy living on the desert planet Tatooine, who yearns for adventure, but seems unlikely to ever find it.

---

## Stage 2: The Call to Adventure

Something happens to alter the stability of the status quo. This can be any one of a number of events but the key element here is that something alters the stability. This stage often involves a Herald.

| |
|---|
| Aladdin is met by Jafar and asked to accompany him to the Cave of Wonders where he is promised untold wealth. |
| A Herald brings an invitation to the Prince's ball for all eligible young ladies. |
| R2-D2 arrives on Tatooine with a message for Obi-Wan Kenobi. Luke's uncle buys the robot, and when Luke cleans it, he discovers the message. He sets out to find Obi-Wan to return the droid to him. |

This stage is sometimes known as the 'Point of Attack'. It is where the status quo is altered and without it there would be no drama. If the invitation does not arrive, Cinderella will never dream of going to the ball. If R2-D2 had arrived on a different planet, Luke would still be a farm boy.

Do not confuse this with another term you may hear: the 'inciting incident'. This often (but not always) takes place before the story begins, and it is the very first moment of the story. The inciting incident in *Cinderella* is that the Prince decides to throw a ball. The inciting incident in *Star Wars* is the capture of Princess Leia (of which Luke is unaware at the beginning of his story).

## Stage 3: Refusal of the Call

When the challenge is issued to the Hero, or the opportunity arises to change his circumstances, the Hero very often hesitates, or lacks self-belief and feels unable to take on the task. In tales where the Hero is particularly keen to undertake an adventure or is very go-getting, this step may be very small, or in some cases, may not appear.

## Stage 4 (Floating Stage): Meeting the Mentor

| |
|---|
| Aladdin questions whether he should go into the cave and is encouraged by Jafar. |
| Cinderella can't believe that she will be able to go to the ball. |
| Having found Obi-Wan and discovered the hologram of Princess Leia, Luke does not believe that he can leave Tatooine to help rescue the Princess. |

The Hero, full of self-doubt, meets the Mentor who helps him move forward with his journey, often giving him a token of some sort, and, if appropriate to the story, using magic to help him.

Special note: I sometimes refer to this as a 'floating stage' because it is not necessarily fixed in this position in the story. It usually appears somewhere between Stage 1 and 8, but often in this position. Sometimes the Hero knows the Mentor and the Mentor's power right from the start, and sometimes the Mentor may appear very late. This stage may occur simultaneously with another stage.

| | |
|---|---|
| Appears at Stage 7 | Aladdin meets the Genie by rubbing the lamp. |
| Appears at Stage 7 | Cinderella meets the Fairy Godmother. |
| Appears between Stages 2 and 3 | Luke meets Obi-Wan Kenobi and goes with him to Kenobi's cave. Kenobi gives him some information about his father and talks about the Rebellion. |

## Stage 5: Crossing the Threshold

The Hero is persuaded to begin the journey required of him. He leaves the stability of his world and ventures forth into the outer world in which his adventure will take place.

| |
|---|
| Aladdin enters the cave, not sure of what will happen therein. |
| Cinderella, believing that she might be able to go to the ball, begins to make preparations. |
| Luke returns to the farm, to find that Stormtroopers have already been there and murdered his relatives. Believing there is no longer anything for him on Tatooine, he joins Kenobi on his quest. Together they travel to Mos Eisley and arrange for a spaceship. |

## Stage 6: Tests, Allies and Enemies

During this section of the journey, the Hero undertakes a number of tests and meets characters that may be Allies or Enemies. Sometimes, which of these they are is not immediately clear.

Sometimes this section is a very substantial section of the story. In *The Wizard of Oz* it lasts from Dorothy landing in Oz and meeting Glinda (a Mentor) right the way through to being caught by the Wicked Witch of the West. In this stage she meets the Scarecrow, the Tin Man and the Cowardly Lion (Allies), the Gatekeeper (a Threshold Guardian), the Wizard (a Trickster), the Wicked Witch of the West (Shadow/Enemy), and the Flying Monkeys (Trickster Enemies). She is tested by the poppy field and by the Wizard's challenge.

> Aladdin moves through the cave, and meets the Flying Carpet (Ally). He is tested in getting the lamp and then by being trapped in the cave by Jafar (Shadow/Enemy).

> Cinderella is tested by the Ugly Sisters (Shadows/Enemies) who challenge her to complete certain tasks before she can go to the ball, and also tell her that she must have something to wear. Disney's version of this story adds weight to this stage by having the mice act as Allies to Cinderella by having them make her a dress.

> Luke meets Han Solo and Chewbacca (Allies). He is tested by Obi-Wan on the journey. The Death Star traps the spaceship and Luke is again tested as he attempts to rescue Princess Leia.

The next two stages are interdependent and are therefore treated together:

*Stage 7: Preparation for the Supreme Ordeal*

*Stage 8: The Supreme Ordeal*

At this point in the story the Hero faces his biggest challenge so far. This is a test that will often threaten his life and will ultimately result in his transformation or rebirth as a new kind of person. This is known as the Supreme Ordeal. Normally the wish the Hero made at the beginning of the tale will play a part in the nature of the Supreme Ordeal. Every Hero's Supreme Ordeal is unique to that Hero. The stage prior to this is known as the Preparation for the Supreme Ordeal, or sometimes The Approach to the Cave (in ancient myths, the Supreme Ordeal often takes place inside a cave such as the labyrinth in which Theseus kills the Minotaur or the Gorgon's lair). The Preparation stage is usually one of self-doubt and recognising the dangers that the Supreme Ordeal threatens. Although the stage is called the Supreme Ordeal it is not necessarily about a major challenge, but about the moment of transformation or rebirth; both Aladdin and Cinderella long for their transformation.

| Preparation for the Supreme Ordeal | The Supreme Ordeal | The Rebirth of the Hero |
|---|---|---|
| Seemingly alone in the cave, Aladdin rubs the lamp and releases the Genie. | The Genie offers Aladdin three wishes. Aladdin wishes to become a prince and is transformed. | Aladdin is reborn from a street urchin imprisoned in a cave to a wealthy prince who is free. |
| The Ugly Sisters rip Cinderella's dress and leave for the ball. She is left desolate, believing her dreams are shattered. The Fairy Godmother arrives. | The Fairy Godmother transforms Cinderella and sends her to the ball, but with a proviso that she must return by midnight. | Cinderella is transformed from a scullery maid into the beautiful princess of her dreams. She attends the ball and the prince falls in love with her. She leaves at midnight, leaving her shoe. |
| Luke enters the Death Star and finds Princess Leia, but there appears to be no way out when they are attacked by Stormtroopers. They dive into a garbage chute and appear stuck there. | In the garbage chute, Luke is attacked by an unseen creature, dragged under the water, and appears to have drowned. He then returns, having killed the creature. This is symbolic of him having become the triumphant Hero he always dreamed he would be. | Luke is transformed from a farm boy into a heroic young man. |

## Stage 9: Reward

Having passed through the rebirth of the Supreme Ordeal, the Hero then receives the Reward. This is the most reflective stage in the journey, and is the time for the Hero to take stock of what they have achieved. Often, at this stage in the story, the Hero appears to have accomplished the objective with which they started their journey.

---

Aladdin, now Prince Ali, goes to meet the Princess and can be accepted at court.

---

The morning after the ball, Cinderella remembers the wonderful time she had, and believes that, her dream having been fulfilled, she is satisfied with her life.

---

Luke Skywalker rescues Princess Leia from the Death Star and they return to the rebel base, but with news that the Empire has a weapon big enough to destroy any planet.

---

Note how, at this stage, there is an unexpected complication arising from the Hero having achieved their initial objectives. Cinderella has been to the ball, but does not expect the Prince to follow her. Princess Leia has been rescued but the news about the Death Star is beyond anything Luke might have considered when he was back on Tatooine. He simply wanted to rescue the Princess. The story has just got a whole lot more complicated.

## Stage 10: The Road Back

Having seemingly accomplished his wish, the Hero realises that there is unfinished business. This stage is often characterised by a chase sequence in which the threat of the Shadow hangs over the Hero, or where the Shadow pursues the Hero. At this stage, the Hero realises that he must resolve the unfinished consequences of the Supreme Ordeal.

Aladdin is unmasked as the street urchin by Jafar whose true intentions are made clear, and he threatens Aladdin with death.

The Prince announces that he will search the kingdom to find the owner of the glass slipper and marry the girl. Cinderella is scared that her sisters will discover her trip to the ball and the sisters lock her in a tower.

Luke agrees to join the rebel forces to destroy the Death Star to make the universe safe.

## Stage 11: The Final Conflict (or Resurrection)

This is the climax to the story. In this stage the Hero uses the lessons he has learned through the journey, draws on the wisdom bestowed upon him by the Mentor and finally defeats the adversary in order that he can return the world to stability. He must resolve any unforeseen consequences of the Supreme Ordeal.

No longer pretending to be Prince Ali, Aladdin uses knowledge he gained from the Genie to defeat Jafar. Because he has been truly heroic, he wins the Princess.

Released from the tower by the mice, Cinderella is able to try on the slipper and, in doing so, is proved to be the Prince's true love.

Using the Force as a guide, Luke Skywalker is able to drop his missile into the small gap required to take it straight to the heart of the Death Star. Darth Vader is defeated and left spinning off into space (leaving the way open for a sequel) and the Death Star is destroyed, leaving the universe safe (until the sequel).

## Stage 12: Return to Stability

The threat defeated, the Hero's world is now returned to a place of stability.

This might be the same stability of the Ordinary World of Stage 1, but if it is, then the Hero will have learned something from their journey. In *The Wizard of Oz*, Dorothy returns to the farm just as it was, but now she has learned that 'There's no place like home'.

It might be a new place of new stability in which the Hero finds their new or real place in the world. Cinderella's breeding and natural class, for example, shine through, making her an ideal Princess, and her new stability is in the castle.

---

Aladdin, proved as a noble young man and having learned his lesson to be himself, becomes the Prince to Jasmine's Princess.

---

Cinderella is chosen to marry the Prince and become his Princess, leaving the Ugly Sisters' house to live in the castle.

---

Luke Skywalker is fêted as a hero of the rebellion for having destroyed the Death Star. The universe appears to be safe.

---

Note how much further each of these characters has come from their initial desire:

---

Aladdin only wanted to be recognised as someone more than a beggar, but he ended up becoming a heroic Prince.

---

Cinderella only wanted to go to the ball, but she ended up becoming a Princess.

---

Luke wanted to rescue Princess Leia but he ended up saving the universe.

---

You sometimes hear films and plays being talked about in terms of a 'three-act structure'. The monomyth correlates to this in roughly four stages per act. Having got to the end of our story, here is a summary of the monomyth, with the three-act structure indicated. We will also use this three-act structure throughout the rest of the book.

Act One runs from the Ordinary World to the point at which the Hero Crosses the Threshold and begins the journey. Act Two runs until the end of the Supreme Ordeal. Act Three runs from the recovery from the Supreme Ordeal to the end of the story. Sometimes these acts go by other names: Beginning, Middle and End!

Please do not believe that these act divisions necessarily have very clear delineation. Often it is difficult to find a clear point where Act One becomes Act Two, or Act Two becomes Act Three.

Similarly, do not believe that these acts have anything to do with where the interval might fall in a regular two-act musical presented with one interval. We will look at interval placement later.

| | | | | |
|---|---|---|---|---|
| **Act One** | 1. *The Ordinary World:* All stories begin at a place of stability. Often the Hero yearns for more excitement, or to change their life in some way. | 2. *Call to Adventure:* Something happens to alter the status quo and challenge the Hero to make a journey. | 3. *Refusal of the Call:* The Hero very often hesitates, or lacks the self-belief to take on the task. | 4. *(Floating Stage) Meeting the Mentor:* The Hero, full of self-doubt, meets the Mentor who helps him move forward with his journey, often giving him a token of some sort, and sometimes using magic to help him. |
| **Act Two** | 5. *Crossing the Threshold:* The Hero is persuaded to begin the journey required of him. He leaves the stability of his world and ventures forth into the outer world in which his adventure will take place. | 6. *Test, Allies and Enemies:* During this section of the journey, the Hero undertakes a number of tests and meets characters that may be Allies or Enemies. | 7. *Preparation for the Supreme Ordeal:* The Hero prepares for his biggest challenge so far. | 8. *The Supreme Ordeal:* The Hero undertakes a task of significant magnitude. His old self dies and he is reborn as a different type of person. |
| **Act Three** | 9. *Reward:* Having passed through the rebirth of the Supreme Ordeal, the Hero then receives the reward. This is the most reflective stage in the journey. | 10. *The Road Back:* Having seemingly accomplished their wish, the Hero realises that there is unfinished business. At this stage the Hero realises that he must resolve the unfinished consequences of the Supreme Ordeal. | 11. *The Final Conflict:* In this stage, the Hero uses the lessons he has learned through the journey, draws on the wisdom of the Mentor and finally defeats the Shadow. | 12. *Return to Stability:* The threat defeated, the Hero's world is now returned to a place of stability. |

When I first read about the monomyth I was filled with scepticism, much as I imagine you may be at present. I could see, as demonstrated above, that it might have some truths for folk tales and some Hollywood films, but I was most interested in seeing if it could be applied to the musical and, if so, what it might tell us about the musical.

I applied it to this diverse group of well-known and successful musicals to see if they contain each of the stages of the monomyth. I have chosen these musicals because many people are likely to have seen them, if only in the film versions. Be warned that the film version of *Little Shop of Horrors* differs wildly from the stage version in Act Three, and it is the *stage* version that we are considering here. Similarly, it is specifically the *film* version of *The Sound of Music* under consideration.

> **Five Musicals**
>
> If you don't know any of these musicals, watch the film versions of *The Sound of Music, Little Shop of Horrors, My Fair Lady* and *Evita*. There is a complete recording of *Miss Saigon*; if you don't know the musical, listen to the recording whilst following it in the enclosed libretto.

| | |
|---|---|
| *The Sound of Music* | Richard Rodgers and Oscar Hammerstein II's 1959 musical based on Maria von Trapp's autobiography. As this piece is rarely performed in its original stage version, I will consider the 1965 film version. |
| *Little Shop of Horrors* | Howard Ashman and Alan Menken's 1982 pop musical based on the Roger Corman movie of the same name. I will use the stage version (the film version uses a different plot in Act Three). |

| | |
|---|---|
| *Miss Saigon* | Alain Boublil and Claude-Michel Schönberg's 1980 musical based loosely on the story of *Madam Butterfly*, reset in the Vietnam War. |
| *My Fair Lady* | Alan Jay Lerner and Frederick Loewe's 1956 musical version of George Bernard Shaw's play *Pygmalion*. |
| *Evita* | Andrew Lloyd Webber and Tim Rice's 1978 musical based on the life of Eva Perón. |

Let's consider the major archetypes for each of these works:

| | *Hero* | *Shadow* | *Mentor* | *Shapeshifter* |
|---|---|---|---|---|
| *The Sound of Music* | Maria von Trapp | The Baroness The Nazis | The Mother Abbess | Captain von Trapp |
| *Little Shop of Horrors* | Seymour | Orin the dentist Audrey II | Mr Mushnik Audrey II | Audrey |
| *Miss Saigon* | Kim | Ellen | The Engineer | Chris |
| *My Fair Lady* | Eliza Doolittle | Henry Higgins (at times) | Henry Higgins Col. Pickering Mrs Higgins | Henry Higgins |
| *Evita* | Eva | Che | Magaldi Perón | Perón |

You will have noted that there is often more than one character in the Mentor and Shadow roles. This is not unusual. Often characters act as Mentors for only a certain period. Higgins in *My Fair Lady* behaves primarily as a Mentor throughout Acts One and Two, only to move more clearly into the Shapeshifter role in Act Three. Similarly, the Baroness in *The Sound of Music* and Orin in *Little Shop of Horrors* are despatched by the end of Act Two, to be replaced by a greater Shadow (the Nazis and Audrey II, respectively) who has spent the first two acts growing in power. The central relationship in each work is between the Hero and the Shapeshifter. This is because musicals tend to deal with emotional terrain.

Sometimes it is very difficult to identify exactly who your Hero is. In the case of *Miss Saigon*, it is also possible to analyse the musical with Chris as the Hero, in which case the casting looks like this:

|  | *Hero* | *Shadow* | *Mentor* | *Shapeshifter* |
|---|---|---|---|---|
| *Miss Saigon* | Chris | Thuy | John<br>The Engineer | Kim |

However, in Act Three of the story, Chris becomes increasingly passive, and is not active enough to be the Hero.

Let's look at each stage of the monomyth for each of these musicals and see how they are relevant. Note how similar the stages are in each musical.

The charts on the next pages are laid out according to the stage of the story, but each is reproduced, musical by musical, later on.

## Stage 1: The Ordinary World

All stories begin at a place of stability. Often the Hero yearns for more excitement, or to change their life in some way.

| | |
|---|---|
| *The Sound of Music* | In the cloistered abbey, the young novice Maria does not fit in. She rebels against abbey rules and is not suited to life as a nun. |
| *Little Shop of Horrors* | The run-down setting of Skid Row is established, along with Seymour's wish for a better life, and his hidden love for Audrey. |
| *Miss Saigon* | The nightclub in Saigon. Although it is Kim's first night working there, she can expect to be there for some time. It is her new 'ordinary world'. She has already met the Engineer, her Mentor (the floating Stage 4). |
| *My Fair Lady* | Eliza works as a flower girl in Covent Garden. This is a completely stable world for her, surrounded by people of her class. |
| *Evita* | Eva lives with her family, as she always has, in the town of Junín, Argentina. Note that the opening funeral sequence has no function within the monomyth, but is important in introducing the audience to the character of Che and in establishing the importance of Eva by the end of her life. If you saw the musical without the opening funeral, you would still be able to follow the story completely. |

## Stage 2: The Call to Adventure

Something happens to alter the status quo and challenge the Hero to make a journey.

| | |
|---|---|
| *The Sound of Music* | The Mother Abbess summons Maria and requests that she leaves the abbey to become governess to the von Trapp children. Note that this stage also contains the first scene between Maria and her Mentor (the Floating Stage 4). |
| *Little Shop of Horrors* | Seymour reveals that he has been given a bizarre small plant, which he has named Audrey II. After work, it becomes clear that the plant will only grow if given blood. |
| *Miss Saigon* | Kim meets Chris, who appears to be nobler than the other Marines. |
| *My Fair Lady* | Eliza meets Professor Higgins who bets his friend Colonel Pickering that he can teach her to speak like a lady and pass her off as a duchess. Although Higgins is her Mentor, he does not begin to act as one until later. |
| *Evita* | Eva desires a ticket to Buenos Aires as the companion to the nightclub singer Magaldi. She is very driven and full of ambition at this point. |

## Stage 3: Refusal of the Call

The Hero very often hesitates, or lacks the self-belief to take on the task.

| | |
|---|---|
| *The Sound of Music* | Maria begs the Mother Abbess to allow her to stay in the abbey, but her argument is rejected. She decides to put on a brave face. |
| *Little Shop of Horrors* | Seymour tries to feed the plant everything except blood. |
| *Miss Saigon* | Kim, coerced by the Engineer, agrees to spend the night with Chris. |
| *My Fair Lady* | Eliza has a very famous Refusal of the Call in the line 'Go-ahn' (meaning 'Go on', or 'I don't believe you'). She does not believe that Higgins could win his bet. They part and Higgins forgets the matter. |
| *Evita* | Eva has no refusal of the call. She is passionately ambitious and has a strong opposition to any of Magaldi's objections. |

## Stage 4 (Floating Stage): Meeting the Mentor

The Hero, full of self-doubt, meets the Mentor who helps him move forward with his journey.

| | |
|---|---|
| *The Sound of Music* | Maria's meeting with the Mother Abbess effectively begins the story at Stage 2. In this scene the Mother Abbess acts as a Herald and Mentor, announcing the Call to Adventure and advising upon it. |
| *Little Shop of Horrors* | Mushnik is quite an ineffective Mentor, providing just enough advice to move the plot forward. Seymour is already working for him at the beginning of the story. |
| *Miss Saigon* | The Engineer, Kim's pimp, is a very controlling Mentor, who she has just met at Stage 1. Rather than advising he demands that she go with Chris, and Kim, recognising Chris's noble spirit, agrees. |
| *My Fair Lady* | The musical is largely about the Hero–Mentor relationship, although this does not become apparent until Stage 5. Later in the story, as Higgins's function morphs from Mentor to Shapeshifter in Act Three, Pickering and Mrs Higgins step into the Mentor role. |
| *Evita* | Magaldi appears to be her Mentor, but is largely ineffective. Eva meets her true Mentor, Perón, in Stage 6. Although he is ostensibly her romantic interest, Perón acts much more as a Mentor than as a Shapeshifter. Their private relationship is only briefly glimpsed in two scenes. The role of Che is much closer to the function of the Shapeshifter and he appears as a number of different characters through the piece. |

Note that in three of the examples (*The Sound of Music, Miss Saigon* and *Evita*), the Hero already knows the Mentor at the beginning of the story. Only in *My Fair Lady* does the Hero meet the Mentor (or first Mentor) onstage. This is not uncommon and illustrates how much of a floating stage the Meeting with the Mentor can be.

## Stage 5: Crossing the Threshold

The Hero is persuaded to begin the journey required of him. He leaves the stability of his world and ventures forth into the outer world in which his adventure will take place.

| | |
|---|---|
| *The Sound of Music* | Maria leaves the abbey and physically travels to the von Trapp family villa where she enters their world. |
| *Little Shop of Horrors* | Seymour gives the plant blood. Whilst he does not physically enter a new place, from this moment on the flower shop begins to physically transform as it becomes more successful. |
| *Miss Saigon* | Waking after their night together, Kim and Chris realise that they are more romantically attracted than a client/prostitute relationship would normally be. They Cross the Threshold into a more committed relationship. |
| *My Fair Lady* | Eliza physically Crosses the Threshold into Higgins's house when she arrives, requesting to take up his offer of lessons. |
| *Evita* | Eva physically Crosses the Threshold to Buenos Aires, which she sees as a place of opportunity. |

Even though this is a diverse sample of musicals, note that in three of the five examples (*The Sound of Music, My Fair Lady* and *Evita*) the Hero makes a physical Crossing of the Threshold. This is more common than might be expected.

## Stage 6: Tests, Allies and Enemies

Having Crossed the Threshold, the Hero now meets new characters in the new world they will inhabit.

| | |
|---|---|
| *The Sound of Music* | Maria meets Captain von Trapp (Shapeshifter), the children (Allies), the Baroness (Shadow), the young Nazi Rolf (Liesl's Shapeshifter), the staff (potential Enemies). She is tested by the children early on, by the Captain and by preparing the children for the Baroness. During this section Maria befriends Liesl and acts as a Mentor to her. |
| *Little Shop of Horrors* | Flushed with the success that Audrey II brings, Seymour's relationships with existing characters change. He is befriended by the previously ambivalent Mushnik, he grows closer to Audrey and he meets Audrey's boyfriend, the sadistic dentist Orin. He is tested by the plant who challenges him to bring more blood, which he manages to do. |
| *Miss Saigon* | Kim and Chris marry in a Vietnamese ceremony in which they are surrounded by friends (Allies). Her betrothed Thuy (Shadow to Chris) enters and curses the ceremony. Chris's friend John tells him that Saigon is falling. |
| *My Fair Lady* | Higgins becomes Eliza's Mentor; Pickering becomes an Ally, as does Mrs Pugh. Eliza meets Freddie, who fulfils the Shapeshifter function. She is tested, firstly by Higgins in the teaching scenes, and then in the Ascot scene: a test that she clearly fails. She returns to Higgins's house for further tuition. |
| *Evita* | Having arrived in Buenos Aires, Eva meets a string of lovers (Allies) who help her climb the social ladder. She meets her Mentor and romantic interest Perón, his Mistress (Eva's Shadow), the aristocracy and army (both Enemies), and she begins to manipulate the Descamisados (Allies) who will sweep her husband to power. |

Note how substantial this section of all of these musicals is. In the case of *Evita*, it is approximately 50 per cent of the first half of the musical. There is generally a lot of material to be covered at this stage in the story and typically this is where key supporting characters will be introduced.

*Stage 7: Preparation for the Supreme Ordeal*

The Hero prepares for his biggest challenge so far.

| | |
|---|---|
| *The Sound of Music* | At the ball, the child Birgitta tells Maria that Captain von Trapp is in love with her, and that it is clear to the children that Maria is in love with the Captain. Horrified, Maria leaves the von Trapp villa and returns to the abbey. |
| *Little Shop of Horrors* | Having grown in weight and having gained the power of speech (and song), the plant Audrey II challenges Seymour to kill Orin in order to free Audrey and to provide nourishment for Audrey II. Seymour doesn't believe that he can do this. |
| *Miss Saigon* | Kim, already pregnant from their short affair, tries to reach Chris as he is evacuated from Saigon. He cannot take her with him and they are separated. |
| *My Fair Lady* | Eliza appears, her training completed, dressed for the Embassy Ball. She doubts that she can carry off the task. |
| *Evita* | As Perón's election campaign picks up momentum, Eva works tirelessly to secure his success and her future role as First Lady. Perón has doubts, which Eva dismisses. |

*Miss Saigon* has a very long second act and a very short third act. It takes a large section of Act Two and plays it as a flashback during Act Three as 'Kim's Dream'. In order to analyse the monomyth in a work with a flashback or flashforward, one must first put the scenes into the order that the *Hero experiences them*, not the order in which the audience experiences them.

The theme of doubt runs through this stage, and there is often a moment of reflection before the Supreme Ordeal.

*Stage 8: The Supreme Ordeal*

The Hero undertakes a task of significant magnitude. His old self dies and he is reborn as a different type of person.

| | |
|---|---|
| *The Sound of Music* | The Mother Abbess advises Maria to follow her heart. Maria returns to the von Trapp villa and is open to the Captain's proposal. Maria the novice/governess is married and is reborn as Maria the wife and mother. |
| *Little Shop of Horrors* | Seymour murders Orin, and also his own innocence. Seymour the mild-mannered assistant florist is reborn as Seymour the murderer. |
| *Miss Saigon* | The theme of rebirth is made explicit. Kim is reborn as a mother by giving birth to her and Chris's son Tam. As the audience sees her child, she sings that she would die for him. |
| *My Fair Lady* | At the ball, Eliza passes her Supreme Ordeal with flying colours, with all believing her to be aristocracy. Eliza the flower girl is now reborn as Eliza the Lady. |
| *Evita* | Perón's campaign is successful and he is elected president. In a rare example, this stage takes place offstage during the intermission. The victory speeches (the Reward) open the second half. Eva the ambitious pauper is reborn as Eva Perón, First Lady, appearing on the balcony. |

All of these Supreme Ordeals are irreversible in the characters' lives. Maria (a strict Catholic) will be married for life, Seymour will always have committed this murder, Kim's child cannot be un-born, Eva Perón will always have occupied the office of First Lady. Only Eliza could conceivably return to the circumstances of her former life, but she is now unrecognisable there. Supreme Ordeals change characters' lives for ever, and when writers talk about whether the 'stakes are high enough' they are often referring to whether the Supreme Ordeal carries enough weight.

*Stage 9: Reward*

Having passed through the rebirth of the Supreme Ordeal, the
Hero then receives the reward.

| | |
|---|---|
| *The Sound of Music* | Maria's reward is the wedding and following honeymoon (during which Max tries to get the children to commit to the singing concert), and her new closer relationship with the children. |
| *Little Shop of Horrors* | Nourished by Orin's corpse, Audrey II grows more impressive and Mushnik can afford to have the shop refurbished. More importantly, Audrey confesses her love for Seymour and he is fêted locally. |
| *Miss Saigon* | Kim escapes from Vietnam to Bangkok where a sex worker with a child is not uncommon. She can begin a new life of stability, and support her child in a peaceful land. |
| *My Fair Lady* | Eliza's reward is short-lived. Higgins claims it for himself. Eliza leaves Higgins's house, stronger and more confident than before. |
| *Evita* | Eva has a substantial reward. She appears in her new guise as First Lady to an adoring public. After the success of the evening she wonders where she can go from here, but she claims a further reward – her tour of Europe. |

The audience of *Miss Saigon* understand that time has passed
because Kim's child is not a babe in arms but a four-year-old
boy.

## Stage 10: The Road Back

Having seemingly accomplished their wish, the Hero realises that there is unfinished business.

| | |
|---|---|
| The Sound of Music | Maria and the Captain appear to have everything they want, except that a new threat appears in the form of the Nazis, who command the Captain to report for duty. |
| Little Shop of Horrors | Audrey II is getting hungry again. Mushnik suspects Seymour and is fed to the plant. Although Seymour is still being offered rewards, he is increasingly distressed by his situation. |
| Miss Saigon | John traces Kim to Bangkok and goes to meet her. Believing that Chris has come to take her and Tam to America, Kim rushes to Chris's hotel room, where she encounters her Shadow, Ellen, and discovers that Chris has an American wife. |
| My Fair Lady | Eliza rejects Freddie's advances and is pursued by Higgins to Mrs Higgins's house. |
| Evita | On her tour of Europe, Eva begins to get sick. A new threat appears in the form of her health. The implication is that her hugely energetic rise to fame has come at a cost to her health. |

*Stage 11: The Final Conflict (or Resurrection)*

The Hero uses the lessons learned through the journey, draws on the wisdom of the Mentor and finally defeats the Shadow.

| | |
|---|---|
| *The Sound of Music* | The von Trapps perform at Max's concert as a diversion to allow them to escape the Nazis. They hide in the abbey where they are discovered by Rolf, whose love for Liesl is stronger than his love for the Nazis. |
| *Little Shop of Horrors* | Audrey II tricks Audrey and eats her. Seymour, enraged, decides to take an axe to the plant from the inside. |
| *Miss Saigon* | Kim decides that stability for her child is more important than her own life and instructs Tam to run and meet his father. |
| *My Fair Lady* | Higgins and Eliza meet at Mrs Higgins's house where Higgins recognises how attached he has become to Eliza, who establishes herself as an intelligent and independent young woman. |
| *Evita* | Eva succumbs to illness. She broadcasts to the nation. |

## Stage 12: Return to Stability

The threat defeated, the Hero's world is now returned to a place of stability.

| | |
|---|---|
| *The Sound of Music* | United as a family, the von Trapps escape to the safety of Western Europe (and eventually to America), their stability assured. |
| *Little Shop of Horrors* | Seymour, having lost the battle with the plant, gets what he always wanted – an eternity with Audrey as they are both reborn as the plant's flowers. |
| *Miss Saigon* | To achieve her objective of securing a stable future for her son, Kim commits suicide, ensuring that Chris must take Tam with him back to America. Kim has not achieved the stability she desired, that is her tragedy, but she has sacrificed her own life to ensure the stability of her son's life. |
| *My Fair Lady* | Eliza, now recognised as a strong and independent woman, returns to Higgins's home, presumably as his lover, but certainly as his equal. Eliza's place in the world and their relationship have both moved to a new stability. |
| *Evita* | Eva dies, but the Prologue has shown how she will be mourned. She is at peace having achieved all that she desired, except longevity. |

Whilst three of these five musicals end in the death of the Hero, all of them bring the story to a place of stability. The Prologue in *Evita* is effectively a flashforward to the end of the story before it has begun.

Obviously the breakdowns above only outline the bare bones of each story, and of the Hero's story at that. Substantial parts of the musicals are not mentioned, such as Liesl's relationship with Rolf, John's commitment to the Bui-Doi, Perón's rise to power and the entire character of Alfred Doolittle, Eliza's father. This is because this is a tool for analysis, not a recipe.

Be aware that if you are adapting a story it is perfectly legitimate to mould the story into a new form as part of the adaptation process, so don't be afraid to be imaginative. The monomyth can help to analyse whether you have the shape of the Hero's journey correct, and whether all the necessary stages carry the correct weight.

Over the next few pages are repeats of the summaries for each musical for each stage. In each of these I have moved the Floating Stage 4 to where it appears in the musical.

| Stage | The Sound of Music |
|---|---|
| 1. The Ordinary World | In the cloistered abbey, the young novice Maria does not fit in. She rebels against abbey rules and is not suited to life as a nun. |
| 2. The Call to Adventure <br><br> 4. Meeting the Mentor | The Mother Abbess summons Maria and requests that she leaves the abbey to become governess to the von Trapp children. Note that this stage also contains the first scene between Maria and her Mentor. <br><br> Maria's meeting with the Mother Abbess effectively begins the story at Stage 2. In this scene the Mother Abbess acts as a Herald and Mentor, announcing the Call to Adventure and advising upon it. |
| 3. Refusal of the Call | Maria begs the Mother Abbess to allow her to stay in the abbey, but her argument is rejected. She decides to put on a brave face. |

| | |
|---|---|
| 5.<br>*Crossing the Threshold* | Maria leaves the abbey and physically travels to the von Trapp family villa where she enters their world. |
| 6.<br>*Tests, Allies and Enemies* | Maria meets Captain von Trapp (Shapeshifter), the children (Allies), the Baroness (Shadow), the young Nazi Rolf (Liesl's Shapeshifter), the staff (potential Enemies). She is tested by the children early on, by the Captain and by preparing the children for the Baroness. During this section, Maria befriends Liesl and acts as a Mentor to her. |
| 7.<br>*Preparation for the Supreme Ordeal* | At the ball, the child Birgitta tells Maria that Captain von Trapp is in love with her, and that it is clear to the children that Maria is in love with the Captain. Horrified, Maria leaves the von Trapp villa and returns to the abbey. |
| 8.<br>*The Supreme Ordeal* | The Mother Abbess advises Maria to follow her heart. Maria returns to the von Trapp villa and is open to the Captain's proposal. Maria the novice/governess is married and is reborn as Maria the wife and mother. |
| 9.<br>*Reward* | Maria's reward is the wedding and following honeymoon (during which Max tries to get the children to commit to the singing concert), and her new closer relationship with the children. |
| 10.<br>*The Road Back* | Maria and the Captain appear to have everything they want, except that a new threat appears in the form of the Nazis, who command the Captain to report for duty. |
| 11.<br>*The Final Conflict (or Resurrection)* | The von Trapps perform at Max's concert as a diversion to allow them to escape the Nazis. They hide in the abbey where they are discovered by Rolf, whose love for Liesl is stronger than his love for the Nazis. |
| 12.<br>*Return to Stability* | United as a family, the von Trapps escape to the safety of Western Europe (and eventually to America), their stability assured. |

| Stage | Little Shop of Horrors |
|---|---|
| 1.<br>The Ordinary World<br><br>4. Meeting the Mentor | The run-down setting of Skid Row is established, along with Seymour's wish for a better life, and his hidden love for Audrey.<br><br>Mushnik is quite an ineffective Mentor, providing just enough advice to move the plot forward. Seymour is already working for him at the beginning of the story. |
| 2.<br>The Call to Adventure | Seymour reveals that he has been given a bizarre small plant, which he has named Audrey II. After work, it becomes clear that the plant will only grow if given blood. |
| 3.<br>Refusal of the Call | Seymour tries to feed the plant everything except blood. |
| 5.<br>Crossing the Threshold | Seymour gives the plant blood. Whilst he does not physically enter a new place, from this moment on the flower shop begins to physically transform as it becomes more successful. |
| 6.<br>Tests, Allies and Enemies | Flushed with the success that Audrey II brings, Seymour's relationships with existing characters change. He is befriended by the previously ambivalent Mushnik, he grows closer to Audrey and he meets Audrey's boyfriend, the sadistic dentist Orin. He is tested by the plant who challenges him to bring more blood, which he manages to do. |
| 7.<br>Preparation for the Supreme Ordeal | Having grown in weight and having gained the power of speech (and song), the plant Audrey II challenges Seymour to kill Orin in order to free Audrey and to provide nourishment for Audrey II. Seymour doesn't believe that he can do this. |
| 8.<br>The Supreme Ordeal | Seymour murders Orin, and also his own innocence. Seymour the mild-mannered assistant florist is reborn as Seymour the murderer. |

| | |
|---|---|
| **9.**<br>*Reward* | Nourished by Orin's corpse, Audrey II grows more impressive and Mushnik can afford to have the shop refurbished. More importantly, Audrey confesses her love for Seymour and he is fêted locally. |
| **10.**<br>*The Road Back* | Audrey II is getting hungry again. Mushnik suspects Seymour and is fed to the plant. Although Seymour is still being offered rewards, he is increasingly distressed by his situation. |
| **11.**<br>*The Final Conflict*<br>*(or Resurrection)* | Audrey II tricks Audrey and eats her. Seymour, enraged, decides to take an axe to the plant from the inside. |
| **12.**<br>*Return to Stability* | Seymour, having lost the battle with the plant, gets what he always wanted – an eternity with Audrey as they are both reborn as the plant's flowers. |

| Stage | Miss Saigon |
|---|---|
| 1.<br>The Ordinary World | The nightclub in Saigon. Although it is Kim's first night working there, she can expect to be there for some time. It is her new 'ordinary world'. She has already met the Engineer, her Mentor (the floating Stage 4). |
| 4.<br>Meeting the Mentor | The Engineer, Kim's pimp, is a very controlling Mentor, who she has just met at Stage 1. |
| 2.<br>The Call to Adventure | Kim meets Chris, who appears to be nobler than the other Marines. |
| 3.<br>Refusal of the Call | Kim, coerced by the Engineer, agrees to spend the night with Chris. |
| 5.<br>Crossing the Threshold | Waking after their night together, Kim and Chris realise that they are more romantically attracted than a client/prostitute relationship would normally be. They cross the threshold into a more committed relationship. |
| 6.<br>Tests, Allies and Enemies | Kim and Chris marry in a Vietnamese ceremony in which they are surrounded by friends (Allies). Her betrothed Thuy (Shadow to Chris) enters and curses the ceremony. Chris's friend John tells him that Saigon is falling. |
| 7.<br>Preparation for the Supreme Ordeal | Kim, already pregnant from their short affair, tries to reach Chris as he is evacuated from Saigon. He cannot take her with him and they are separated. |
| 8.<br>The Supreme Ordeal | The theme of rebirth is made explicit. Kim is reborn as a mother by giving birth to her and Chris's son Tam. As the audience sees her child, she sings that she would die for him. |
| 9.<br>Reward | Kim escapes from Vietnam to Bangkok where a sex worker with a child is not uncommon. She can begin a new life of stability, and support her child in a peaceful land. |

| 10.<br>*The Road Back* | John traces Kim to Bangkok and goes to meet her. Believing that Chris has come to take her and Tam to America, Kim rushes to Chris's hotel room, where she encounters her Shadow, Ellen, and discovers that Chris has an American wife. |
|---|---|
| 11.<br>*The Final Conflict*<br>*(or Resurrection)* | Kim decides that stability for her child is more important than her own life and instructs Tam to run and meet his father. |
| 12.<br>*Return to Stability* | To achieve her objective of securing a stable future for her son, Kim commits suicide, ensuring that Chris must take Tam with him back to America. Kim has not achieved the stability she desired, that is her tragedy, but she has sacrificed her own life to ensure the stability of her son's life. |

| Stage | My Fair Lady |
|---|---|
| 1.<br>The Ordinary World | Eliza works as a flower girl in Covent Garden. This is a completely stable world for her, surrounded by people of her class. |
| 2.<br>The Call to Adventure | Eliza meets Professor Higgins, who bets his friend Colonel Pickering that he can teach her to speak like a lady and pass her off as a duchess. Although Higgins is her Mentor, he does not begin to act as one until later. |
| 3.<br>Refusal of the Call | Eliza has a very famous Refusal of the Call in the line 'Go-ahn' (meaning 'Go on', or 'I don't believe you'). She does not believe that Higgins could win his bet. They part and Higgins forgets the matter. |
| 4.<br>Meeting the Mentor | The musical is largely about the Hero–Mentor relationship, although this does not become apparent until Stage 5. Later in the story, as Higgins's function morphs from Mentor to Shapeshifter in Act Three, Pickering and Mrs Higgins step into the Mentor role. |
| 5.<br>Crossing the Threshold | Eliza physically Crosses the Threshold into Higgins's house when she arrives, requesting to take up his offer of lessons. |
| 6.<br>Tests, Allies and Enemies | Higgins becomes Eliza's Mentor; Pickering becomes an Ally, as does Mrs Pugh. Eliza meets Freddie, who fulfils the Shapeshifter function. She is tested, firstly by Higgins in the teaching scenes, and then in the Ascot scene: a test that she clearly fails. She returns to Higgins's house for further tuition. |
| 7.<br>Preparation for the Supreme Ordeal | Eliza appears, her training completed, dressed for the Embassy Ball. She doubts that she can carry off the task. |
| 8.<br>The Supreme Ordeal | At the ball, Eliza passes her Supreme Ordeal with flying colours, with all believing her to be aristocracy. Eliza the flower girl is now reborn as Eliza the Lady. |

| 9.<br>*Reward* | Eliza's reward is short-lived. Higgins claims it for himself. Eliza leaves Higgins's house, stronger and more confident than before. |
|---|---|
| 10.<br>*The Road Back* | Eliza rejects Freddie's advances and is pursued by Higgins to Mrs Higgins's house. |
| 11.<br>*The Final Conflict*<br>*(or Resurrection)* | Higgins and Eliza meet at Mrs Higgins's house where Higgins recognises how attached he has become to Eliza, who establishes herself as an intelligent and independent young woman. |
| 12.<br>*Return to Stability* | Eliza, now recognised as a strong and independent woman, returns to Higgins's home, presumably as his lover, but certainly as his equal. Eliza's place in the world and their relationship have both moved to a new stability. |

| Stage | Evita |
|---|---|
| 1.<br>The Ordinary World | Eva lives with her family, as she always has, in the town of Junín, Argentina. Note that the opening funeral sequence has no function within the monomyth, but is important in introducing the audience to the character of Che and in establishing the importance of Eva by the end of her life. If you saw the musical without the opening funeral, you would still be able to follow the story completely. |
| 2.<br>The Call to Adventure<br><br>4.<br>Meeting the Mentor | Eva desires a ticket to Buenos Aires as the companion to the nightclub singer Magaldi. She is very driven and full of ambition at this point.<br><br>Magaldi appears to be her Mentor, but is largely ineffective. |
| 3.<br>Refusal of the Call | Eva has no refusal of the call. She is passionately ambitious and has a strong opposition to any of Magaldi's objections. |
| 5.<br>Crossing the Threshold | Eva physically Crosses the Threshold to Buenos Aires, which she sees as a place of opportunity. |
| 4.<br>Meeting the Mentor<br><br><br>6.<br>Tests, Allies and Enemies | Eva meets her true Mentor, Perón, in Stage 6. Although he is ostensibly her romantic interest, Perón acts much more as a Mentor than as a Shapeshifter. Their private relationship is only briefly glimpsed in two scenes.<br><br>Having arrived in Buenos Aires, Eva meets a string of lovers (Allies) who help her climb the social ladder. She meets her Mentor and romantic interest Perón, his Mistress (Eva's Shadow), the aristocracy and army (both Enemies), and she begins to manipulate the Descamisados (Allies) who will sweep her husband to power. |
| 7.<br>Preparation for the Supreme Ordeal | As Perón's election campaign picks up momentum, Eva works tirelessly to secure his success and her future role as First Lady. Perón has doubts, which Eva dismisses. |

| | |
|---|---|
| 8.<br>*The Supreme*<br>*Ordeal* | Perón's campaign is successful and he is elected president. In a rare example, this stage takes place offstage during the intermission. The election campaign ends the first half. The victory speeches (the Reward) open the second half. Eva the ambitious pauper is reborn as Eva Perón, First Lady, appearing on the balcony. |
| 9.<br>*Reward* | Eva has a substantial reward. She appears in her new guise as First Lady to an adoring public. After the success of the evening she wonders where she can go from here, but she claims a further reward – her tour of Europe. |
| 10.<br>*The Road Back* | On her tour of Europe, Eva begins to get sick. A new threat appears in the form of her health. The implication is that her hugely energetic rise to fame has come at a cost to her health. |
| 11.<br>*The Final Conflict*<br>*(or Resurrection)* | Eva succumbs to illness. She broadcasts to the nation. |
| 12.<br>*Return to Stability* | Eva dies, but the Prologue has shown how she will be mourned. She is at peace having achieved all that she desired, except longevity. |

## Two-Hero and Multi-Hero Stories

Some stories contain more than one Hero. Stories with two Heroes are not uncommon and there are stories with three or more Heroes. A two-Hero story automatically gives you a plot and subplot, which Engel considers one of the Needs of the musical. In this case you will be able to analyse a Hero's journey for the Hero of the plot and of the subplot. Sometimes these plots run simultaneously, and sometimes one begins considerably later than the other.

*Case Study:* Les Misérables *by Alain Boublil and Claude-Michel Schönberg**

Les Misérables is a good example of a two-Hero monomyth. In this musical the two Heroes' stories do not run simultaneously, as they would if this were a simple plot and subplot musical, but they overlap part way through the story. The two Heroes are Jean Valjean and Marius. Within a two-Hero story it is not uncommon for certain parts of one journey not be included, or for them to happen offstage.

Jean Valjean's Ordinary World is established as being on the chain gang, as a thief. His Ordinary World is removed from him by Javert (his Shadow). Notice how alike Jean Valjean and Javert are – they are both strong, active men of the same age, convinced of their ability to do the right thing. Valjean robs the Bishop of Digne (his Mentor) who challenges him to do good and 'buys' his soul for God (Call to Adventure). Valjean determines to start his life anew, as a good man. He Crosses the Threshold to a life on the right side of the law. The Prologue to Les Miz is therefore Act One of Jean Valjean's story.

Eight years have passed and Valjean is now living as Monsieur Madeleine and is the mayor of the town. He is tested in a number of ways and meets his Allies and Enemies. He is tested by Fantine (Ally), who asks him to look after her child Cosette (Ally). He is tested by Javert, who discovers his true identity and threatens to bring him to court. He is tested by the Thénardiers (Enemies) who make him pay a good deal of money for Cosette.

---

* Seen in Paris in 1980, and in London, in the famous RSC production, in 1985.

Nine further years pass (this certainly is not a musical that has time compression!). Valjean, Javert, the adult Cosette and the Thénardiers (with the daughter Eponine) are all now living in Paris. The Thénardiers have fallen on hard times and run a street gang. The gang sets upon Valjean and Cosette and they are rescued by Javert (who does not recognise Valjean). The character of Marius (the second Hero) is introduced, and is immediately attracted to Cosette (Marius' Call to Adventure). Marius' Ordinary World is with a group of students who are distressed by General Lamarque's death. Lamarque has been the only government minister to show feeling for the poor. Enjolras (Marius' Mentor) leads the group of students on to the streets to try to start a revolution.

Marius leaves the students to see Cosette. She is equally in love with him and Marius Crosses the Threshold from being a student to being a lover. Note that as with *My Fair Lady* and *The Sound of Music*, he literally Crosses the Threshold into Valjean's estate. Valjean believes that Javert has found him and prepares to flee (Preparation for the Supreme Ordeal).

As the students build their barricade, Marius' thoughts are only for Cosette and he sends a letter to her (a Test). Valjean intercepts the letter and at the barricade Javert is exposed a spy and kept hostage (Javert is now an Enemy to both Valjean and Marius). Eponine is killed by the army (Enemies) and Marius shows compassion for her (a Test).

Valjean arrives at the barricade and is given the chance to kill Javert. This is Valjean's Supreme Ordeal. He has a choice and he can remove the threat of Javert by killing him. This would be the logical choice. But Valjean has promised God to make the right decision. He sets Javert free and in doing so he is now truly reborn as the good person he has been striving to be since the Prologue (this is illustrated in the hymn-like 'Bring Him Home').

The students prepare for a battle (Marius' Preparation for the Supreme Ordeal) and all except Marius are killed when battle commences. Jean Valjean rescues Marius, badly injured. This is Marius' Supreme Ordeal, his near-death.

Valjean meets Javert and pleads for time to deliver Marius to medical care. Javert, unable to understand such goodness, commits suicide and achieves the same end as if Valjean had killed him, but crucially leaving no stain on Valjean's soul. This is Valjean's Reward.

Marius recovers in Cosette's care and their relationship grows stronger (his Reward). Unaware of the suicide and concerned that Javert will find him, Valjean confesses the truth of his broken parole to Marius and insists he must leave. (Valjean's Road Back). As Marius and Cosette wed, the Thénardiers try to blackmail Marius about Valjean, claiming he is a murderer who stole a ring from a corpse. (Marius' Road Back). The ring proves to Marius that it was Valjean who saved him and the Thenadiers are ejected from the wedding, and Marius' life (Marius' Final Conflict).

Valjean confesses the truth of his life and of Cosette's history to Cosette. As he dies, he is visited by the ghosts of Fantine, Eponine and the students in a clear message that he has achieved enough to enter Heaven (Valjean's Final Conflict).

The Return to Stability is achieved: Valjean has entered Heaven (the ultimate place of Stability) and is no longer haunted by his past. The revolution is over (for now) and Marius and Cosette are in the stable world of their marriage.

## Same-Sex Relationships and Shapeshifters

The notion of the Shapeshifter as the romantic interest for the Hero is built upon the heterosexual orthodoxy that men and women lack an emotional understanding of each other. How, then, does a same-sex relationship function within the notion of the monomyth? Is a Hero's same-sex lover his Shadow or a Shapeshifter? The answer might be either. He is only likely to be his Shadow if he is working in opposition to him. The chances are that he is likely to be his Shapeshifter. In any work of a romantic nature it is a general rule that the writer needs to keep the lovers from reaching stability until the end of the story, even if they have been in a previously stable place. As a result, it is likely that the lover needs to operate as a Shapeshifter in order to keep the drama in play throughout the story.

*Case Study:* La Cage aux Folles *by Jerry Herman and Harvey Fierstein*

Nightclub owners Georges and Albin are probably the most famous same-sex couple in musical theatre. Who is the Hero? At first it might appear that it is Georges' son Jean-Michel, but actually the Hero is Georges. The musical is the story of how Georges has to reconfirm his relationship with Albin in spite of his son's choice of fiancée and her parents. The entire musical comes down to Georges, not Albin, finally being prepared to say 'I Am What I Am'. Georges is the Hero; Eduard Dindon, the homophobic politician, is his Shadow; and Albin is the Shapeshifter. The role of Mentor is taken by a number of different characters at different points throughout the musical; by Albin, by the butler Jacob, and by the stylish, friendly restaurateur Jacqueline. Georges also acts as Mentor to his son Jean-Michel and, in doing so, proves to the audience that he has learned through the process; he is effectively self-mentoring.

The Ordinary World is the St Tropez nightclub and living quarters in which gay couple Georges and Albin have their comfortable, stable existence. The Call to Adventure is that Jean-Michel has decided that he has met his future wife and has invited her and her right-wing parents for dinner. Georges Crosses the Threshold by agreeing that this can occur and that Albin, his partner of many years but a camp drag queen who headlines the show, will be compromised or hidden in order not to shock the future in-laws, the Dindons. Georges undergoes a number of Tests, which include trying to 'train' Albin in the art of masculinity, with the help of the St Tropez townspeople (Allies), in refitting the apartment in severe Catholic design, and in dressing and behaving conservatively. One of his tests is to tell Albin that he is no longer invited, despite Albin having raised Jean-Michel as his own son. This leads to Albin storming out of the club with a rip-roaring rendition of the show's theme song 'I Am What I Am'.

Georges' Supreme Ordeal is to be reborn as 'heterosexual' Georges for the dinner party with the Dindons, and his reward is that it appears to be passing relatively smoothly until Albin arrives dressed as Jean Michel's 'mother' (Georges' Road Back

– Albin on the scene is definitely a new threat). After 'Mother' sings in Jacqueline's restaurant where they have gone for dinner, Albin reveals himself to be a man and Eduard Dindon is outraged and refuses to give his blessing to the marriage. Despite this, Georges proves to Albin how much he loves and appreciates him when both he and Jean-Michel sing 'Look Over There' to Albin. Dindon relents, allowing the lovers to wed and Georges and Albin head into the sunset singing the romantic 'Song on the Sand', the farce of the past twenty-four hours played out, their relationship strengthened through facing the adversity, and stability restored.

In this musical, Albin is literally a Shapeshifter, he appears in three different guises: the male Albin, the female hostess of the nightclub Zaza, and the domestic female Mother.

## Further Considerations

The monomyth is not always easy to understand. These are some commonly asked questions about it:

1.  *What is the maximum number of Heroes you can have?*

    Whilst there is no definite maximum to the number of Heroes you could have, it is rare to find three and very rare to find more than three. Stephen Sondheim and James Lapine's *Into the Woods* effectively has The Baker, Jack, Cinderella and Little Red Riding Hood, but this is a rare example. It is no accident that they are the four characters that are still in play at the end of the story.

2.  *What about* Cats, *which does not seem to follow this at all, but is a hugely successful musical?*

    Not every musical can be analysed using the monomyth – and Andrew Lloyd Webber's *Cats* is one example. *Cats* does not follow a linear narrative of any kind. It has a very simple framing device, of the cats having to nominate one cat to be reborn, but this is not a narrative. Most of *Cats* is a series of character songs, which for narrative purposes could be performed in any order. This is not a criticism: that the creative team were able to fashion such a successful show without a real narrative is testament to the quality of the work they did. Structurally, *Cats* is closer to a revue than a book musical, as are other musicals like *Godspell*, or the revue-style musical *Working*.

3. *Must there be a Hero, Mentor, Shadow and Shapeshifter?*

   Not every musical has all four of the major archetypes. Bear in mind that characters can shift their function during the story, as Professor Higgins does in *My Fair Lady*, or that a very minor character might appear simply to perform a very major function, such as the Bishop of Digne in *Les Misérables*. Whilst a musical does not necessarily need all four, it is important to consider the function of each of them. *Into the Woods*, for example, has many Heroes and Mentors but few Shadows. The major Shadow, the Giant's Wife, operates as a Shadow to the entire community, but only appears in the second half.

4. *Do all stages have equal weight and stage time?*

   Definitely not. This will depend on the story being told and the manner of the telling. Some stages, such as Refusal of the Call, may disappear completely from some types of stories where the Hero is particularly ambitious (such as *Evita*). Some stages may take a long period of stage time. The Tests, Allies and Enemies stage of *The Wizard of Oz* takes nearly sixty of the film's ninety-eight minutes.

---

### Twenty-Five Questions

Complete this exercise in pencil – you may well want to change your initial answers as you go through. Take a musical you know well and ask yourself the following questions. These questions are not asked in the order that they occur in the monomyth structure, but in the order that is most likely to be easiest and most useful. Write it in pencil and alter it later if you need to.

1.  Who is the Hero?
2.  What is the Ordinary World? How is it stable?
3.  In Act One, what is it that the Hero wants (his objective)?
4.  Who is the Hero's Mentor?
5.  When does the Hero meet the Mentor? (Write the answer in the box relevant to that stage in the story.)
6.  Is there a Shadow? If so, who is it?
7.  When does the Hero become aware of the Shadow? What is the Shadow's objective?
8.  What is the threshold that the Hero has to cross to undertake his journey? Is it a physical threshold, or is it an emotional threshold?
9.  How is the Call to Adventure delivered to the Hero?
10. Is there a Shapeshifter? If so, who is it?
11. What are the Tests that your Hero undergoes?
12. What characters are introduced in the Tests, Allies and Enemies Stage?
13. Are new Allies or Enemies introduced?
14. What is the Supreme Ordeal? How is the Hero reborn at this point?
15. How is the Supreme Ordeal connected to the Hero's original objective?
16. In what way does the Hero Prepare for the Supreme Ordeal?
17. By the Preparation for the Supreme Ordeal, does the Hero have a choice about whether to proceed?
18. Having been reborn in the Supreme Ordeal, what is the Hero's reward?
19. What are the consequences of the Supreme Ordeal and do they lead to the Final Conflict?
20. What is the Final Conflict? What must the Hero accomplish here?

21. How is the Final Conflict revealed in the Road Back stage?

22. Does the Hero 'win' in the Final Conflict or not?

23. How does the resolution to the Final Conflict lead to a new stability?

24. Is the stability returned to at the end of the story the same as that at the beginning, or different?

25. What Heralds, Threshold Guardians and Tricksters does the musical have, if any?

## Planning a Monomyth

Draw a 4 x 3 grid on a large piece of paper, as follows.

| 1.<br>The<br>Ordinary<br>World | 2.<br>Call to<br>Adventure | 3.<br>Refusal of the<br>Call | 4.<br>Meeting the<br>Mentor<br>(floating stage) |
|---|---|---|---|
| 5.<br>Crossing the<br>Threshold | 6.<br>Test, Allies<br>and Enemies | 7.<br>Preparation<br>for the<br>Supreme<br>Ordeal | 8.<br>The Supreme<br>Ordeal |
| 9.<br>Reward | 10.<br>The Road<br>Back | 11.<br>The Final<br>Conflict | 12.<br>Return to<br>Stability |

Take the story that you found easiest to work with in the earlier exercise. In each box write the major elements of the story that are relevant to each stage. Keep your descriptions brief.

## Using the Monomyth

I have stated before that the monomyth is not a recipe. It is all very well being able to analyse other musicals, but what is the function of the monomyth in creating your own musical? The monomyth will allow you to analyse your own story, and to determine whether the stakes are high enough at the major turning points of the story, such as the Call to Adventure, the Supreme Ordeal and the Final Conflict.

Firstly, proceed no further until you have your story. Do not use the monomyth to write a story from scratch, or the piece that you write will be dull and formulaic. Consider how the monomyth refracts through different stories, like light through different crystals: always light, but always different.

Once you have your story, which will probably be about 1,000 words, you can begin to analyse it using the monomyth. The monomyth will allow you to clearly see your Hero's journey, to see if the tests and ordeals that he must undertake are sufficiently onerous and to see what functions your other characters are performing.

The monomyth allows you to begin to see what kind of shape your musical will have. It also allows you to make choices about how to adapt the material you have into a strong narrative structure. If you have areas of the story that you think are weak, think about how you can strengthen them. If, for example, your Supreme Ordeal is a little limp, how might you raise the stakes? Use the monomyth as a way of being able to see the strengths and weaknesses of the story you are telling. Rewrite the story, strengthening the aspects that you think are weakest, then go back and analyse it again and again. Do this by rewriting and expanding your synopsis until you are happy that each stage carries sufficient weight.

Be aware that not *all* scenes in your musical must relate to the monomyth structure. In fact, it is very rare that they do. Think of the monomyth aspects of your story as the foundations or floorplan, a guide to the shape that will rise above it, but not the entire shape. A floorplan exists in two dimensions, but you must create something that lives in three dimensions.

In *My Fair Lady*, Lerner and Loewe added scenes that do not appear in *Pygmalion*, the play upon which it is based, and that do not have roles in the monomyth of Eliza's story. These are the two scenes featuring Alfred Doolittle and the chorus singing 'With a Little Bit of Luck' and 'Get Me to the Church on Time'. They perform an important function in the musicalisation of the story – they provide large-scale production numbers that are practically impossible to include if the adaptation remains close to the monomyth structure of Eliza and Higgins's relationship, and they give a strong sense of what Eliza will lose if she changes her social position. This kind of work is known as 'opening up'. This is the term given to spotting an opportunity for a production number, which is not immediately obvious from reading the source material. For example, Lerner and Loewe also 'opened up' the tea-party scene from the original play by re-setting it at Ascot. To all intents and purposes, the scene fulfils the same function (it is one of Eliza's Tests) but has been re-imagined to allow for more choral musical possibilities.

---

### Twenty-Five Questions for You

Take your 1,000-word story and repeat the Twenty-Five Questions exercise for your own work. You may find that you are missing good answers for some of the twenty-five questions – and this may be perfectly acceptable, depending on your story. At this time, don't worry about it. As you will have found when you ran the exercise with an existing story, some stages will be stronger and carry more time than others. For example, you almost certainly won't have a full set of seven different archetypal characters, but I would be surprised if you have less than four.

---

## Outside the Monomyth

If you are choosing a pre-existing story (i.e. an adaptation of some kind), the chances are that you will be able to identify a monomyth structure within it. Stories as diverse as Greek myths, the work of Jane Austen or Charles Dickens and countless Hollywood movies all have a monomyth structure at their heart. That is what makes them enduring stories.

If you are genuinely unable to find the monomyth structure, even after reading this chapter and completing all the exercises, then it may be that you are writing a revue, such as *Cats*. There is nothing wrong with this; you will be working on a different kind of show that, at heart, will not be a book musical, even if it appears to be. If so, you will need to ensure that each individual moment of the show is successful within its own terms, and exciting to the audience.

For me, it is when dealing with biographical musicals that the monomyth is most useful. You must unlock the dramatic story within the biographical material and I find that the monomyth can be a useful tool in helping me analyse the key dramatic moments that I wish to focus upon. Successful musicals based on biographical material, like *The Sound of Music* or *Evita*, have an inherent monomyth structure.

---

### Create a Synopsis

Now write out your 1,000-word story as a single document, seamlessly moving through all the key moments. Don't worry about how long this document becomes – it might be 2,000 or 3,000 words long. This is your synopsis.

---

## A Warning

Whatever you do, *never ever* mention the monomyth structure when out on a date. Nothing kills romance or passion quicker than 'In the movie we just saw, I think there were real weaknesses in the Crossing the Threshold stage, and as for the Supreme Ordeal...'

Believe me, I know from bitter experience!

# 6
# *Song Spotting*

# Song Spotting

When I began to use the monomyth to help structure my work, I was particularly interested in the role that it might have in song spotting; the art of deciding where the songs might come in any musical. Many people think that where the songs come is a random set of choices, like a parlour game, but, by analysing a number of musicals, and their songs, against the monomyth, it is possible to see the very different functions that songs have at specific moments of storytelling. Just as the monomyth does not prescribe the style of the musical, nor does this kind of analysis.

Have you considered *why* there are songs in a musical and *what* they are doing there? In all musicals there are certain songs that form the backbone to the score and are integral to the story. Often these are the more memorable songs. Are they more memorable because they are better songs, or because they are more important in the overall musical? It is a question that can be debated in relation to every song.

In a through-sung musical it is equally important to address the question of the function of the songs, even though the language of the musical is that it is entirely sung. Often, it is not the quality of the song that gives it longevity, but the dramatic position of the song within the show.

Consider the major songs in the five musicals analysed in the previous chapter:

| Stage | The Sound of Music | Little Shop of Horrors | Miss Saigon | My Fair Lady | Evita |
|---|---|---|---|---|---|
| 1. The Ordinary World | 'Maria' | 'Prologue' 'Skid Row' | 'The Heat is on in Saigon' | 'Wouldn't It Be Loverly?' | 'Eva, Beware of the City' |
| 2. The Call to Adventure | 'My Favourite Things'[1] | 'Da Doo' | 'The Trans-action' | 'Why Can't the English?' | 'Eva, Beware of the City' |
| 3. Refusal of the Call | | 'Grow for Me' | | | |
| 4. Meeting the Mentor | 'My Favourite Things' | 'Mushnik and Son' | | 'Poor Professor Higgins' | 'Eva, Beware of the City' |
| 5. Crossing the Threshold | 'I Have Confidence' | 'Grow for Me' | 'Sun and Moon' | | 'Buenos Aires' |
| 6. Tests, Allies and Enemies | 'My Favourite Things'[2] 'Do-Re-Mi' 'Lonely Goatherd' 'So Long, Farewell' | 'Ya Never Know' 'Mushnik and Son' 'Dentist' 'Somewhere That's Green' 'Get It' | 'The Deal' 'The Wedding' | 'Just You Wait' 'Poor Professor Higgins' 'The Rain in Spain' 'I Could Have Danced All Night' 'Ascot Gavotte' 'On the Street Where You Live' | 'Goodnight and Thank You' 'I'd Be Surprising-ly Good for You' 'Perón's Latest Flame' |
| 7. Prepara-tion for the Supreme Ordeal | | | 'Kim's Nightmare' | | 'A New Argentina' |

1. In the stage version only.
2. In the film version.

| Stage | The Sound of Music | Little Shop of Horrors | Miss Saigon | My Fair Lady | Evita |
|---|---|---|---|---|---|
| 8. The Supreme Ordeal | 'Climb Ev'ry Mountain' | 'Now (It's Just the Gas)' | 'I'd Give My Life for You' | 'Embassy Waltz' | |
| 9. Reward | 'Something Good' 'Wedding Sequence' | 'Suddenly Seymour' | | 'You Did It' | 'Don't Cry for Me, Argentina' 'High Flying, Adored' |
| 10. The Road Back | | 'Supper-time' 'The Meek Shall Inherit' | 'Please' 'Chris is Here' | 'Show Me' | 'Rainbow High' 'Rainbow Tour' |
| 11. The Final Conflict (or Resurrection) | 'So Long, Farewell' (concert version) 'Edelweiss' | 'Sominex / Suppertime II' | 'Room 317' | 'Without You' 'I've Grown Accustomed to Her Face' | 'Waltz for Eva and Che' 'She is a Diamond' 'Eva's Final Broadcast' |
| 12. Return to Stability | 'Climb Ev'ry Mountain' (reprise) | 'Finale' | 'Finale' | | 'Lament' |

As you can see from this table, not every stage of the story necessarily contains a song. There are, however, certain key stages that commonly do contain songs. These tend to be the major stages of the story:

1. The Ordinary World
2. The Call to Adventure
4. Meeting the Mentor
6. Tests, Allies and Enemies
8. Supreme Ordeal
11. Final Conflict
12. Return to Stability

It should not be a surprise that in a piece of musical theatre, the major stages of the storytelling are musicalised. That is one of the defining characteristics of the art form.

This chart identifies the stages, and gives the songs that occur at these stages certain names. Some of these names are in very common usage throughout the musical-theatre world.

| | | | | |
|---|---|---|---|---|
| Act One | *1.*<br>*The Ordinary World*<br><br>Opening number | *2.*<br>*The Call to Adventure*<br><br><br>←——— 'I Wish' song | *3.*<br>*Refusal of the Call*<br><br>———————→ | *4.*<br>*Meeting with the Mentor*<br><br>Mentor's number |
| Act Two | *5.*<br>*Crossing the Threshold* | *6.*<br>*Tests, Allies and Enemies*<br><br>Allies and Enemies' numbers (often production numbers) | *7.*<br>*Preparation for the Supreme Ordeal* | *8.*<br>*Supreme Ordeal*<br><br>Major song (often for Hero and company) |
| Act Three | *9.*<br>*Reward*<br><br>Celebratory song | *10.*<br>*The Road Back* | *11.*<br>*Final Conflict*<br><br>11 o'clock number | *12.*<br>*Return to Stability*<br><br>Finale |

Let's look at each of the stages of the monomyth, with particular reference to the five musicals we looked at in the last chapter and at the defining characteristics of the songs at each stage.

## Openings: The Ordinary World

Not surprisingly, Ordinary World songs are often 'opening numbers'. They establish the very stability that is key to this stage and they 'set the scene', allowing everything that comes after to be a contrast to this opening number. 'The Circle of Life', 'The Heat is on in Saigon', 'Skid Row', '(How Do You Solve a Problem Like) Maria?' and 'Food, Glorious Food' all have very different sounds, but they all have exactly the same function: they all establish the stability of the situation, a stability that will be rocked by the story that is about to unfold.

Sometimes there will be more than one song in the Ordinary World, and in a through-sung show this will almost certainly be the case. In *Jesus Christ Superstar* the Ordinary World stage of the story contains four numbers: 'Heaven on their Minds', which establishes Judas's concerns about Jesus's situation; 'What's the Buzz' and 'Strange Thing Mystifying' in which Judas expresses those concerns to Jesus's followers; and 'Everything's Alright' in which Jesus's disciples attempt to calm the situation.

## Outside the Ordinary World: Prologues

Sometimes a writer wants to establish a theme, a musical or dramatic style that does not establish the Ordinary World. An example of this is Sondheim's brilliant 'Comedy Tonight' in *A Funny Thing Happened on the Way to the Forum* which delightfully informs the audience of what is to come and, vitally, gives them licence to expect a light-hearted night during which they can expect to laugh. Having been given such a licence to laugh, they are much more willing to do so. Sondheim also creates a brilliant Prologue for *Sweeney Todd*, in which the storytelling role of the chorus is established, along with the musical language, but in which the Ordinary World is not established. We have also noted that Andrew Lloyd Webber and Tim Rice's *Evita* opens with a Prologue, a flashforward to the end of the story, which establishes the importance of Eva Perón to the nation, but again contains no plot.

What each of these Prologues does is to establish the *dramatic, physical* and *musical language* of the work – the forthcoming hilarity of *A Funny Thing...*, the brooding ballad opera of *Sweeney Todd* and the operatic sweep of *Evita*.

## 'I Wish' Songs and the Call to Adventure

The Call to Adventure is the Hero's first inkling that the stability of the Ordinary World is about to be shaken. The songs that occur at this stage fire the dramatic engine of the piece. You will notice in the chart that the 'I Wish' song is in the Call to Adventure, but also has arrows that point across Act One. The 'I Wish' song can occur at any point in Act One, but is most common at the Call to Adventure or the Refusal of the Call stages; it is one of the cornerstones of any score. The 'I Wish' song is about *who* the Hero is and *what he wants*. Audiences don't need to want the same thing as the Hero, but they understand the very human emotion of wanting (or wishing). So when the Hero states that they wish for something, every member of the audience *empathises* because every member of the audience has wanted something in their own lives. As a result, the audience wants the Hero to achieve their wish and will back them during their journey to achieve it. It is a simple dramatic rule: if nobody wants anything, why should the audience care about whether they get anything, or whether anything happens? Audiences want and need to care about the characters; if they don't, they lose interest.

'I Wish' songs are sometimes known as 'I am/I want' songs, but I find this clumsy and don't feel that it truly captures the dynamism these songs should have.

'I Wish' songs come in every style:

*My Fair Lady* contains one of the most famous classic Broadway examples: Eliza's 'Wouldn't It Be Loverly?' contains the specific wish of a more comfortable life: 'All I want is a room somewhere, far away from the cold night air'.

*Miss Saigon* contains a group 'I Wish' number, 'The Movie in My Mind', in which the prostitutes sing of their wish to leave Vietnam and make a better life in America. Kim's personal wish is combined here with the community wish.

*Little Shop of Horrors* also reveals the joint wish of the Hero and Heroine, as they sing of their desire to get out of their current circumstances in the opening number 'Skid Row (Downtown)'. This fires the story expertly right from the start. Later, once Seymour (the Hero) has Crossed the Threshold and is feeding the plant blood, Audrey (the Shapeshifter love interest) reveals her wish for a quiet suburban life in the classic 'I Wish' number 'Somewhere That's Green'. This song makes the audience empathise with her, whilst they are already empathising with downtrodden Seymour. It also reveals that both Audrey and Seymour have wishes and, as a result, the audience wants them to be together.

Eva Perón's 'I Wish' number is contained in her strident demanding refrain in 'Eva, Beware of the City': 'I want to be a part of BA, Buenos Aires, Big Apple'. She repeats this again and again, echoed by her family, in reaction to every barrier Magaldi puts in her way. Having left home for the city at the end of the number, the next song, 'Buenos Aires', is full of Eva stating her wishes.

But what of *The Sound of Music*? Uniquely, among these five musicals, the stage show's Hero, Maria, does not have an 'I Wish' song. This is because Maria, more than any of the other Heroes under consideration, is a reluctant Hero. She does not want to leave the abbey and has to be persuaded to by the Mother Abbess. She does not desire to leave the stability of the Ordinary World but is forced from it. For the film version, Richard Rodgers added the number (with his own lyrics) that comes close to being an 'I Wish' number, 'I Have Confidence', in which Maria expresses her wish to succeed in her new role.

Other 'I Wish' numbers of note, and in different styles, include:

- 'One Song Glory', the rocky 'I Wish' song from *Rent*.
- Leo Bloom's 'I Want to be a Producer' from Mel Brooks's *The Producers*.
- 'Maybe' from *Annie*.
- The Siamese twins' duet 'Like Everyone Else' from *Sideshow*.
- Mama Rose's barnstorming 'Some People' from *Gypsy*.

- 'The Wizard and I' from *Wicked*.
- 'Waiting for Life' from *Once on This Island*.
- 'Something's Coming' from *West Side Story*.
- 'I Got a Marble and a Star' from Kurt Weill's *Street Scene*.
- 'Corner of the Sky' from *Pippin*.
- Both 'A Room in Bloomsbury' and the title song from *The Boyfriend*.
- *The Lion King*'s boisterous 'I Just Can't Wait to Be King'.
- 'I Hope I Get It' from *A Chorus Line*.
- 'Part of Your World', *The Little Mermaid*'s classic 'I Wish' song in which nearly every line begins with the words 'I want...'
- The opening to *Into the Woods*, in which each of the major characters uses the words 'I wish...' to begin their story.

You can see here there is a huge range of styles and structures to 'I Wish' songs, but they all have one thing in common: they all exhibit characters wishing and thereby forcing the audience into empathy.

Notice how the characters' 'I Wish' songs sing about what they *want*, not about what they *don't want*, or about how their lives stink. Eliza Doolittle doesn't sing about how awful it is to be a flower-seller in Covent Garden; she sings about the 'warm face, warm hands and warm feet' she wants. Annie doesn't moan about being in an orphanage; she sings about how wonderful her parents may be. The dancers in *A Chorus Line* don't sing about how terrible a dancer's life is; they sing about how they *want* the job. I have seen a few musicals, all of which flopped, in which the Hero's 'I Wish' song was about how terrible their life was; audiences don't like whingers and whiners, they like positive characters. Negative characters turn them off because they are difficult to empathise with.

The wishes of the characters directly relate to the stories that follow. At the time of writing (Spring 2011), one of the issues I had with the musical *Betty Blue Eyes* was that the main

'I Wish' song, 'A Place on the Parade', didn't really relate to the story that followed. For the audience it felt like an irrelevance, even though it was a charming song.

## Refusal of the Call

The 'I Wish' song might also be placed during a moment of doubt for the Hero in the Refusal of the Call stage. But these songs should not become negative.

There are also songs of doubt that can occur at this stage. In *Little Shop of Horrors*, Seymour's solo 'Grow for Me' begins with him wondering what is wrong with the plant. It captures the moment where the plant responds to blood and Seymour's doubt about feeding it, and then Seymour Crossing the Threshold as he bleeds into the plant. This is an excellent example of one song moving forward the dramatic content of the story.

Doubts that the Hero has are often expressed non-musically. Maria von Trapp argues with the Mother Abbess and Eliza Doolittle has her famous 'Go-ahn'. Eva Perón, the fiery, driven, ambitious girl, has no doubt at all. The weight of this stage of the story will depend on the attitude of the Hero – a reluctant Hero (like Maria von Trapp) might have quite a substantial Refusal of the Call, whilst an ambitious Hero (like Eva Perón) may have none at all.

## Mentor and Teaching Songs

Although the Meeting the Mentor stage of the story can move across Act One and Act Two of the story, the function of the stage is always the same: to impart important knowledge to the Hero from the Mentor. In a musical this is often expressed musically in a teaching song.

Just as 'I Wish' songs come in many styles and forms, so do teaching songs. Remember also, that many characters can perform a Mentor function when they teach the Hero an important lesson. Most musicals has a teaching song at some point, and just as the Meeting the Mentor stage can move around the story, so the placement of the teaching song(s) can vary.

Rodgers and Hammerstein made the Mentor song a central feature of their musicals, usually writing for a middle-aged woman in the most operatic song of each score, in outstanding numbers that have become standards: 'Climb Ev'ry Mountain' from *The Sound of Music*, 'Happy Talk' from *South Pacific*, 'Something Wonderful' from *The King and I* and 'You'll Never Walk Alone' from *Carousel*.

Some musicals (and plays) are built almost entirely around the relationship between the Hero and Mentor. One of these is Jerry Herman's *Mame* in which Mame Dennis sings three phenomenal teaching songs to Patrick: 'It's Today', 'Open a New Window' and 'We Need a Little Christmas'.

In another musical where the Mentor-Hero relationship is central, *My Fair Lady*, the teaching song is used as a montage to illustrate Higgins tutoring Eliza over a period of time. The song 'Poor Professor Higgins' is sung as a commentary by Higgins's staff and is interspersed with spoken scenes between the major characters. The song itself does not contain the teaching, which takes place during the scenes.

Here are just a few examples of teaching songs, showing the range of styles and types:

- 'Men of Hareford' from *Me and My Girl*.
- 'Find Your Grail' from *Spamalot*.
- 'When You're Good to Mama' from *Chicago*.
- 'Mama Will Provide' from *Once on This Island*.
- In *Oliver!*, Oliver Twist has three Mentors, the Artful Dodger, Fagin and Nancy, who each have a teaching song: 'Consider Yourself', 'You've Got to Pick a Pocket or Two' and 'It's a Fine Life'.
- 'Look Over There' from *La Cage aux Folles*.
- 'Today 4 U' from *Rent*.
- 'No Time at All' from *Pippin*.

The Land of Oz has thrown up many teaching songs in its various musical incarnations:

- Glinda is a classic Mentor and her sequence with the Munchkins and Dorothy is a classic of the genre in

'Come Out, Come Out' and 'Ding Dong the Witch is Dead'.

- *The Wiz* has the same character, but now named Addaperle, and a similar number, 'He's the Wizard'.
- *Wicked* has a darker take on the Mentor song with Doctor Dillamond's 'Something Bad'.
- And Andrew Lloyd Webber added a new teaching song to his 2011 London Palladium production, 'Wonders of the World'.

## Crossing the Threshold

As Heroes Cross the Threshold into the unknown, they may have a song, which often reflects their doubt or wonder, or their new maturity. Kim and Chris in *Miss Saigon* have their first love duet, a reflective number, 'Sun and Moon', which elevates their relationship from the squalid reality to a celestial plane.

Sometimes characters Cross the Threshold during a number. In the film version of *The Sound of Music*, 'I Have Confidence' illustrates Maria's physical journey from the abbey to the von Trapp mansion and also her emotional journey from novice nun to novice governess (and surrogate mother). Similarly, Seymour Crosses the Threshold during 'Grow for Me' from hapless florist to feeder of a blood-drinking plant.

In some musicals it is a non-musical stage, such as Eliza's arrival at Professor Higgins's house, or Bill Snibson's arrival at Hareford in *Me and My Girl*. Note how similar those two musicals are; Stephen Fry even specifically referenced *My Fair Lady* in his revisions to the *Me and My Girl* book for the successful 1984 revival.

## Production Numbers, Tests, Allies and Enemies

Having Crossed the Threshold, the Hero then experiences the substantial Tests, Allies and Enemies stage of the story, musical numbers abound. In addition to teaching songs, there are also character songs, situation songs, and plot songs. this is also a point in the show that is likely to contain 'production numbers' which may be any of the types of songs above, or any others.

A production number is a song with spectacular staging that includes the chorus or ensemble and generally involves dancing and choral singing, usually led by a leading character. A musical with a chorus will generally include anything from three to ten of these.

*Cats*, for example, has nine numbers which might be classed as production numbers ('Jellicle Songs for Jellicle Cats', 'The Gumbie Cat', 'Rum Tum Tugger', 'The Jellicle Ball', 'Growltiger's Last Stand', 'Skimbleshanks', 'Macavity', 'Mr Mistoffelees' and 'The Ad-Dressing of Cats').

The placement and function of production numbers will vary according to the style and story of the piece. For example, *Fiddler on the Roof* has four production numbers in Act One ('Tradition', 'To Life', 'Tevye's Dream', 'The Wedding Sequence'), but none in Act Two.

Musicals that have diegetic songs, especially those with backstage settings, tend to have a high number of production numbers. The stage version of *42nd Street* has fourteen numbers of which only three ('Young and Healthy', 'About a Quarter to Nine' and the 'Finale') are *not* production numbers.

It is common that the Opening Number will be a production number, setting the scene, but the other numbers in Act One tend to focus the audience on the Hero, and to do this, tend towards solos and duets. In Act Two, as the Hero's journey really gets going, production numbers delight the audience, and any of the songs found at this stage in the story may be production numbers.

Audiences love production numbers; for many audiences, they are what make a musical. When considering source material for your musical, ask yourself about production numbers. Where are the opportunities for them? How many will you have? How many do you want? How will you need to change to the story or relocate moments in the story to allow for production numbers? Remember that you cannot shoe-horn production numbers in to a story and if you can't see a way to open up your story, ask yourself if you are writing a chamber musical, or if this is a suitable story for a musical at all.

Character songs are simple to describe. As the Hero meets new characters, be they Allies or Enemies, these characters may have introductory songs. Character songs come in many forms and may be solos, duets or production numbers, but their defining feature is that they demonstrate the distinctive characteristics or point of view of a character or group of characters.

*The Producers* contains a number of character songs as Leo and Max meet various off-beat characters that populate the cast, including Nazi Franz Liebkind's 'In Old Bavaria', Roger De Bris' production number 'Keep it Gay' and Ulla's 'When You've Got it, Flaunt it'. All of these numbers occur during the Tests, Allies and Enemies stage of the story.

*The Wizard of Oz* has three character numbers set to the same music at this stage, as Dorothy meets the Scarecrow, Tin Man and Lion. Each of them has their own 'I Wish' number that introduces them ('If I Only Had a Brain/Heart/the Nerve').

Situation songs are those songs that explore the moments in time or place where the Hero finds himself. Think of them as character songs for places or situations. 'The Merry Old Land of Oz' (from *The Wizard of Oz*) or 'Lonely Town' (*On the Town*) or 'Bali Ha'i' (*South Pacific*) are all examples of songs about places, but a situation song might just as easily be 'If My Friends Could See Me Now' (*Sweet Charity*) or 'We Can Do It' (*The Producers*). Situation songs are often celebratory, such as *Fiddler on the Roof*'s 'To Life' or *Beauty and the Beast*'s 'Be Our Guest' and a celebratory situation is always a good excuse for a production number.

Plot songs are those songs in which the plot is moved forward as a result of the number. These are often songs in which decisions have to be made or invitations delivered. The difference between plot songs and situation songs is that situation songs *describe* the moment and plot songs *develop* the moment. In *Blood Brothers*, Mrs Johnstone, the single mother of twins she cannot afford to raise, gives up one of her babies during the song 'Easy Terms'. In *Dreamgirls*, Curtis, CC and Wayne decide to use underhand techniques to secure record sales in the song 'Steppin' to the Bad Side', and in *Sweeney Todd*, Sweeney re-establishes himself as a premier barber in the area in the 'Shaving Contest'. Each of these numbers takes place in the Tests, Allies and Enemies stage of the story and each significantly develops the plot.

Let's have a look at the songs in this stage of the story in each of our five case-study musicals:

| | The Sound of Music | Little Shop of Horrors | Miss Saigon | My Fair Lady | Evita |
|---|---|---|---|---|---|
| Tests, Allies and Enemies | 'Do-Re-Mi' 'Lonely Goatherd' 'So Long, Farewell' | 'Ya Never Know' 'Mushnik and Son' 'Dentist' 'Some-where That's Green' 'Get It' | 'The Deal' 'The Wedding' | 'Just You Wait' 'Poor Professor Higgins' 'The Rain in Spain' 'I Could Have Danced All Night' 'Ascot Gavotte' 'On the Street Where You Live' | 'Goodnight and Thank You' 'I'd Be Suprisingly Good for You' 'Perón's Latest Flame' |

The songs in *The Sound of Music* reflect Maria's role new role as Mentor to the von Trapp children. In this musical, the role of the ensemble is played by the children. 'Do-Re-Mi' and 'The Lonely Goatherd' are the closest *The Sound of Music* comes to production numbers as it is a surprisingly intimate musical. 'How Can Love Survive?' is a situation song that reveals the worldly cynicism of Max and the Baroness, in contrast to Maria's naivety (it was cut from the score for the movie).

In *Little Shop of Horrors*, 'Ya Never Know' is a situation song in which the girl group tells of Seymour's new situation; 'Somewhere That's Green' is Audrey's 'I Wish' number, which indicates how much closer she is emotionally to Seymour than we had guessed before; 'Closed for Renovation' is a situation song; 'Dentist' is a character song for Seymour's Shadow, Orin the Dentist; and 'Mushnik and Son' is a plot song in which Seymour agrees to be adopted by Mushnik.

The through-sung style of *Miss Saigon* requires more plot songs than a book musical might need. 'The Telephone Song' is a situation song in which Chris sings of the situation with Kim, and John sings of the political situation. 'The Deal' is a plot song in which the Engineer haggles with Chris for Kim. 'The Wedding' is a situation song in which Kim and Chris marry. 'Thuy's Arrival' is a character song for Chris's Shadow, Thuy. And 'The Last Night of the World' is a situation song for Chris and Kim in a state of high emotion.

*My Fair Lady* begins this stage of the story with a character number for Higgins, 'I'm an Ordinary Man'. Eliza then has a character number, 'Just You Wait', revealing her to be much more feisty than 'Wouldn't It Be Loverly?' might have led the audience to believe. 'Poor Professor Higgins' is a teaching montage, and a situation number. 'The Rain in Spain' is a celebratory situation number as Eliza masters Received Pronunciation and 'I Could Have Danced All Night' is another celebratory situation number, which reveals Eliza's romantic feelings for Higgins. The 'Ascot Gavotte' is a situation number about Ascot and a production number, and 'On the Street Where You Live' is a character song for Freddie (Higgins's Shadow). Using Bernard Shaw's original play to carry the plot, Lerner and Loewe concentrate on exploring situation and character in the songs.

Eva Perón's Tests, Allies and Enemies stage begins with 'Buenos Aires', a situation song and the second major production number, describing her joy in the big city. 'Goodnight and Thank You' is a plot number in which Eva uses her bedroom skills as a means of social climbing. 'The Art of the Possible' is a character song for Perón, revealing him to be the most ruthless of the Argentinian generals. 'I'd Be Surprisingly Good for You' is a plot number in which Eva and Perón meet and are attracted to each other. 'Another Suitcase In Another Hall' is a character number for Perón's Mistress (Eva's Shadow), and 'Perón's Latest Flame' is a situation number and a production number, which reveals that neither the military nor the aristocracy are fond of Eva.

At this moment, in the stage of the story where the Shadow is typically revealed, the Baroness, Orin the Dentist, Thuy, Freddie and Perón's Mistress all have their first songs. This is not surprising when you consider that the Hero's discovery of an opposing force to himself is a key element of this stage.

As you write your musical, carefully consider the songs in this stage of the story. You will certainly have songs here: I can think of no musical that has no songs at this stage. You can use them to introduce new characters, further plot or reveal situations. A tip here is to be careful that when writing situation songs about places, you do not simply describe the scenery. This is all too common and makes for dull writing. Describe who the characters are, why the characters are there and what it means to them, but don't describe the setting – that is a job for the set designer.

## Preparation for the Supreme Ordeal

After the packed incidents of the Tests, Allies and Enemies, the furthering of the journey and the production numbers that the audience can revel in, it can be a relief to find that the Preparation for the Supreme Ordeal is often not musicalised. Sometimes it is a moment of beautiful underscoring, as it is in *My Fair Lady*. With Eliza's entrance, dressed for the Embassy Ball, the orchestra strikes up 'I Could Have Danced All Night' in a beautiful romantic arrangement. Similarly, *The Sound of Music* also uses only orchestral sounds at this stage as the von Trapp party is in full swing (mostly offstage). Often it is a book scene, as it is in *Little Shop*, as Seymour wrestles with his conscience in the dentist's chair. Of the five case-study musicals, only the two through-sung shows fully musicalise this stage. In *Evita*, Eva leads the charge for Perón's presidency in the production number, 'A New Argentina'.

In an unusual structure, the audience does not see the Preparation for the Supreme Ordeal of *Miss Saigon* until they are watching the second half of the show. This is the whole flashback sequence of 'Kim's Nightmare', as she, already pregnant with Chris's son, cannot leave the country with him.

## Supreme Ordeals

The Supreme Ordeal is the central dramatic incident of the story, the moment when the Hero metamorphoses and is reborn. In a musical, not surprisingly, this moment is often musicalised and this number is commonly a keystone of the musical score. There is generally a moment of decision or drive as the Hero begins the transformation, but bear in mind that the rebirth is not necessarily a positive step.

In *Sweeney Todd*, Sweeney transforms from a man bent on specific revenge to a mass-murderer determined to slaughter as many members of the human race as possible. He is reborn as a serial killer, and the song 'Epiphany' charts his emotional journey between the two states.

In *Oliver!*, Oliver Twist is restored to his genetic family and reborn as an upper-class boy, his relief and joy being illustrated in 'Who Will Buy?'. *Wicked*'s Elphaba is reborn as an independent young woman unafraid to question those she has held in esteem, and mastering her new powers in 'Defying Gravity'.

*Little Shop*'s Seymour undergoes a transformation similar to Sweeney Todd's in the number 'Now (It's Just the Gas)' in which he negligently allows the Dentist to die in order to provide food for the plant. Like Sweeney, he becomes a killer (albeit a reluctant one).

*Miss Saigon*'s Kim is reborn as a self-sacrificing mother in 'I'd Give My Life for You', in a premonition of the end of the story.

Maria von Trapp experiences a similar transformation as the Mother Abbess sings the iconic 'Climb Ev'ry Mountain' and Maria decides to return to the von Trapps' villa as a wife and mother. It is not Maria who sings this number, it is the Mentor, but it is ultimately Maria's decision.

*My Fair Lady* owes much to the Cinderella story, and it is the same transformation that Eliza undergoes in her Supreme Ordeal, the Embassy Ball. She enters looking like a beautiful princess and then dances with royalty and aristocracy at the ball. Although this is not a song, it is a piece of musical storytelling. Eliza triumphs over all, including the laser-like scrutiny of Zoltan Karpathy, to prove herself a true lady.

The Supreme Ordeal of *Evita* is interestingly handled. 'A New Argentina', the montage of the election campaign, is the Preparation for the Supreme Ordeal, and then comes the intermission and as Act Two begins, 'Don't Cry for Me, Argentina' is Eva's Reward. It is a strange lyric, much more suitable to when it is first heard in the 'Prologue' after Eva's death and late in Act Two as Eva suffers the ravages of cancer. There is no reason for Argentina to cry for Eva at all in this, her most powerful moment. Eva's Supreme Ordeal is a rebirth, from the ambitious actress of Act One to First Lady – again a kind of Cinderella story, and it is no accident that in the remarkable original production by Hal Prince she was dressed in a white ballgown, straight out of a fairytale, rather than a more historically accurate costume. Eva is undeniably reborn at this point in the story, and has supremely achieved her objective of social climbing.

## The Interval (or Intermission)

You might, if you have an eye for such things, have spotted that many of the numbers discussed in relation to the Supreme Ordeal are also commonly thought of as Act One finales. 'Climb Ev'ry Mountain', 'Now (It's Just the Gas)', 'I'd Give My Life for You' and the 'Embassy Ball' are all the ends of the first half of their respective shows. This is no coincidence, for there is something very satisfying for an audience to see a story begin with a character receiving the Call to Adventure, and then undergoing the rebirth of the Supreme Ordeal, during a single act, in one sitting. Many novice writers presume that there must be a cliffhanger at the end of the first half of the evening to ensure that the audience returns, but this is not necessarily so. It is more important to see the Hero achieve the rebirth necessary for their success and then to wonder what might happen next.

The interval, or intermission as it is known in the USA, commonly falls between Act Two and Act Three of the structural three-act model, which is why many musicals have significantly longer first halves than seconds. *Fiddler on the Roof*, for example, runs approximately ninety minutes before intermission and forty-five after. You must take your audience to a satisfying place in the story before releasing them from the onward thrust of the story and allowing them a rest.

The interval is a crucial time for the success of a musical. Audiences undergo a transformation at interval for a number of reasons. Firstly, it is the first time that audiences are allowed to talk to each other and it is at intermission that they put their personal and private feelings about the experience they are having into a more public forum. The strongest feelings in the group will colour those of the rest of the group. How many times have you been at the theatre with friends and discovered to your relief that those friends love or loathe the show as much as you do?

It is at the interval that audiences actually talk about the experience they are having, and if they love it they decide which of their friends and relations they should recommend it to. Surprisingly, audiences do not talk much about the musical after the show. They talk about where they left the car, where to go for dinner and whether the babysitter and children are at war, but they don't talk about the show very much. They will talk about it again, and at more leisure; but at the interval they talk about the show in a way that colours how they feel for the second half.

The interval is also the one time you allow your audience the chance to leave the theatre. Even in performances that some people find offensive, it is a bold audience member who walks out whilst the company are performing. More commonly audience members wait until the interval and then do not return for the second act. As a writer, keep the question 'The second act or dinner?' in your mind. That is the question the audience will be asking at the interval, subconsciously or not.

Ask yourself if you want or need an interval in your story. Increasingly popular is the long one-act show and this can be a very valid form for certain stories. On *Let Him Have Justice*, we decided very early on that the atmosphere, tension and tragic inevitability of the story required that the audience stayed through the ninety-minute running time in one sitting. Similarly, Sondheim's *Passion* and *Follies*, Stephen Dolginoff's *Thrill Me* and the international hit *A Chorus Line* all had original productions without an interval. There are two thoughts to ponder if you are thinking of not having an interval. The first is the total running time of the show. Ninety minutes is acceptable. Two hours is pushing it – and any longer and you are likely to get resistance. Audience members' bladders have a time limit! (Incidentally, if you are writing for children or a family audience never run more than an hour without a break.) Secondly, in Europe (especially the UK), the interval is an important time for the theatre to make money through bar sales. In these territories, to mitigate the loss in sales, theatre managers generally impose a surcharge on the rent paid by producers for a show with no interval.

If the interval is such an important moment, it is obvious that the moments of the play immediately before and after are also of great importance. Some of the finest writing in musical theatre is found in Act One finales. The numbers might be thrilling like 'Defying Gravity', chilling like *Cabaret*'s 'Tomorrow Belongs to Me', stirring like 'Climb Ev'ry Mountain', amusing like *Me and My Girl*'s 'Lambeth Walk', emotional like *Side Show*'s 'Who Will Love Me as I Am?', darkly humorous like *Sweeney Todd*'s 'A Little Priest', romantic like *The Phantom of the Opera*'s 'All I Ask of You' or inspiring like *Les Misérables*' 'One Day More'. Most importantly, it should capture the essence of the musical and the story you are telling. Some musicals, such as *Les Misérables* and *Me and My Girl*, are made by brilliant Act One finales.

The Act One finale occurs, as we have seen, at the end of the first half of the performance, but commonly at the end of Act Two of the storytelling (I told you it would get confusing!).

The Act One finale is one of the cornerstones of the musical. It doesn't necessarily muscialise the last moments of the act, and it doesn't necessarily need to be a production number. It should capture the essence of your show. If the story is epic in scale and involves many characters with their own stories, then it should be a number with many of them in. If your story is about one man and his struggle, you might want to focus on that. Remember that the Act One finale will be the impression that your audience will be left with as they begin to discuss the musical with colleagues over a glass of wine at interval. What will they be talking about?

Having released your audience from the story for a short break, you will now need to re-engage them with the opening of Act Two. The audience has already voted with its feet by returning to the auditorium for the second act.

Act Two openings come in every shape and size imaginable and may be spoken text, a song or a production number. Often this decision will depend on the Act One finale and will provide a contrast to it. *Les Misérables* ends Act One with a production number in which the entire cast state their point of view, and opens Act Two with a duet for Marius and Cosette, upon whom most of the second half of the show focuses. Similarly, *Mame* ends Act One with a hymn of praise to its leading lady and uses the beginning of Act Two to focus back on the tale of Patrick and his aunt. *Fiddler on the Roof* re-establishes the relationship between Tevye, God and the audience, and begins straight off with a dialogue scene.

*Little Shop* starts Act Two with probably the weakest song in the score, 'Call Back in the Morning', which establishes how successful the shop has become. *The Sound of Music* begins Act Two in a low-key fashion, with a dialogue scene in which the von Trapp children do not want to sing for Max. *Miss Saigon* shifts the focus from Kim and on to John's work in the USA on behalf of the Bui-Doi; a new strand of the plot that will drive Act Two to its tragic conclusion. This is a supremely effective production number that reaffirms the epic scale of the story after the intimacy of 'I'd Give My Life for You'.

*My Fair Lady* begins Act Two with 'You Did It', in which Higgins and Pickering praise each other (but not Eliza) for the success at the Embassy Ball, and *Evita* goes one stage further and uses 'Don't Cry for Me, Argentina', its most famous song, which was firmly established as a popular hit at the time of the opening of the show, to create one of the most famous openings to Act Two in all of musical theatre.

Many musicals use an orchestrated entr'acte to settle the audience and remind them of some musical themes. This can be a useful mechanism to re-establish the musical content of the show, especially if you are going to begin the second half with a dialogue scene. An entr'acte is commonly written after the bulk of the score is completed and may not even be drafted by the composer, but by the musical arranger, to the composer's instructions.

Now, having had our interval, let's return to the monomyth...

# Rewards

The drama of the Supreme Ordeal played out, the Reward stage of the story tends to bring more reflective musical moments in which the Hero is given a chance to enjoy, and become comfortable with, their new role. This stage of the story might be quite extensive, as it is in *Sweeney Todd*, in which Mrs Lovett celebrates new success in 'God, That's Good' and then Sweeney enters a calm, dreamlike reverie as he kills many customers in the number 'Johanna'. Killer Seymour Krelborn finds all his dreams coming true as the Little Shop of Horrors experiences new success and then Audrey confesses her love for him.

Like Sweeney Todd, Eva Perón has two numbers in her Reward stage. 'Don't Cry for Me, Argentina' is a scene of her finally securing her position as First Lady. The second number, 'High Flying, Adored', is a typical Reward-stage number, a reflective ballad, and a moment for all to draw breath, take a look back at what has happened and to prepare for the next stage of the drama.

Most of *The Sound of Music*'s Reward stage is played out in four scenes. Maria returns to the von Trapp villa, the Baroness withdraws and the way is clear for the Captain to wed Maria. In the original stage show, the couple had a song, 'An Ordinary Couple', which is far below top-drawer Rodgers and Hammerstein. This was replaced in the movie version with 'Something Good', a typically reflective Reward ballad. Maria's Reward continues with the wedding sequence in which she finally becomes a wife and stepmother.

*My Fair Lady*'s Reward section is also celebratory as Higgins and Pickering joyfully break into 'You Did It', and then a reprise of Act One's 'Just You Wait' illustrates just how much Eliza has grown. Having triumphed at the Embassy Ball, she is no longer in awe, nor passive, and the audience is taken straight into the drama that will occupy Act Two: what will Eliza do now that she has been transformed?

Reward sequences tend to celebrate the changes in the character undergone in the Supreme Ordeal, allow the Hero to enjoy them in some way and open the way for the unforeseen consequences of the transformation to be played out. The Hero, having often achieved their initial goal, as stated in their 'I

Wish' song, and arrived at what might appear to be a new place of stability, discovers that life is a whole lot more complicated and that the stability is only an illusion. Now it is time for the drama of Act Three of the story.

## The Reprise

A common feature in the third act of a musical (and sometimes earlier) is the reprise. This is where a song already sung is repeated, sometimes with slightly altered lyrics, for dramatic, sometimes ironic, effect. Reprises may occur at any time during the musical, but are most usually found later in the story, when a range of musical themes has been established, and so the one featured is chosen for maximum effect. Think, for example, of the poignancy of Eliza's walk through Covent Garden as the costermongers sing 'Wouldn't It Be Loverly?', or Eva Perón's pathetic 'Final Broadcast'.

Rodgers and Hammerstein knew the value of the reprise and used it extensively. In their first collaboration, *Oklahoma!*, they gave their Hero and Shapeshifter Heroine an ambivalent song of romantic denial, 'People Will Say We're in Love', only to reprise it when they have agreed to marry with the lyric 'Let people say we're in love'. This is a classic example of a reprise with a lyric alteration that changes the meaning of the song. They used the same technique to maximum effect in *Carousel*. In their first meeting, Billy Bigelow and Julie Jordan sing the classic 'If I Loved You'. In the third act of the story, as Billy returns to earth in a ghostly form, he sings a slightly altered lyric as Julie feels his presence but cannot see him, in one of the most emotional scenes in musical theatre.

In *South Pacific*, they used the technique of changing the context of the lyric to change its meaning, in their use of reprises of 'Some Enchanted Evening'. When Emile first sings it to Nellie, it is a song of opportunity: they might be each other's great loves. When they meet again on the beach, it is a song of affirmation, they are clearly in love, but when Nellie rejects him because she finds out that his children are of mixed race, he repeats the song, as the Act One finale, as a song of determination. Finally, it is reprised musically as part of the finale ultimo (see below) in which the theme becomes a song of stability. The different context of each situation alters the meaning of the lyric.

In *The Sound of Music*, they used the technique of changing the character singing to create the effect. The song 'Sixteen Going on Seventeen' first appears as a romantic duet for the von Trapps' eldest daughter Liesl and her beau, Rolf. This also demonstrates that he is her Mentor figure and that she is not able to communicate intimately with either her father or his betrothed, the Baroness. Later in the story, once Rolf joins the Nazis and her father marries Maria, her new stepmother reprises the song, which illustrates how Liesl now has a new Mentor, and how easily Maria fulfils the maternal role.

In *The King and I*, they used a different technique (twice): that of changing the character being sung *to* in order to change the meaning of the song. Early in the piece, when Anna has Crossed the Threshold and arrived in the Siamese court, she sings 'Hello, Young Lovers' to indicate how she has loved, but does not expect to love again. Later, as Lun Tha and Tuptim plan their escape, she sings the same lyric to them to indicate her solidarity with them. Similarly, as she arrives at the dock with her son Louis, she sings 'I Whistle a Happy Tune' to raise their spirits, and this is reprised as the final sung item, when she tries to raise the spirits of the royal children as they face an uncertain future on the death of their father, the King.

Reprises tend to be shorter than the original song, but can be remarkably effective and create truly musical theatre. They are one of the advantages that musicals have over non-musical theatre because they act as a form of recall for the audience. As we will see, some musicals have extensive sequences made up entirely of reprises.

Not surprisingly, you are more likely to find reprises in a through-sung musical than in one with dialogue scenes, and in these musicals one must use reprises carefully for maximum effect. When Andrew Lloyd Webber's *Aspects of Love* opened, many critics felt that the anthem 'Love Changes Everything', which opened the show, reprised too many times, and often in circumstances that did not demand such an anthem. As a result they felt that the show lacked variety in the score and it only had one major song. I think this point of view underestimates that score, but it is a useful lesson: the power of the reprise is diminished by overuse and it can overpower other elements of the score. The reprise is a potent ingredient: be prudent with its use.

## The Road Back

The Road Back, when the drama of Act Three becomes a reality, is one of those stages, like the Preparation for the Supreme Ordeal, that is just as often carried in dialogue scenes as in songs. If there are songs in this section they are often not major songs in the score.

In *The Sound of Music*, the Nazi threat and summoning of Captain von Trapp is handled through book scenes. Maria sings her reprise of 'Sixteen Going on Seventeen', which demonstrates her new maternal role, but the entire plot at this stage is carried through dialogue.

In *Miss Saigon*, the song 'Please' is a beautiful ballad, but most of the plot of the Road Back is carried in the recitative-style 'Chris is Here' (that develops on into the Preparation for the Supreme Ordeal flashback, 'Kim's Nightmare').

*My Fair Lady*'s Road Back is concerned with how the relationship between Eliza and the other characters (notably Higgins) will play out now that she is a lady. The song 'Show Me' signifies a change in her relationship with Freddie (it is, in fact, their only substantial scene together), but her real dilemma is captured in the flower market scene where the costermongers reprise her 'Wouldn't It Be Loverly?' 'I Wish' song whilst treating her as a lady. In a classic piece of 'opening up', Lerner and Loewe lighten the dramatic tone of this stage with the production number 'Get Me to the Church on Time', and then Higgins's 'A Hymn to Him' is an Act Three counterpoint to his Act One 'I'm an Ordinary Man', emphasising how little he has changed. Of these songs, only the interpolated, dramatically unimportant 'Get Me to the Church on Time' has become a classic.

*Evita*'s Road Back sequence similarly includes numbers that are not cornerstones of its score. 'Rainbow High' and 'The Rainbow Tour' are concerned with the preparations for, and execution of, Eva Perón's tour of Europe. It was during this tour that she showed the first signs of the illness that would kill her. Having returned from Europe, the musical has its last full-scale production number, 'And the Money Kept Rolling In', in which Eva takes a small role and the Argentinian people take centre stage. From here on, the music takes a markedly fragmented tone as the show focuses on her decline.

*Little Shop of Horrors* begins this stage with a classic Road Back moment: the discovery. Mushnik suspects Seymour's role in Orin's death, and in the number 'Suppertime' is lured to his own demise. This is followed by the montage number 'The Meek Shall Inherit', in which Seymour's entrapment in his Faustian pact becomes all too clear to him. Both numbers propel the plot forward; neither is a classic.

It is clear that the Road Back is a stage of the story in which the Hero learns of the new threat from the unforeseen consequences of his actions leading up to the Supreme Ordeal. Musicalised or not, it is the turning point between the celebrations of the Reward section and the climax of the drama in the Final Conflict.

## The Final Conflict

This is the climax of the musical, the moment when everything must be resolved to take the characters to a new place of stability. Just as with the Supreme Ordeal, it is likely that the climax of your story will be musicalised.

In *The Sound of Music*, the Final Conflict is a combination of song and scenes. The music festival is the first scene and the songs are diegetic. First, the Captain sings the faux folk tune 'Edelweiss', and then the von Trapps sing 'So Long, Farewell', which is used to cover their exit from the stadium and their escape to the abbey. In a non-musical scene at the abbey, they are nearly caught by the Nazis but Rolf does not betray them. The only question then is how to escape from Austria and Nazi-controlled territory.

The Final Conflict of *Miss Saigon* is made up of two scenes both concerning Chris's American wife Ellen, a Shadow who is completely unknown to Kim. In the recitative scene 'Room 317',

Kim comes to Chris's hotel room and is mistaken by Ellen for the maid. As they realise that they both think they are married to Chris, Kim's world falls apart and she leaves. Ellen sings of her own dilemma in 'Now That I've Seen Her' and then Chris and John return from searching for Kim. In 'The Confrontation', Chris has to choose between Kim and Ellen, but Kim has already come to her own conclusion.

In *My Fair Lady*, a long dialogue scene between Higgins and Eliza at Mrs Higgins's house forms the core of the Final Conflict. Eliza proves herself a match for Higgins and sings her own Act Three counterpoint to her Act One 'Just You Wait': 'Without You'. Rather than resenting him, she now discards him, proving herself an independent freethinking young lady. Higgins is astonished by his own reaction, 'I've Grown Accustomed to Her Face', in which he finally realises that he has fallen in love with Eliza, only when she no longer needs him.

*Evita* and *Little Shop* share a similarity in their Final Conflict sequences in that the Hero must die in order to resolve the plot; the threat to them is greater than their ability to resolve it. Throughout this sequence of *Little Shop*, song and dialogue are mixed. The score makes excellent use of the reprises to bring the story to its close. The Plant (Audrey II sings a reprise of 'Suppertime' as it attacks Audrey, and then, fatally wounded, she sings a reprise of 'Somewhere That's Green' before Seymour feeds her, and then himself, to the plant.

The climactic stage in *Evita* begins with her abstract battle with Che in the 'Waltz for Eva and Che'. A reprise of the army's song, showing that they have not changed their attitude to her, follows. Perón answers them with his biggest solo of the show, 'She is a Diamond', and then Lloyd Webber uses reprises of many themes from the show, most notably 'A New Argentina', but now Eva cannot rabble-rouse; she is dying. As she collapses, Perón echoes his Mistress's song from Act One; 'So What Happens Now?' he asks, and then Eva is plunged into a montage sequence of her life flashing before her in which phrases from many of the songs of the score are repeated.

The hurtling of the plot towards its conclusion often leads to sequences that are made extensively of reprises. Sondheim's *Sweeney Todd* has a thirteen-minute sequence that contains almost no new music. This is roughly a third of the second half of the show. Reprise follows reprise as the characters hurtle towards the conclusion of their stories, usually their deaths.

## The Eleven O'Clock Number

The term 'Eleven O'Clock Number' was coined during the period when all Broadway curtains rose at 8.30 p.m. Two and a half hours later the musical would climax with a showstopping number that would send the audience home with a memorable performance lodged firmly in their hearts.

The eleven o'clock number is often concerned with the Hero making the final decision that will return his life to a form of stability. The most famous of these is undoubtedly 'Rose's Turn' from *Gypsy*, possibly the finest eleven o'clock number in musical theatre, and composed of new material and quotes from the score. Just as 'I Wish' songs vary according to the subject matter and style of the show, so do eleven o'clock numbers, but what is true of all of them is that they are showstoppers.

I use the term 'showstopper' in its theatrical sense, to mean a number for which the applause is so great that the show stops whilst the audience goes wild. It means something that is wonderful, delightful, admirable and massively pleasing. During the bumbling, illiterate presidency of George W. Bush his administration began to use the term 'showstopper' as a term to mean a breakdown, or a massive problem that would 'stop the show'. In the theatre, the correct term for that is a 'show stop' not a 'showstopper'.

Eleven o'clock numbers vary according to the show, but if you are going to 'save the best till last' it is in this stage of the story that you should unveil the glorious showstopper you have up your sleeve, and that means that it is likely, but not necessarily, tied into the Final Conflict. Depending on your Final Conflict stage, it might come slightly earlier, as it does, for example, in *La Cage aux Folles* (in which it comes during the Road Back stage).

Some great eleven o'clock numbers include:

- 'Rose's Turn' from *Gypsy*.
- 'Memory' from *Cats*.
- 'The 42nd Street Ballet' from *42nd Street*.
- 'Shall We Dance?' from *The King and I*.
- 'Cabaret' from the show of the same name.
- 'Next to Normal' from the show of the same name.
- 'Being Alive' from *Company*.
- 'The American Dream' from *Miss Saigon*.
- 'For Good' from *Wicked*.
- 'No One is Alone' from *Into the Woods*.
- 'Back to Before' from *Ragtime*.
- 'The Best of Times' from *La Cage aux Folles*.
- 'What I Did for Love' from *A Chorus Line*.
- 'Time Heals Everything' from *Mack and Mabel*.
- 'Leaning on a Lamp Post' from *Me and My Girl*.
- 'Fifty Per Cent' from *Ballroom*.
- 'Oklahoma!' from the show of the same name.

Shows that make extensive use of reprises in the Final Conflict stage are unlikely to have eleven o'clock numbers. You will notice that all of the numbers listed above (with the exception of 'Memory') are songs that have not yet been heard in the show. A show that has a strong sense of community might have a choral eleven o'clock number, such as 'What I Did for Love', 'No One is Alone' or 'Oklahoma!', and a story that focuses strongly on an individual's struggle will probably have one in which that character makes a final plea or decision, such as 'Being Alive' or 'Fifty Per Cent'. Your eleven o'clock number must relate to the theme or central dilemma of the story or it becomes an irrelevance.

Whether you decide to make use of reprises, or you write an anthemic eleven o'clock number, or you decide to write some other conclusion to your story, you need to resolve the plotting of your story at this point. If you have a central relationship between the Hero and the Shadow, this must now be resolved, such as *The Lion King*'s final fight between Simba and Scar. More commonly in a musical will be the resolution of any difficulties in the relationship between the Hero and the Shapeshifter, such as the relationships between Emile and Nellie in *South Pacific*, or Cliff and Sally Bowles in *Cabaret*. Your central relationships need to reach a place of stability: *Wicked*'s Elphaba and Glinda recognise the value of their relationship in 'For Good'; *Company*'s Bobby resolves to commit in 'Being Alive'; and in *Cats*, Grizabella's relationship with the community is finally resolved as she is nominated for the Heaviside Layer.

## The Finale and the Return to Stability

The final stage of the Hero's journey will certainly have a musical element, and the way in which the music functions in this stage of the story breaks down, broadly, into three methods, each of which is often known as the finale, or finale ultimo (literally, the 'final last', to distinguish it from an Act One finale or an Act Two finale). In order for the story to be satisfying there needs to be a Return to Stability, with a lesson learned. The finale is normally composed of:

- A spoken scene with underscore; or
- A reprise; or
- A new song.

The spoken scene with underscore was very common in the Golden Age of Broadway. *My Fair Lady*, *The King and I*, *South Pacific* and many others end with dialogue scenes in which the Return to Stability is clearly indicated. As this is established, the orchestra swells and the curtain falls. Think, for example, of the final scene of *The King and I*, in which the King lies dying and, in a state of serenity, passes power to his son. Prince Chulalongkorn begins to proclaim Anna's long-wished-for reforms. The monarchy, the court and the country are restored to a place of stability. The musical underscore for all of this is the beautiful melody of 'Something Wonderful', which indicates that the King is at peace and that it is his parenting that brought the reform. As the scene continues, the music crescendos, drowning out any further speeches as the curtain falls.

Similarly, in *My Fair Lady*, Higgins – having just sung 'I've Grown Accustomed to Her Face' and through it realised just how deep his feelings are for Eliza – plays recordings of Eliza's cockney voice as the orchestra gently plays 'I Could Have Danced All Night', her musical theme of attraction to him. Eliza enters, stops the recording and continues the text. Higgins realises she is there and the orchestra strikes up a fully orchestral fortissimo rendition of 'I Could Have Danced All Night' as the curtain falls. There is a clear choice for the director here, in how Higgins and Eliza behave towards each other as the music swells. George Cukor's film version, which owes a massive debt to Moss Hart's original stage production, indicates that their relationship will go on as before; Trevor Nunn's National Theatre production had Higgins and Eliza laughing together as the curtain fell; and the Danish National Theatre mounted a production in which the director made the mistake of having Higgins and Eliza passionately kiss through the music, which completely misunderstood the nature of their relationship.

The spoken scene with underscore can be particularly effective, especially if you have a large orchestra, but these are very expensive. As a result, in recent years this style of finale has fallen from fashion, although Andrew Lloyd Webber used it to great effect at the end of *Sunset Boulevard*. Oftentimes, this form of finale was not recorded as part of the original cast recording, particularly during the Golden Age when forty-five minutes' worth of material was pretty much the limit that could be squeezed on to a twelve-inch vinyl recording. A number of more recent complete recordings, notably on the JAY label, have made these finales available, including those of *South Pacific*, *The King and I* and *My Fair Lady*.

*Fiddler on the Roof* takes this one step further and largely does away with the dialogue. The village that the audience met in the opening 'Tradition' is now fragmented and scattering across the world. As Tevye and his family leave Anatevka, themes from the opening appear in the orchestral underscoring against a mournful trombone drone, emphasising the bleakness of the characters' plight. Strangely, *Fiddler on the Roof* does not take its audience to the Return to Stability stage, it only implies it. Tevye announces that the family are leaving for America; for the audience of the original production, America was a code for stability and freedom from religious intolerance. The stability is implied.

The reprise is probably the most common form of Finale. The easiest way to indicate the Return to Stability is to reprise the opening number, in the manner of 'The Circle of Life' in *The Lion King*, and if your story lends itself to it, this can be an effective Finale. Think of the delightful ending of *On the Town* as Gaby, Ozzie and Chip return to the stability of their ship, only to find three new sailors disembarking, singing excitedly of their day ahead in New York.

If a Prologue has opened the musical, an Epilogue is often the finale, such as in *Sweeney Todd* or *A Little Night Music*. If you have a diegetic Prologue, especially one that welcomes the audience, such as 'Comedy Tonight' in *A Funny Thing Happened on the Way to the Forum* or 'Willkommen' in *Cabaret*, then reprising this to take leave of the audience can be the most logical step, but you must make sure that you have returned your characters to a place of stability beforehand.

Another common finale is to reprise one of the major songs, and rather than a direct repeat, which is often the case with the reprise of the opening number, this can use any of the techniques of the reprise to alter or magnify the meaning of the song. In *The Sound of Music*, the Mother Abbess sings 'Climb Ev'ry Mountain' at the end of Act One to encourage Maria to face any obstacle in life with courage, and specifically to return to the von Trapp villa and face up to her emotions for the Captain. At the finale, the nuns sing literally and figuratively 'Climb Ev'ry Mountain' as the von Trapps begin their journey over the mountains to safety. As with *Fiddler on the Roof*, the Return to Stability is implied, but as this is a real-life story, we know that the von Trapps eventually settled in America. Actually, if they had gone over the mountains from Salzburg they would have ended up further into Nazi territory, but Oscar Hammerstein never let fact get in the way of a good image!

Similarly, in *Carousel*, the song first sung by Nettie to Julie to help her through her grief, 'You'll Never Walk Alone', is reprised as a college graduation hymn advising young adults, and as an expression of the show's guiding principle that the dead watch over us.

Other songs that might prove effective finales, depending on your story, are the 'I Wish' song, the Act One finale or the title song (if you have one).

If you use the 'I Wish' song, it is likely that this will now feature in a choral arrangement, just as it does as the finale of *The Little Mermaid*. 'I Wish' songs that can act as finale songs are actually quite rare as the character's point of view at the beginning of the story is often so naive compared to where they finish. It also reminds the audience of the driving wish of the protagonist.

Reprising the Act One finale is another choice, particularly if the relationship between Act One and Act Two is distinctive, or if the relationship between the Supreme Ordeal and the Return to Stability is strong. In *Sunday in the Park With George*, Sondheim uses the parallels between the lives of Georges Seurat and his (fictional) grandson, George, to explore the creation of art. At the end of Act One, the chorus sing 'Sunday' as Seurat paints his most famous work, *Sunday Afternoon on the Island of La Grande Jatte*. At the end of the Act Two, whilst his grandson is on the island and has been visited by the ghost of his grandfather's muse, Dot, the chorus return, reprising 'Sunday' as George resolves his creative block.

Finally, a title song, wherever it might appear in the show, is always a strong choice for reprising at the finale. Examples of this are the ending of *Guys and Dolls* or *42nd Street*. Of course, it is possible – even desirable – that by changing the characters singing, you will change the meaning of the song, as Jerry Herman does at the end of the *Hello, Dolly!* when Vandergelder begins to sing the title song before proposing to Dolly.

*Miss Saigon* uses reprises of 'This is the Hour' (previously sung by the chorus) and 'Sun and Moon' to create a Finale scene in which Kim decides to commit suicide, thereby securing her son a stable, more prosperous future in America with his father. The strains of 'Sun and Moon', almost entirely orchestral, remind the audience of the strength of their relationship as the curtain falls.

Often a score contains a new song at the finale, and it is here that the function of the finale can be truly examined. Reprises or underscored scenes can return the characters to a place of stability, but the new number can go one step further. When thinking about your musical, you should think about the experience that the audience will undergo. This is to do with the shape of the play.

At the beginning of the performance the audience settles into its seats, its thoughts are all about the outside world – whether the mobile phone is turned off, a last check of text messages, where the car was left, the troubles at the office – and they must be taken through the opening minutes into the world of the play. At the end of the play, the audience is released back into the outside world. The most obvious ritual of this is when they applaud the actors, thank them for their work and release the actors from their roles and back to their lives.

Think of it like this:

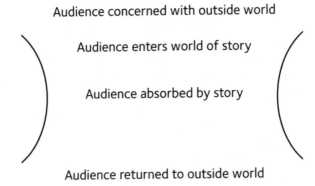

Audience concerned with outside world

Audience enters world of story

Audience absorbed by story

Audience returned to outside world

In a musical, a finale song can relate the musical back to the outside world of the audience's lives, relating the story they have seen to the world beyond the theatre. Examples of this are *Avenue Q*'s 'For Now', *Cats*' 'The Ad-Dressing of the Cats' and one of the most beautiful finales ever, Leonard Bernstein's 'Make Our Garden Grow' from *Candide*. It may be late in the show for introducing new material, but if you have a song as good as this, it is never *too* late.

*Evita* uses this kind of finale, with the 'Lament', in which Eva, at the point of death, justifies her own life and sings of choices we all have to make. As she dies, Che steps forward to give a little narration to end the story. *Little Shop of Horrors* also uses this kind of finale, a warning to the audience, 'Don't Feed the Plants', which is a metaphor for 'Don't give into temptation'.

Think carefully before committing to a form for your finale. Remember that it is the last moment of the show and the one that will leave a lasting impression on the audience. What is the moral or the philosophy in your tale? Be careful of getting too didactic. As Sam Goldwyn said, 'If you want to send a message, call Western Union.' Let your story speak, and having brought your characters to a place of stability, or at least implied stability, think about what you want the audience to remember. Then think about your finale.

---

### Song Function

Take a musical you know well and make a list of the songs in the order they appear. If you have access to a complete recording or a libretto, then list all of the songs, including reprises. Then go through the list and mark at what stage of the story the songs appear and the function of the song – is this an 'I Wish' Song, a character song, etc. Also, note if the song is a production number, a solo, a duet, a trio, etc., and whether it contains dance music (a production number will invariably contain dance music, but a number with dance music is not necessarily a production number).

---

You will have seen in this chapter that, depending on where a song comes in the story, its place will determine the function of the song in the show. You should always think about the function of the songs before beginning to write them. Most importantly, the function of any song will be determined by your story and your approach to the story. Every musical is different because every character's journey through every tale is different. The choices that you make about the songs in your musical will be determined by the characters' journeys through the story. There are similarities between songs at certain stages of the musical, but there is no formula.

---

### Spotting Your Synopsis

Take your synopsis and go through it, spotting the moments for the songs. Use the notes you have made on each stage of the story to work out whether you need, or want, a song at each stage, and to work out the function of the songs. Refer to the songs only by the type of song they are and who will sing them (e.g. 'I Wish' song – Solo – Cinderella), but make notes in the synopsis about what is being sung about and what the point of the song is. How much music are you going to use? Will it be through-sung or contain book scenes? Where are your production numbers? Which songs are solos? Which reprises are you going to use and how are you going to change the function of the song when it is reprised?

---

If twenty writing teams got together and each of them was asked to create five songs for a musical version of *Cinderella*, then each writing team would choose to musicalise different moments of the story in different ways. Each would write in a different style, so there might be an urban rap *Cinderella* or an operatic *Cinderella*, and each team would make different choices about which stages to musicalise and how. You would end up with twenty different takes on the tale, and one hundred songs, all of which would be related to the *Cinderella* story. Each team would write in its own unique style, and the choices they make is what makes each team's work distinctive. Now it is time to begin to make those choices to make your own work distinctive.

---

### Spotting a Story

Choose a very well-known story, like *Little Red Riding Hood* or *Goldilocks*. Imagine you have been commissioned to write a new musical version of the story. Decide on five moments in the story that you would musicalise and the type of song that you would choose to use at each stage.

---

# 7
# *Theatrical Language*

# *Theatrical Language*

Every musical or play has its own theatrical language. This is made up of many components, primarily narrative, time, location, characters, musical style and physical style and a number of other key decisions, which largely fall, in some way, into each of these categories.

These elements of theatrical language are interrelated:

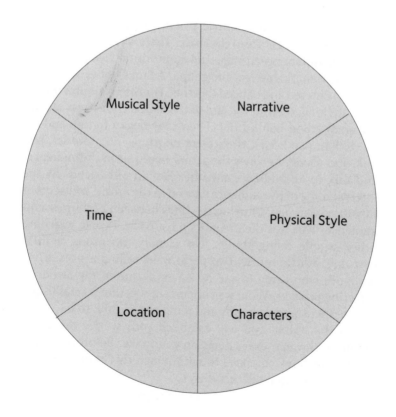

Peter Brook wrote that the simplest act of theatre is that one person walks into a space whilst another person watches. He is describing a very simple theatrical language. Think of it like this: if you sit and tell a child a fairytale, you are making a piece of theatre; you are doing something and the child is watching. If you introduce puppets into your telling of the story you would be creating a theatrical language, because you are making a decision about how you are going to tell this story. If you then introduce a different voice for each puppet, you are creating a more complex theatrical language, and this language increases in complexity the more elements you introduce until you have a full-scale theatrical experience. At each stage you have asked yourself, 'How am I going to tell this story?'

Every decision you make about your piece of theatre affects and defines its theatrical language. When I created my production of Peta Murray's play about a ballroom-dancing couple, *Wallflowering*, I took inspiration from Brook's definition of theatre. In a room that had been built as a ballroom, the audience sat around a central playing space. One chair was positioned in the centre of the space. There was no other set and no distinction between stage and auditorium. Two people (the cast: the remarkable real-life couple Adam Cooper and Sarah Wildor) entered and danced together. For three minutes no one said anything, then, at the end of the dance, the actress sat and the actor stood behind her. Then they began to talk and for more than two hours, there were no props, no more set, just talk, and dance. At times the actors would sit in the audience, and talk to an audience member like an old friend. At the interval some of the audience danced to the music, whilst other members watched, blurring the lines between performer and audience. This was theatre at its most basic. People watching other people doing things. No scenery, no props, a little costume, a little music, two performers telling a story to an audience who came to see it. It is still one of my favourite directing projects. What was important was that it established its theatrical language early and remained faithful to it.

As the writer, you will establish your work's theatrical language through every decision you make. Before you start writing the book you need to ask yourself this basic question: 'How am I going to tell this story?'

Some of these decisions are not for the writer to make. They belong to producers, directors, designers, and all the other members of the creative team; but the writer makes more decisions about the theatrical language than anyone else, and most of the decisions that the other creatives can make are dependent on those original decisions made by the authors.

You need to define your theatrical language for yourself. Think about each of the elements mentioned above and answer the following questions, as well as any others you can think of that come under these headings. You will know the answers to many of these questions with barely any thought if you have already written your synopsis, but still ask the questions. If you are working in a group, make sure you talk about all of these aspects, even if it is only to dismiss them.

*Narrative*

How is your story going to be told? We have already considered the story of the musical, but there are other questions. Are you going to have a narrator? Or narrators? If so, do you need them? If not, you are generally better to do without. Will any required narration be carried out through song, as it is in *Children of Eden*? Is the narrative told entirely through music (through-sung) or are there book scenes?

*Time*

What is the time frame for your story? Does your play take place over hours, days, months or years? If so, how is this communicated? Is it a play in which the time taken to perform the play is the same as the time the characters experience (this is called a time=time play)? *West Side Story* takes place over three days, but Marsha Norman's play *'Night, Mother* is a time=time play. If there are 'time gaps' between scenes, what has happened offstage during these periods that the audience doesn't see? Is time told chronologically or are there flashbacks and flashforwards? What period is your story set in?

## Location

Is this a single-location story that all takes place in one space or room? Or does it have multiple locations? If so, how many locations are involved? What locations are offstage from your major locations? Where have characters come from when they enter a scene and where are they going to when they exit a scene? What is the relationship between the onstage action and the audience? Is there a 'fourth wall'?

The 'fourth wall' refers to a convention in naturalistic plays and musicals in which there is an imaginary wall onstage where the proscenium arch is. The audience are looking through the 'fourth wall' at the stage. In productions where the fourth wall is 'dropped', both the actors and the audience believe that the actors can see the fourth wall and that the characters the actors are playing are not aware that they are in a theatre. In a production where the fourth wall is 'broken', the characters and the audience are aware of each other. For example, *Guys and Dolls* and *My Fair Lady* have the fourth wall dropped and *Godspell* has a fourth wall that is broken.

Location is created onstage through settings (or 'the set') and these come in four types:

1.  Realistic: in which locations such as rooms are recreated onstage in detail.
2.  Abstract: in which no specific period or location is depicted.
3.  Suggestive: in which only certain elements are realistically represented to create the suggestion of a space.
4.  Functional: in which nothing is realistically presented and only those elements that are required for the performance are onstage, e.g. a circus, in which the scenic elements are derived from performance requirements.

## Characters

What is the relationship between the actor and his role? Does every actor play only one role, or many roles through the performance? In a musical, it is common for leading actors to play one role, but for ensemble performers to play multiple roles. How many actors do you have/need? Is an actor's performance diegetic? That is, is the actor aware that he is performing as a character, or are we asked to believe that the actor is the character? Do some characters play other characters?

In, for example, *The Sound of Music* or *The Phantom of the Opera*, the audience believe that the actors are those characters for the duration of the performance, whereas in *The Fantasticks* the actors play actors putting on a performance of the story, and in *Once on This Island* most of the cast play storytellers who relate the tale (the characters are diegetic). What is the relationship between the characters and the audience? If the fourth wall is firmly in place, then there will not be a relationship, but in many musicals the fourth wall is completely, or partially removed. The characters in *Godspell* or *Barnum* interact with, and are aware of, the audience; in *Fiddler on the Roof*, there is a complex arrangement whereby Tevye 'breaks through' the fourth wall and talks directly to the audience, but no other character can. In Kander and Ebb's *The Rink* and *The Scottsboro Boys*, some characters play a range of important characters (not ensemble roles) through the performance.

## Musical Style

The style of the songs, their function and the musical genre in which you write are a key element of the theatrical language of your musical. Are the songs diegetic or non-diegetic? These are not mutually exclusive: there are many musicals that mix the two, such as *South Pacific* or *The Sound of Music*. Is the musical style rock, pop, jazz, classic musical theatre, operatic or rap? There are as many different styles in musical theatre as there are in music, from the operetta of *The Phantom of the Opera* to the rap of *In the Heights* and the children's TV music of *Avenue Q*. Does every character have the same musical style? In *South Pacific*, for example, Emile's musical style is notably more operatic than Nellie's, indicating his more cultured, sophisticated European character. If the musical is through-sung, is there recitative, or does number follow number? If there are book scenes, how much underscore is there? Some musicals, such as *Ragtime* and *Show Boat*, have an almost continuous musical score under the spoken scenes. How many production numbers, solos, duets and trios are there? What is the role of any ensemble singing? Will the musicians and/or singers be amplified or acoustic?

## Physical Style

You will need to consider the physical style of the work. This doesn't mean the physical set, but the physical language that the cast will use, which may be written into the musical from its earliest stages. One major question here is the function of dance in your piece. Some musicals, such as *Les Misérables* and *Sweeney Todd*, have practically no dance; others, such as *Cats*, *A Chorus Line* and *Chicago*, each have a hugely important and distinctive dance style that defines the entire performance style of the show. A physical style is not only about dance. A show like *Sunday in the Park with George* has very little dance, but the combination of the actors' movement, the set and the costumes creates a highly distinctive physical style for the show.

The musical style and the physical style are closely related to each other. The balletic style of Bernstein's music for *West Side Story* is interdependent with Jerome Robbins' choreography. The hip hop and rap of *In the Heights* led choreographer Andy Blankenbuehler to create a remarkable physical style for the show that drew on the movements of street dance. Think about each character's physical style, and about their physicality, at each important moment of the musical. In *West Side Story*, it is Tony's stillness contrasted to the dance-based movements of the Sharks and Jets that indicates his maturity and his unwillingness to get involved in the gangs' disputes. Tony doesn't dance until the gym scene, and when he does it is almost immediately with Maria. In some cases, such as Robbins' work in *Fiddler on the Roof* and *West Side Story*, the physicality of the choreography has become so important to the theatrical language of the show that it became part of the authorship, and the choreographer receives a percentage of all licensing receipts. This is, however, the exception and not the rule.

Different directors and creative teams in different productions will reinvent some of the theatrical language of the musical. Director John Doyle excised Hal Prince's neo-Brechtian social commentary from *Sweeney Todd* when he reinvented it as a piece for actor-musicians, and Trevor Nunn created two different productions of *Chess*, one for London which was through-sung and one for Broadway which contained spoken dialogue. But most of the theatrical language of any piece is woven into the fabric of its writing. *Cats* may not be performed using Gillian Lynne's choreography for 'Now and Forever', but it will always be a dance musical, as will *On the Town*, *Chicago* and *A Chorus Line*. Tevye will always break the fourth wall and *Barnum* will always be set in a circus. It is the physical language of those musicals.

Having seen how the elements of theatrical language are defined, remember that a decision made in one element of the theatrical language will affect all the others. If the story has a certain time or location, this may affect the musical style, which will affect the physical language, etc. With this in mind, there are aspects to both time and location that should be considered...

## The Three Dimensions of Time and Location

There are three dimensions to time and location: those of story, plot and performance.

*Time*

There is the time that the story takes place in. Then there is the time that the plot takes place in. Finally, there is the time the performance takes place in.

So, *Mrs Warren's Profession* has a story that takes place over about thirty years. It has a plot that takes place over five days, in four scenes. It has a performance running time of about two hours (do not include intermissions).

Similarly, *Wicked* has a story that takes place from the landing of the Wizard in Oz to the faked death of Elphaba, a plot that runs through the same time frame and a performance time of about two hours, ten minutes.

Now, you might think about the relationship between the three times as follows.

Story time is always greater than, or equal to plot time, which is always greater than or equal to performance time. Time is compressed in theatre like this:

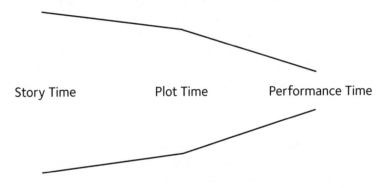

Story Time          Plot Time          Performance Time

If you were thinking about a time=time play, like Terrence McNally's *Frankie and Johnny in the Clair de Lune* or Marsha Norman's *'Night, Mother*, then plot time and story time would be equal and it might be drawn like this:

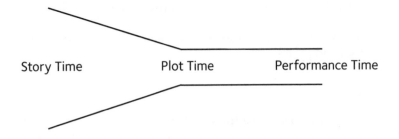

Story Time          Plot Time          Performance Time

It would be rare to find a play where the whole of the story takes place onstage. This would have to involve two characters who had never had any relationship prior to their first moment onstage and then the play follows that relationship right through to the end. Even though *Frankie and Johnny* is about a one-night stand and the plot time is the same as the performance time, the story began when they first met earlier in the evening.

In a musical, however, you can bend time in the musical numbers, and actually alter the relationship between plot time and performance time. Listen, for example, to 'He Wanted to Say' from *Ragtime*. Here is a song in which a number of possibilities are explored about what might be said, and then exactly what is said is revealed at the end of the song; the song has taken longer in performance time than it does in the plot time. Similarly, 'Home' at the end of *The Wiz* is three-and-a-half minutes long, but is supposed to take place in the time it takes Dorothy to click her heels together three times. Again, the performance time is longer than the plot time. In fact, most fantasy numbers operate in this way, and it is possible, therefore, to have a musical that has a performance time that is longer than the plot time. A musical that comes close to this is *The 25th Annual Putnam County Spelling Bee*, a piece that almost takes place in real time, but in which many of the characters have fantasy numbers that take longer than the plot moment. Musical theatre makes time travel possible!

It is, of course, possible to do this in non-musical theatre. Shakespeare comes close with some of the soliloquies in his plays, but it is much easier to accomplish and much more common in musical theatre because the music allows for moments to be explored, and for time to be stretched, altered and compressed much more easily than in a non-musical play.

## Location

There are the locations that the story takes place in, the locations that the plot takes place in and the performance location(s).

*Mrs Warren's Profession* has a story that takes place in many locations throughout London, the south-east of England and across Europe. The major locations mentioned in the story are slums near the Mint, the Temperance Restaurant, Waterloo Bridge, the brothels of Budapest, Brussels and Ostend, Newnham College, Cambridge, a cottage near Haslemere, the rectory garden near Haslemere and the Chancery Lane chambers of Honoria Fraser. The plot takes place in the garden of the cottage near Haslemere, inside the cottage, the Rectory Garden and Honoria Fraser's chambers in Chancery Lane. The performance location is the theatre that the play is being performed in. The performance location for any production is usually a theatre, except in the case of site-specific work.

*Wicked* has a story that takes place in various locations in Oz, including Munchkinland, Elphaba's childhood home, the university at Shiz, the Emerald City, the Throne Room of the Emerald City and Fiyero's castle. The plot of *Wicked* takes place in most of these locations, being a multiple-location show, with a largely suggestive setting (in which elements of the locations are onstage but not entire naturalistic rooms). The Broadway production has approximately thirty specifically realised locations. The performance location is a large-scale theatre.

---

**Analyse Time and Place**

Analyse the story time, the plot time and the performance time of three or four musicals you know. Which has the greatest difference between the story time, the plot time and the performance time? Then consider the same questions for the locations.

---

Playwrights often don't need to think much about theatrical language. Naturalistic playwrights think about it least. Let's consider the theatrical language of a basic naturalistic drama. A narrative told by a group of characters acting in ways completely in line with those in which people normally act. A story that unfolds chronologically and where plot time=performance time. A single set, with the fourth wall dropped. No music unless it appears diegetically and a physical style based entirely on the natural movement of the characters at any given moment. Many time=time plays will fulfil all of these credentials. Of course, these playwrights have made a conscious decision to work within a naturalistic framework. It is a deliberate decision, but having made it, lots of the other decisions about theatrical language are irrelevant. Interestingly, the jukebox musical *Million Dollar Quartet* comes close to this (before it goes into its fantasy encore finale). Audiences accept this theatrical language very easily, almost without explanation, because this is a very common language. It is even more common when you change it just slightly to mean that acts of a play can have different time periods and locations, but within each act there is one location and chronological time movement.

The further you move from this naturalism, the more you need to ensure that your audience can understand your theatrical language. For all the faux naturalism of musicals like *My Fair Lady*, simply by having characters sing, the audience understands that this will not be naturalism and then looks to the writer to be their guide.

## Theatrical Language and Film Versions

The various theatrical languages that musical-theatre creators have utilised over the years have translated with greater or lesser success to the more naturalistic medium of film. As a general rule, the more theatrical the language, the more problematic the transfer to film – except in a few rare cases, where an inspired director has entirely re-imagined the theatrical language as a cinematic language with its own coherence and logic. Bob Fosse's film version of *Cabaret* is a brilliant example of such re-imagining, in which he edited the score and treated all the musical numbers in a diegetic fashion. The very theatricality of some pieces, such as *A Chorus Line* and *Nine*, have led to disastrous film versions; some have had multiple false starts and never made it into production, such as *Cats* (although the stage production was later filmed for video). I mention this only to point out that in the transfer to a movie version, any musical necessarily has to change its theatrical language to a cinematic language, and this may happen with greater or lesser success. Therefore, if you are analysing the theatrical language of a musical, refer to the original stage version, not the movie version, as there may be considerable differences.

*Case Study:* Godspell *by Stephen Schwartz and John-Michael Tebelak*

*Godspell* has proved itself one of the most adaptable and flexible musicals, and has been presented with varying cast sizes and directorial concepts. This study is largely about the style of the original production and concept (directed by the bookwriter, Tebelak, in 1971), but certain directors have used very strong concepts to alter some of the theatrical language of the piece.

The setting is an abstract area of a playground. The narrative of the work is based on the Gospel According to St Matthew, and the show is a collection of parables, rituals and songs. It begins with the baptism of the Jesus character and ends with the resurrection, but the bulk of the show is concerned with the teachings of Jesus, interpolated with contemporary (1970s) pop settings of hymns and religious songs.

The nature of time in *Godspell* is quite unclear. It appears that Jesus and the group of disciples are together for months, but the piece also works as a time=time piece in which the entire experience is about two hours. Each parable and song is presented as an entity unto itself, and so the revue-style nature of the work means that the concept of time is not important because it is not telling a linear narrative.

The location is both in the theatre and in the playground of the setting, and it is quite abstract. Again, the revue style of the narrative means that an abstract setting is appropriate. The actors interact with the audience and walk among them at certain moments in the play. There is only one location and there is no fourth wall.

The notion of character in *Godspell* is interesting. The original (and most common) cast size is ten. Two male actors play easily identifiable roles. One plays the Jesus figure and the other plays a character based first on John the Baptist and then on Judas Iscariot. All of the roles, including these two, are named after the real names of the original cast members, so the Jesus figure is actually a character called Stephen. Roles are not mentioned in a programme (or 'playbill'), only the actors' names are listed, and the actors use their own names during the performance where necessary. In the Prologue, each of the cast (except the Jesus and John the Baptist figures) sings the roles of historical philosophers, but these roles are never referred to again. Within each parable, actors take on different roles depending on the requirements of each story, and often play non-human roles (sheep, goats, etc.) if the parables demand. There is great flexibility for the director and acting company to tell these stories.

The musical style is that the songs are not directly related to the scenes, nor are they performed by the characters of the parables. The songs sometimes comment on moments in scenes and sometimes act as interludes between the parables. The relatively small size of the cast means that the size of any singing ensembles is limited. The musical style is 1970s pop, but it also draws on vaudeville ('Turn Back, O Man' and 'All for the Best') and folk music. The lyrics make use of many traditional hymns or prayers, such as 'All Good Gifts' and 'Day by Day', and some songs have original lyrics. The crucifixion scene has a strong rock style, and a shofar, a traditional instrument used in Jewish services, is incorporated at certain moments, most notably to summon the cast.

The physical style varies wildly from production to production, but in the original was largely built around clowning. The cast wore clownish outfits and the Jesus figure, famously, wore a Superman T-shirt. The physicality of the cast was very free and quite 'hippyish'. Most of the numbers have a dance or staging element, and the challenge for a choreographer is to create a dance style that is exciting and appropriate, yet keeps the freedom of spirit that is so vital to the experience. Whatever your own religious beliefs, the aim of *Godspell* is to celebrate the joy that Christians find in their religion, and the physical style of any production needs to reflect this.

Let's compare the theatrical languages of each of the five musicals we studied previously. In the following table, *The Sound of Music* is considered in its stage version, not the film version.

Do not be confused by having non-diegetic characters with diegetic songs. In *The Sound of Music*, the characters are not aware of the audience (except in the concert scene), but they often perform diegetic songs for each other, such as when Maria arranges for the children to sing to the Baroness.

|  | The Sound of Music | Little Shop of Horrors | Miss Saigon | My Fair Lady | Evita |
|---|---|---|---|---|---|
| Narrative | Book scenes and musical numbers. There is no narrator; the story unfolds in scenes in realistic settings. | Book scenes and musical numbers. A three-girl group acts as a narrator, breaking the fourth wall. | Through-sung with recitative. The story unfolds in scenes, and the character of the Engineer comments on the action. | Book scenes and musical numbers. There is no narrator and the story unfolds in scenes. | Through-sung with limited recitative. Che is the narrator and the piece is performed in a non-realistic setting. |
| Time | The story unfolds chronologically. The story takes place in 1937 and 1938, although the exact timings are vague. | The story unfolds chronologically, over a few days, then the song 'The Meek Shall Inherit' covers a period of a week, and the remaining scene takes place in one night. | The story unfolds chronologically, with a substantial flashback sequence. The story takes place in 1975 and 1978. | The story unfolds chronologically. The story takes place in a little over six months. | The show begins at the end of the story and then flashes back to the start and unfolds chronologically. |
| Characters | The characters are non-diegetic. The ensemble play nuns, Nazis and party guests. | The characters are non-diegetic, but the three girls break the fourth wall to narrate. No other characters break the fourth wall. There is no ensemble. | The characters are non-diegetic, although the character of the Engineer sometimes breaks the fourth wall to comment on the action. The ensemble play marines, bar girls, Vietnamese, Thais and Americans. | The characters are non-diegetic. No character breaks the fourth wall. Ensemble play servants, operagoers or market-dwellers, Ascot crowd and ball guests. | Che is the only character that breaks the fourth wall. Che narrates the story and is aware of the diegetic nature of the performance. All the characters are non-diegetic. Three principal actors play the leading roles; there are two smaller roles and all others are ensemble playing a wide range of Argentinian and non-Argentinian roles. |

| | | | | | |
|---|---|---|---|---|---|
| *Location* | Takes place in realistic settings in Salzburg, notably the abbey and the von Trapp villa and grounds. In the singing competition, the audience is treated as the audience for the competition, but not interacted with. | Takes place in realistic settings inside and outside Mushnik's florist's shop, with one additional scene, Orin's dental practice. | Takes place in a wide range of suggestive settings in Vietnam, Bangkok and America. Original production made use of large-scale set design including a statue and a helicopter. | Takes place in a range of realistic settings in London, notably Higgins's study. The scenes with extensive stage time tend to be more realistically produced. | Takes place in a very wide range of locations in Argentina and abroad. Settings are not realistically produced and the basic setting is abstract, with suggestive elements used as required. |
| *Musical Style* | A 1960s Broadway style that is influenced by Austrian folk song and Catholic liturgical music. Songs are often diegetic. The children mainly fulfil the ensemble role. There is very little singing by the male ensemble. Female ensemble sing in their roles as nuns. Original orchestrations designed for acoustic singing. | A pastiche score of early 1960s rock'n'roll, doo-wop and Motown. No ensemble. The three-girl group narrate only in song. Pop orchestrations designed for amplification. | Large-scale resources with considerable production numbers and extensive ensemble writing. 1980s through-sung musical-theatre style. Some Far-Eastern influences in orchestrations and entire work designed for amplification. | Classic 1950s Broadway style. Higgins's music is designed for sprechgesang.* Eliza's vocal music is written in chest voice and changes once she becomes a lady. Substantial ensemble material. Original orchestrations designed for acoustic singing. | Large-scale resources with a number of production numbers. Role of Eva is a considerable musical challenge with a wide range. |
| *Physical Style* | Natural physical movement for all characters. Little dance, usually generated from the movement of the children. Ball scene contains short dance sequence. | Movement derived from 1950s 'B-movies' for many characters. Pastiche Motown-style movement for the girl group. | Natural physical movement for all characters. Some major production numbers use presentational dance. Considerable amount of movement derived from the sex-trade showgirls of Far East. | Natural physical movement for most characters. Some stylised sequences (e.g. Ascot). Substantial production numbers. | A combination of natural physical movement and, in the original production, some heavily stylised movement for certain ensemble sequences. |

* A German word, which directly translates as 'speech singing' and describes a vocal technique between the two.

**Analyse a Theatrical Language**

Take a musical that you know well and consider the six aspects of the theatrical language of the story. Use a stage version of the musical for this exercise. Next time you see a stage musical, briefly analyse the theatrical language soon after you have seen it.

**Plan a Theatrical Language**

Draw a grid box like this for your own musical project:

|  | *My Musical* |
| --- | --- |
| Narrative |  |
| Time |  |
| Characters |  |
| Location |  |
| Musical Style |  |
| Physical Style |  |

Now fill in details of the theatrical language that your musical will employ. Make as many notes as possible using the information in this chapter to help you consider the necessary questions.

## Teaching the Theatrical Language

The theatrical language of any play is about encouraging the audience to suspend their disbelief. You are creating a compact with them. As a writer, you are saying to the audience, 'I have a tale to tell and I am going to tell it to you like this...' The audience want both the tale you tell and the way in which you tell it to be exciting, stimulating, thought-provoking and entertaining.

You can tell your story to the audience in any fashion you like. You can do anything onstage, but you *must* teach the audience the theatrical language you are going to use, and once you have taught them, you must be consistent. A theatrical language is a common language you create with the audience. As the writer, you teach them the language in the first fifteen to twenty minutes of the performance. Once they have learned it, that is all they want to understand for the duration of the performance. From the moment the curtain goes up, an audience starts to understand your language. They make sense of it for themselves and they want to be led by you, into the wonderful world of your theatrical imagination. Whatever you do whilst teaching them will be fine with the audience, they will go along with it. So you can break the fourth wall, you can keep the fourth wall, you can tell them jokes, you can impress them with amazing dancing, you can have a soloist belt out a fantastic showstopper, you can even have all the cast perform naked. That's all fine. You may, or may not, give them certain permissions: the permission to laugh, the permission to applaud, the permission to empathise with your Hero. That's all fine too. But once you get to about twenty minutes in, the audience starts to believe that they understand your language and from then on you have to have a very good reason to start changing the language you are communicating in. You *can* change the language, but if you are not very careful you will shock, surprise and alienate your audience. It will be like waking a dreamer; they will be disorientated and disturbed. Audiences don't express it that way; they simply decide they don't like your show.

Imagine you were the finest language teacher in all history. You encounter someone with whom you have no common language, but because you are the finest language teacher, you teach them your own language in fifteen minutes. Having taught them, would you then tell a joke and then change to a different language for the punchline? No, that would be lunacy. But that is exactly what many inexperienced playwrights do.

So how do you teach the audience the language of your play? You begin to tell them the story. After all, in this language, in *your* language, you are the finest language teacher in all history.

*Case Study:* Fiddler on the Roof *by Jerry Bock, Sheldon Harnick and Joseph Stein*

The opening twenty minutes of the stage version of *Fiddler on the Roof* is a textbook example of teaching an audience a sophisticated theatrical language that is then carefully adhered to for the rest of the performance.

In the first seconds, a solo violin plays, stating that this is a play in which music will play a key role (i.e. it is a musical). After about thirty seconds, Tevye enters and begins to speak directly to the audience, immediately smashing the fourth wall for his relationship with them. Within the first minute of the show, Tevye explains the title of the musical (and it is an *odd* title), and how it is a metaphor for the lives the characters lead. He tells the audience that the thing that binds the community together is tradition, and the rest of the villagers enter and begin to sing the opening number, 'Tradition'. This number describes every character that will appear in the play (except Perchik). The ensemble sings, describing each character type in the third person (so the Papas sing of 'the Papa', not 'I' or 'me'). The fourth wall is nearly broken through, but the villagers might be singing for themselves at a festival. Only Tevye continues to talk directly to the audience. The villagers dance, and their dance is built on traditional Jewish dances like the Hora, and is very distinctive. The fact that they dance in circles indicates the unity of the village, and the dancers ignore the audience as they dance – this is not the opening to *42nd Street* where the style is all played towards the audience. Tevye introduces specific characters, including those who threaten the village. There are many jokes during Tevye's speech, giving the audience permission to laugh. The number lasts eight minutes and is a production number – it includes singing, dialogue and dancing and it ends with a 'button', a musical and staging climax which prompts the audience to applaud. Eight minutes into a two-and-three-quarter hour* show and look how much has already been established.

The scene changes to Tevye's kitchen and the language of the show changes too. We are in a domestic setting, among the

---

* *Fiddler on the Roof* has a stage running time of approximately two hours, twenty-five minutes, excluding the intermission.

family, and now the fourth wall is firmly in place. Golde and the daughters have no notion of the audience. This is a naturalistic scene of a Jewish family preparing for the Sabbath supper. Yente (the matchmaker) and Motel (the tailor) arrive, both comic Jewish characters. Yente brings the first notion of something that will upset the stability of the Ordinary World of the family, in that she has arranged a marriage between Tzeitel, the eldest daughter, and Lazar Wolf, the butcher. Motel brings the first notion that this will not run smoothly as it is clear that he and Tzeitel have a burgeoning relationship. This immediately engages the audience in the plot. This is a six-minute scene (quite long compared to many others in the musical) and indicates to the audience that there will be some substantial dialogue scenes. Thirteen minutes into the show and the story is already beginning to motor. Yente and Golde having exited, Tevye's daughters enter and tease each other about husbands before singing 'Matchmaker', their joint 'I Wish' song. This number is non-diegetic and the fourth wall is firmly in place. This is the second number of the show and is in a different theatrical language to the first, 'Tradition', indicating that there will be both diegetic and non-diegetic numbers with the fourth wall dropped or broken. As soon as 'Matchmaker' ends, the scene changes to Tevye's yard and Tevye enters. He breaks the fourth wall again, but is now speaking to both God and the audience. Now it is clear to the audience, having witnessed the previous scene and song, that *only* Tevye can break the fourth wall, and that when he speaks to God, he is also breaking the fourth wall. There is a short scene with Golde, the first time we have seen them interact, which establishes their relationship, and in this scene Tevye engages with Golde with the fourth wall in place. As soon as she exits, he smashes the fourth wall again and then leads almost immediately into his solo 'I Wish' number, 'If I Were a Rich Man', ostensibly singing to God, but by implication breaking the fourth wall again. During this number, the show reaches its twentieth minute.

See how complex the language of this show is, and consider how easy it is to understand when you see it onstage. Throughout the remainder of the stage time this theatrical language is religiously reinforced: the Jewish dances, Tevye's smashing of the fourth wall, the production numbers, the book scenes with the fourth wall in place. Only one episode might appear to be outside this language, 'Tevye's Dream', in which he tricks Golde into agreeing to Tzeitel's marriage to Motel, but Tevye is established with Trickster characteristics and so, when the moment becomes an elaborate production number, the audience is delighted.

Now, I never saw the original production of the infamous Broadway flop *Carrie*, but everything I have ever read about it seems to lead back to this issue of theatrical language and teaching it to the audience. Those who saw it (and I am convinced that if everyone who claims to have been at the opening night had actually been there, it could only have played at Madison Square Gardens) have described how they thought they understood what they were watching, only to have the rug pulled from under them as the show took each completely bizarre turn. This wasn't about plot, it was about the fact that sometimes the show was gaudy disco and sometimes it was Jacobean tragedy – and it never found its own theatrical language.

---

### The First Twenty Minutes

Analyse the first twenty minutes of a stage musical you know well and consider the ways in which the writer teaches the audience the language of the show. Are there any major aspects of the musical that are not addressed in the first twenty minutes?

---

Teach the audience your theatrical language and they will thank you for it. Use the first fifteen to twenty minutes to establish this language and use it to tell your story. If you want to throw any curveballs, throw some early and they will accept them as part of the language. Don't leave it too late. You can teach this language. You know it.

**Plan the First Twenty Minutes**

Look at the grid you created earlier. Ask yourself how the first fifteen to twenty minutes of your musical are going to teach the audience the language they will need.

# 8

# *Characters and Scenes*

# *Characters and Scenes*

The two basic components of any play are scenes and characters. In a musical, one must also consider the trickier questions of how the songs work within the scenes and how the characters are motivated to sing. Scenes are, of course, the building blocks of plot, they allow the story to move forward. Whether character or plot is the primary mainspring of drama, neither exists without the other; a scene with no characters is not a scene and a character without a scene is not a character. They are interdependent.

## Characters

All great theatre contains vibrant, compelling characters, and musical theatre is no different. If the characters aren't engaging, the audience won't be engaged, however great the plot, and as a writer your aim must be to create characters that will fascinate the viewers. Remember that your audience is going to give up their money to spend two to three hours in the company of these people – they had better be interesting.

By now you probably have a good idea of the plot that your characters are going to be involved with, and how they behave within that plot gives you a lot of information about them.

## Creating Characters

Before you can begin writing your book, you need to get a clear idea of who will be populating your work. By now, you probably have an idea about what they are going to do, but not necessarily *who* they are.

I always had difficulties with how to develop characters and how to get a handle on their characteristics, so I created something I call a 'Character Bug'. This turns creating characters into a logical format, helps to organise your thoughts, and eventually allows you to be able to see all the characters you have in the scene at once.

Character bugs are created for each of the characters at the point in the journey when the audience first meet them. The journey they take during the course of the story may change their character, but the character bug must be created for the earliest point that the audience see.

The basic template looks like this:

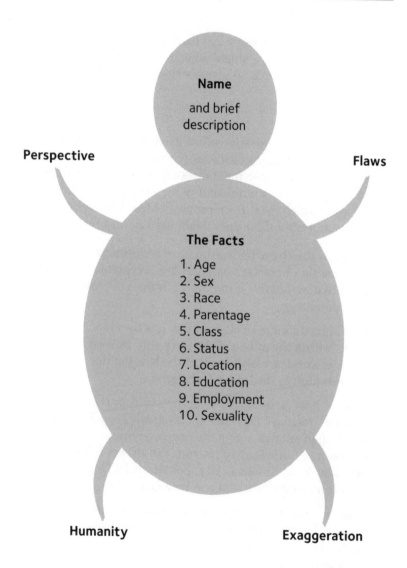

Secondary Objective

Primary Objective

Name

and brief
description

Perspective

Flaws

The Facts

1. Age
2. Sex
3. Race
4. Parentage
5. Class
6. Status
7. Location
8. Education
9. Employment
10. Sexuality

Humanity

Exaggeration

I generally create a character bug for each character on a different piece of paper.

As you can see, it looks like a bug crawling across the page, towards two walls, each of which represents an objective. Each part of the body contains different information:

### Head

Here are the character's name and the briefest description. This should be two words: a single adjective and the other their archetype or function (e.g. an arrogant Hero or a foolish Shadow).

### Body

Here are ten factual questions that need very short answers. When you are creating the character, you need to remember that there are the facts for when the audience first meet them, so if the story takes place over a number of years, write the facts for the earliest age at which the character appears. Most of these facts are self-explanatory, but these ones might need clarification:

*Parentage:* Is the character legitimate or illegitimate? Who are the character's parents? It is acceptable to put 'unknown' here – if the *character* does not know their parentage.

*Status:* This is different to class, in that it is the character's status within the milieu of the story. Riff, in *West Side Story*, is working-class like all of the Jets, but his status is high as the leader of the gang.

*Location:* Where is the character in the world, or the world of the play? This answer is factually geographic, rather than relative – so in the case of Seymour Krelborn in *Little Shop of Horrors*, the answer is 'On Skid Row in an American city', not 'At work.' This answer may inform accent and language.

*Employment:* This relates to what the character generally does all day, and is not necessarily a job. Answers might also include child, student, pensioner, unemployed, etc.

*Legs*

The legs relate to characteristics. These tend to be unchanging and each answer should be as many words as you need, but do not overcomplicate it: you need to be able to keep a grasp on the information.

*Perspective:* This is how the character sees the world around him, and his place within it. This might be something like:
- Tiny aspirations but a huge heart.
- A romantic, she believes everything will be solved by love.
- Believes that life is there for the taking.
- A young girl on the brink of adulthood.
- Downtrodden florist with heart.

*Flaws:* Everybody has their flaws and your characters are no different. In fact, it is what makes them human. This is a list of all the things that are wrong with your character. Don't be afraid of overloading your character with flaws, and whilst they can be negative qualities like 'arrogance' or 'greed', they can be gentler flaws like 'easily influenced'.

*Exaggeration:* Most theatrical characters are exaggerated in some way; it is part of what makes them compelling to the audience. Eliza Doolittle is not just a cockney flower girl; she is *very* cockney, *very* working class, *very* uneducated. Professor Higgins is not just arrogant, sexist or intelligent; he is *very* arrogant, *very* sexist and *very* intelligent. Exaggeration is particularly important when writing comedy.

*Humanity:* All characters have to possess humanity, even the non-human ones. In fact, the non-human ones tend to need *more* humanity than the human ones, so that the audience can identify with them. The opposite of a character's flaws is their humanity; it is what is loveable and positive about the character. This is why 'flaws' and 'humanity' are on diagonally opposite parts of the bug. Without the humanity we cannot care for them, or understand why other characters interact with them. Positive words like 'loyal', 'charming', 'strong' and 'witty' might be found here. The serial killer Hannibal Lecter is charming; in *Kiss of the Spiderwoman*, the titular character is sensuous and seductive, even though kissing her is death; and *Oklahoma!*'s Jud Fry is a lonely man who just wants to be loved by a woman.

It is quite possible to have the same answer for more than one leg, because it may be appropriate to their character. 'Ambition', for example, might be a perspective, a flaw and the humanity of a character such as Macbeth.

As a general rule, it is worth concentrating on the aspects of the character that are the least obvious. Concentrate on the flaws in your positive characters, like the Heroes, and concentrate on the humanity in your characters with negative energy, such as your Shadows. This will allow you to create much more rounded characters.

## Objectives

Characters have primary objectives and secondary objectives. Normally they have to achieve the primary objectives to discover the secondary, which is why on the character bug diagram the primary looks like a wall the bug has to smash through to reach the secondary. When the story begins, Cinderella wants to go to the ball (her primary objective), not to find love and change her life circumstances (her secondary objective). Luke Skywalker wants to save Princess Leia (his primary objective), not save the universe by destroying the Death Star (his secondary objective).

Primary objectives are immediate, specific and conscious. Secondary objectives are broader, generalised and often subconscious. Secondary objectives often hit one of a few broad themes:

- To save the earth/universe (very popular in the action and sci-fi genres).

- To find love (very popular in romantic genres).
- To find their place in the world (popular in all genres).

So, Elle in *Legally Blonde* goes to Harvard to follow her love (primary objective) and finds her place in the world (secondary objective).

In *Guys and Dolls*, Sky Masterson wants to win a bet (primary) and finds love (secondary).

Oliver Twist wants to escape from the cruelty of the orphanage (primary) and finds his place in the world (secondary).

Eliza Doolittle wants to improve her speech (primary) and find her place in the world (secondary).

Aladdin wants to improve his life by getting the lamp for Jafar (primary) but ends up finding love (secondary).

Secondary objectives are not limited to these three but are always broader than the primary. For example, Eva Perón wants to escape to Buenos Aires (primary) but also wants power and status (secondary).

In stories where the Hero dies at the end, the secondary objective will remain either unfulfilled, or his death will fulfil it. Kim wants to build a relationship with Chris in America (primary) but then wants to secure a future for her son (secondary).

By creating character bugs you will have to face questions about the characters that you may not have previously considered. This is how they are helpful in creating dramatic characters that are multifaceted. Create character bugs and you will have a much fuller sense of who your characters are.

As an example, here is a character bug for Eliza Doolittle:

**Find her place in the world**

**Improve her speech**

**Eliza Doolittle**

Cockney
Flower girl
Hero

**Perspective**

She can do better in
life with the right
circumstances

**Flaws**

Headstrong, fiery,
wilful

**The Facts**

Age: 18
Sex: Female
Race: Caucasion
Parentage:
   Father Alfred, dustman;
   Mother unknown
Class: Very working-class
Status: Low
Location:
   Covent Garden, London
Education: Little, if any
Employment: Flower girl
Sexuality: Heterosexual

**Humanity**

Caring, dignified,
warm, witty,
innocent, naturally
intelligent

**Exaggeration**

Working class,
uneducated, very
cockney, defiant,
innocent

Now, you might not agree with all of these qualities that I have included, and I am sure that both George Bernard Shaw, who created the original character, and Alan Jay Lerner, who altered her for the musical, would disagree with some, and would be able to provide more accurate insights. That is all very well, because once a character has been brought into being by the writer, other people, like you and I, will interpret the character through their own perspective.

The character bug is a tool for creation, not a tool for analysis. You can see how, if a writer had started with this character bug, he might end up writing a character like Eliza Doolittle.

---

### Character Bugs

Create a character bug for each of the major characters in your story. Make sure you fill in as much detail as possible: the more you create now, the more you have to draw on later. Stick all the character bugs on a wall where you can see them together. They are great to refer to when working on the script.

---

## Character Voice and Fantasy Casting

The different ways in which different characters speak is known as 'character voice'. Just as each of us speaks in an individual style that is affected by accent, education, status and age, so must characters, or they will not feel like real human beings. Writing character voice can be quite a challenge for writers. Often students tell me that they feel as if all their characters are speaking with the same voice and ask me how they can make each one distinctive. Listening to different voices is important, but I also use fantasy casting as a way of creating character voice.

It is a very simple kind of game. Take your list of characters and decide who should play them in your all-time 'fantasy cast'. The people you choose do not have to be alive, and they don't have to be actors, and they don't even have to be real! It is a case of you being able to hear what they sound like.

Working on *The Railway Children*, we 'fantasy-cast' the lead roles:

| | |
|---|---|
| *Perks* | Brian Conley |
| *Mother* | Marin Mazzie (but English) |
| *Roberta* | The young Hayley Mills |
| *The Old Gentleman* | Albert Finney |

Brian Conley is a popular cheeky-chappie style of comedian, actor and singer with enormous charm, who has played Bill in *Me and My Girl* and Potts in *Chitty Chitty Bang Bang*. Marin Mazzie is a Broadway leading lady who originated the role of Mother in *Ragtime*.

We were never going to get these four people in the show, but this casting gave us:

For Perks, the cheeky, paternal style of Brian Conley and the sense of a character with huge charm who could relate to an audience.

For Mother, the maternal style of Marin Mazzie and the vocal sound we envisaged for the singing. Also, the dignity that Mazzie can have onstage. As the role is British, we considered various British actresses, but felt Mazzie told us more about the role than anyone else. We imagined Marin Mazzie with an English accent and it seemed just the sound we wanted for her. In a strange quirk, the role was first played by the American-born Susannah Fellows.

For Roberta, the sense of a very English girl becoming a woman. We also borrowed from Rodgers and Hammerstein the convention of using a young professional actress (rather than a child actor) for the role. In the novel *The Railway Children*, Roberta seems to be about twelve; we raised her age to fifteen.

In Albert Finney, we found the slightly gruff, no-nonsense grandfatherly sense of the Old Gentleman. Someone who would bring gravitas and grace to the role, but not allow it to become sentimental.

Sometimes fantasy casting comes true: *Liberace Live from Heaven* is a comedy I wrote about what happened when the titular pianist arrived at the Pearly Gates, only to find that St Peter barred him entry on the grounds of his hypocrisy for not admitting his homosexuality. Liberace has to convince the audience of angels gathered in judgement (the theatre audience) to let him into Heaven, and at the end of the play the audience vote and he either goes to Heaven or Hell.

I had perfect fantasy casting for the role of Liberace, the man himself. I could watch and listen to concerts and interviews of him and absorb his speech patterns. I was also writing the play for Bobby Crush, a well-known performer who had played Liberace before.

For the role of St Peter, which was to be played in voice-over, I wanted someone who had gravitas, intelligence, a sense of humour, but who could also sound rather put-upon, because God has lumbered him with all Heaven's admissions administration! My fantasy casting was Stephen Fry. It happened that the producer of the play knew him and Stephen agreed to do it!

There is a third role in the play: God, also played in voice-over (*Liberace Live from Heaven* is 'a one-man show for three people'.) As this is a comedy I took my initial inspiration from a 1960's joke: 'What's God like?' 'She's black'. I wrote the role as a gospel-style female, but rewrote it when one of Britain's most popular comediennes, Victoria Wood, agreed to play God. Victoria Wood is one of my comedy idols, a woman who has given me more laughs than should be legal, but her style is very specific, and I was more than a little daunted by writing for a comic goddess. As I sat down to rewrite, I played her stand-up routine on DVD in the background, over and over, absorbing her specific speech patterns. I rewrote and revised the role, altering the ethnicity and transforming it into a role suitable for Victoria Wood. When she came to record it, she changed one word, and through its London and Edinburgh runs and the tour of New Zealand, she always got great reviews whilst sitting at home! Talk about a dream actress and fantasy casting.

**Fantasy Casting**

'Fantasy-cast' your musical. Discuss it with all your collaborators until you can all agree. It is a great game, but more importantly, it really helps to define the voices of the characters. Put Marilyn Monroe, Quentin Tarantino and Homer Simpson all in the same cast if need be. Don't be hampered by performers you might think are real potential casting. Add pictures of your fantasy cast to your character bugs.

## The Ensemble

When writing a musical, you will probably need to consider the role of the ensemble. I use the term 'ensemble', rather than 'chorus', for two reasons. The first is that the term 'chorus' is also used in songwriting to mean the refrain, which can lead to confusion. Secondly, the term 'chorus' tends to indicate a group of people singing without individuality, whereas the term 'ensemble' indicates a group of individual characters singing together. I much prefer the idea that ensembles are made up of characters, and so do the actors playing the roles.

If you haven't considered it yet, now is the time to work out exactly whom the ensemble will play in any scene they are in, and exactly what their role will be in the musical.

In the twenty-first century, the rule with an ensemble is 'use them or lose them'. In earlier decades, musical theatre could afford to employ an ensemble for only a few scenes. Ensemble members were paid poorly and usually had to pay for their own costumes. In operas, it is not uncommon to find the chorus appearing in only one scene, as they do in *Tosca* or *La Bohème*. In opera, the economics are different as full-time opera companies have full-time choruses who appear as and when required. In the more commercial economics of modern musical theatre, a producer is going to want to see an ensemble used throughout the piece, or excised from it, to save money.

If you completed the exercises in theatrical language in the previous chapter, you will already have considered the role of the ensemble. Now you need to consider their role in each scene, thinking through some of the practicalities, such as how they enter and exit. This sounds trite, but it prompts the question: 'What is the situation in which all these people happen to be in this location?' This leads you to set your scenes in more public places than you might set other scenes, but this will also depend on the theatrical language you create for your work. For example, in *My Fair Lady* the ensemble only appear in scenes set in public or semi-public settings (Covent Garden Market, Ascot and the Embassy Ball). A smaller ensemble appear as servants, and the forums in which they appear are distinct from the bulk of the action that takes place in Higgins's study. In *Sweeney Todd*, the ensemble appears throughout, in both public and private settings, as narrators commenting upon the action.

Within the ensemble you may well have 'featured roles'. These will be small parts played by ensemble members who might have a few lines or solo singing. These roles are useful because they add colour to the ensemble and make it feel like a collection of characters, not a nebulous group. They can also be very useful for comic relief. *Fiddler on the Roof* is full of these roles, such as Avrahm (the bookseller), Shaindel (Motel's mother) and Reb Nachum (the beggar). Each of these roles has just a few lines, but each helps to give colour to Anatevka and make it feel like a real shtetl.

If you are adapting your story, you might also be able to 'open it up' by adding featured ensemble roles. With *The Railway Children*, we opened up the novel by inventing a number of inhabitants at the family's new village, all of whom became featured ensemble roles. Some of them were drawn from the original novel, such as Mrs Ransome the postmistress, and some, such as Lord Fleet, were original creations. When creating featured ensemble roles, you do not need to create entire character bugs for them – unless you are very keen!

## Casting the Ensemble

Write a list of all the scenes that will feature the ensemble. What roles will they play? What characters do you need to invent for featured ensemble roles?

## Scenes and French Scenes

Plays progress through their plots by a series of scenes. Many people think of a scene as a period of a play that takes place in a specific location through a continuous and chronological progression of time, but the definition of 'scene' also varies depending on context.

The definition of a scene as something happening in a specific location through time is true, but there is a more important definition of a scene, and that is by defining it through what is happening. All scenes have an action, a combination of an objective and an obstacle (sometimes called a project and a reversal). This is what is *happening* in the scene.

All plots are made up of a character trying to achieve something (the objective) and a character in opposition in some way (the obstacle). The bigger, more important, more strongly expressed the obstacles, the more drama there is in the scene. If two characters simply agree to do something, then there is no drama, and the play is over. The scene is over when this conflict is played out.

There is another concept of a scene, which is very useful to writers. A 'French scene' is where a scene is determined by a change in the characters onstage, rather than a change of location or time. If a new character enters or exits, then that is a new French scene. So, when Dolly Levi enters at the top of the stairs in *Hello, Dolly!*, that is a new French scene, and when Judge Turpin is murdered and sent down the chute by Sweeney Todd, that is the end of a French scene. Of course, the beginnings of any scenes in which characters are already onstage is automatically the beginning of a new French scene and the ending of any scene with the lights or curtain going down with characters still onstage is automatically the end of a French scene. When considering French scenes in musical theatre, I treat members of the ensemble who enter simultaneously, or nearly simultaneously, as one character, and if two characters are leaving the stage together and one character makes a slightly delayed exit (maybe with an exit line), then I would treat that as the ending of *one* French scene. French scenes are generally shorter than scenes, as they are normally shorter units within a scene.

French scenes are incredibly useful to writers when planning a scene, because they can help to break a complex scene into smaller units, especially if there are lots of entrances and exits. The busier the show, the more French scenes you will have. *A Funny Thing Happened on the Way to the Forum* must have at least a hundred, as it is stuffed full of entrances and exits; whereas a musical like *Godspell* would have very few because the entire cast enter very near the beginning of the show and largely stay onstage for the duration. Both *A Funny Thing...* and *Godspell* take place in a single-unit setting, a piazza and a playground respectively, but the number of French scenes they have varies wildly.

I find it useful to work in French scenes when planning out a script. When I was writing the libretto for *The Railway Children* we decided very early on in the process that one of the concepts for the musical was that it would be a 'memory play', in which the Stationmaster Mr Perks remembered the events of the story. From this moment I was freed from many of the usual constraints of writing scenes, and it became easier to move freely from location to location as Perks remembered only the scenes that were important to the story. As a result, I wrote most of this libretto in French scenes. It was only when I was preparing the script for publication that it became divided up into scenes based on locations, so that other companies producing the show could easily understand the different locations required. The original production had a very 'suggestive' setting in which simple scenic elements were introduced for the locations.

---

### French Scenes

In a libretto for a musical, number the French scenes in pencil in the margins. How many do you count?

---

## Location and Format

All scenes have a location, even if it is abstract. Locations also carry with them all kinds of baggage, and different locations can mean different things to different characters. For example, the Harmonia Gardens Restaurant in *Hello, Dolly!* is a workplace to the waiters, a place to eat, socialise and celebrate to the patrons, and a place that Dolly used to visit but has not been to for many years.

Writers need to choose the locations carefully in order to maximise the impact of the scene. There is the specific location of the scene, but there is also the context of the location. Key to deciding on a location is the immediate offstage location: where do the exits *from* the stage lead *to* in the lives of the characters. (Incidentally, this is a good question to ask any set designer for your work. A good designer will always know the answer.) Then there is what that location means to the character. Is it a work location? A domestic location? A public location? Some of these locations will carry with them ideas about certain activities: a restaurant or a changing room are good examples; we expect to see people eating, working, dressing, etc. Sometimes these choices of locations are key to the play. Richard Greenberg's play *Take Me Out*, for example, explored racism and homophobia in sport, and much of it was set in a changing room. The physical action of the play, with the characters dressing and undressing in and out of their team kit, was a metaphor for the ways in which characters made choices about being part of a team (community), individuals, or at their most individual and intimate – naked. In the British musical *Betty Blue Eyes* there is a key scene (and song) which takes place in a gent's lavatory: an excellent location for a writer to bring together characters from any class at a given time in the plot.

Another type of location comes with more than an expectation of what will happen there: it comes with a 'format'. This is a location in which certain types of activities always take place. Examples of these are places of worship, courts, sports stadia, and the most common one in musical theatre, a theatre (both backstage and onstage). Formats can be of excellent use to musical-theatre writers as they allow a writer to use the format to treat the moment of the story imaginatively. Rodgers and Hammerstein use the format of the location of the wedding scene in *The Sound of Music* to, firstly, condense the ceremony into a few minutes of music, and then to create the entertaining moment of the nuns singing their reprise of 'How Do You Solve a Problem Like Maria?' Similarly, there is an imaginative response from Kander and Ebb in the courtroom scene in *Chicago*, in which one member of the cast plays all twelve jurors.

Musicals have an innate advantage over many plays with regard to time and place. The introduction of music, and therefore a non-naturalistic theatrical language, means that travelling through time and space in a musical can be very easily accomplished. A verse, a chorus or some instrumental music can easily make this transition. James Goldman's libretto for *Follies* is all set in a closed theatre, but constantly shifts between the past and the present, and around different character groupings in different areas of the theatre, with just a few bars of music. The second-act song 'Johanna' in *Sweeney Todd* constantly shifts location between Mrs Lovett's pie shop, Sweeney's barbershop and Anthony's journey through London. Similarly, when we wrote *Let Him Have Justice*, we introduced one song, 'Another Appeal', which took place over two weeks of story time and in twelve different locations; all encapsulated into eight-and-a-half minutes. Of course, it is possible for non-musical plays to do this, but music acts as a kind of lubricant to the storytelling that makes this travel through time and space much easier. Remember, though, that each scene, however short, must be a scene; it must develop plot and/or character and will usually have an objective and an obstacle, or must deliver exposition.

---

### Analyse Location

Take a libretto of a musical with multiple locations and look at the list of all the locations required. How many of these are public? Private? How many of them have formats?

---

> ### Locations in Your Musical
>
> Examine your story synopsis and make notes of all the locations you need as you reach them. Put together a list of these locations and note whether they are private, public and have formats.

## Exposition

Exposition is the term used for speeches or scenes that tell the audience what has happened or what is happening. Because the plot normally starts part of the way through the story, the audience need to be brought up to speed. There are two types of exposition: presentational and representational. Presentational exposition takes place when a character breaks the fourth wall and steps forward to tell the audience the information they need, as Tevye does in 'Tradition' at the opening of *Fiddler on the Roof*. Representational exposition is when the fourth wall is dropped and the characters tell each other the information, unaware that they are also giving it to the audience. An example of this is *A Chorus Line*, in which the character of Zach gives the necessary information to the cast, but is unaware of the audience. As a general rule, any time the fourth wall is dropped, then the exposition is representational, and when the fourth wall is broken, then the exposition will be presentational. The danger with representational exposition is ensuring that the speeches *need* to be made within the logic of the play. It is all too easy to write a play in which two characters give speeches of exposition when both of them are likely to know all the information. These normally run along the lines of:

JACKIE. Do you see that Mrs Jones has moved back into the neighbourhood?

JILLY. Really? Do you remember how she murdered her husband and ran off with his best friend and hasn't been seen for twenty years?

This is the worst kind of exposition because it is lazy and unrealistic, but sometimes whole scenes take place full of this kind of information.

When it comes to presentational exposition, the issue is slightly different: it is not that two characters talking are giving each other information they already have, but that *telling* an audience information is so much less interesting for the audience than *showing* them. The playwright Jeffrey Hatcher likens theatre to striptease: the audience want to discover the thrill of the strip as each scene unfolds and they get to see more and more. You might hint at what is going to come, but you don't want to take all your clothes off at once! Some characters end up as barely characters at all, but their primary function is to give exposition directly to the audience, such as Che in *Evita*.

At worst, too much exposition becomes what is known as 'information dumping', and that is boring, boring, boring. Greg Kotis and Mark Hollmann's meta-musical *Urinetown: The Musical* actually has a song called 'Too Much Exposition', in which Officer Lockstock tells Little Sally that 'Nothing can kill a show like Too Much Exposition'.

## Characters' Objectives

What do characters *do* in scenes? What makes up the moment-to-moment action of a scene? At the beginning of the twentieth century, the great acting teacher Konstantin Stanislavsky spoke of character objectives and super-objectives, which relate to scenes and plays respectively, and actors still use his work today. It is useful for actors to think about what each character is trying to achieve in each scene. Are they looking to further their own objective, or looking to block another character's objective?

When two or more characters appear onstage in a scene, then the progress of the scene usually follows the objective being thwarted, compromised or changed by the obstruction. This then allows the character to progress to the following scene with a changed objective, a realised objective or the same objective to be achieved in a different way. Not all objectives are thwarted; usually one character achieving their objective requires the obstructing of the other character's objective. If both characters achieve their objective and no one obstructs, where is the drama?

Look at the three scenes in *Fiddler on the Roof* in which Tevye's daughters ask for his permission to marry:

In the first, Tevye tells Tzeitel that he has arranged her marriage (Tevye's objective). Tzeitel, rather than reacting in the joyful way Tevye expects, begs him not to make her marry Lazar Wolf (Tzeitel's obstruction). Tevye agrees (his objective is thwarted). Motel enters and asks Tevye for Tzeitel's hand (Motel's objective). Tevye refuses (obstructs), but when Tzeitel tells her father that she and Motel have made a pledge to each other and love each other, Tevye agrees (Motel's objective fulfilled). Here, Tevye fails in his first objective, but Motel succeeds in his.

In the second scene, Perchik asks for Hodel's hand in marriage (Perchik's objective) and Tevye refuses (obstructs). Perchik and Hodel inform Tevye that they will marry anyway and Tevye, finding he has no option except to cut his daughter off, agrees. Here, Perchik succeeds in his objective.

In the third scene, Fyedka wants to talk to Tevye about marrying Chava (Fyedka's objective); Chava persuades Fyedka that it will be better if she talks to her father (she obstructs). Chava tries to persuade Tevye to allow her to marry Fyedka (Chava's objective) but he completely refuses (obstructs). Here, neither Fyedka nor Chava succeeds in their objective, and Tevye's obstruction stands.

These changes of heart in one character's objective (such as Tevye agreeing to Tzeitel and Motel's marriage) are called 'reversals'.

Not all scenes are as obvious in their character objectives as this. Scenes that are very heavy on exposition, or characters whose main function is exposition, may end up with very weak objectives, or seemingly no objective at all, other than to give that exposition. Some scenes near the beginning of plays, especially in the Ordinary World stage of the story, might well be made of little more than exposition and behaviour as the story begins to crank up.

Not every character onstage will necessarily have a strong objective in every scene. Characters might be observers in a scene (such as Tevye's family who are in the scene with Tzeitel), but this may well inform their own journeys in later scenes.

You need to think about who are the leading characters in any scene you are writing, and what they are trying to achieve in that scene. If they are not trying to achieve *anything at all* (i.e. they have no objective), what are they doing onstage? Of course, their objective can simply be one of exposition, support or ritual (such as characters who are wedding guests).

## Planning the Beats, Actioning and Reverse Actioning

Some people think that writers, having decided on a plot, simply sit down and begin writing dialogue. Sure, there may be some writers who work like that, but much more common is to plan the scenes carefully beforehand. When I am working on a scene, I begin very simply. Taking the synopsis (which must be, by now, agreed by any and all co-writers), I begin to work on each individual scene, by creating a synopsis for it. This is usually a simple cut-and-paste job from the show's synopsis and I consider whether there is anything that has been left out, or is ill-defined. There nearly always is, as it is now time to make the characters move the plot forward. Writing *Twang!!*, I once spent a whole afternoon trying to figure out how to take one line of my own synopsis and make it happen onstage.

I make sure that I have listed the cast for that scene and then break the scene down into as many French scenes as I need, listing each one. For each French scene, I ensure I know exactly what needs to be accomplished onstage and I write these beats down in chronological order. In this context (and it is another of those multiple-definition words), a 'beat' is a change of subject or idea within a scene and I write these out. Having sorted out the beats, I rely on an acting technique called 'actioning' to take me towards dialogue.

Actioning is a technique that actors use to unwrap subtext in any line, in any scene, to ensure that the line is played with the right meaning (in their interpretation of the role). It heightens spontaneity and enforces specificity. It is the enemy of 'generalised' acting and is an extension of the work of

Stanislavsky. The best thing about actioning for actors is that they can use it as a technique on their own, even when working as part of a cast.

The central premise is that what we say and what we mean are two distinct ideas. Take, for example, the question 'Would you like a drink?' Depending on the context, this line might mean many things: 'I care for you', 'I think you need to relax', 'I am trying to seduce you', 'I want you to wake up', to name just a few. Actioning provides a way for actors to decide on the specific meaning of the line in the specific situation of the scene, and of their objective in the scene. Each line of the play (and by 'line' I mean sentence rather than speech) is assigned an action, which the actor then uses to say/play the line.

An action is always a transitive verb: a verb that one person can do to another, and is always about the character's intention on that line. A transitive verb can be inserted between the words 'I' and 'you' to create a clause. So, in the examples above, 'Would you like a drink?' might be actioned as 'I comfort you', 'I relax you', 'I seduce you' or 'I wake you'. Actions change with each sentence, because each sentence is a change of thought. Actors attach an action to each line and try to communicate the action whilst speaking the line from the text, giving them a clear map through the objectives of a scene.

### Actioning

This exercise is best done with a partner, so if you are working with a collaborator get him to do it at the same time. Take a short duologue scene from a play or libretto – it only needs to be about ten lines. Assign yourselves the roles. Mark the beats of the scene (the changes of thought). These will normally be where there is a full stop and are unlikely to be more than one per sentence. Sometimes it takes more than one sentence to create one beat. Then, imagine that you are an actor playing the role. For each beat find an action for what you think the character is intending to do to the other character with the line. Remember the *intention* is the action, not the success of the intention. There are no wrong answers: the

> choices of actions you make become your performance. Now, trying to communicate your intentions, read the lines of the script to each other. You might find it easy to say the action before each line (e.g. '*I greet you...* Good morning, Mr Smith'). See how the actions change your reading of the line as you change the action, such as '*I threaten you...* Good morning, Mr Smith'.

This isn't the place for a long exploration of actioning,* but I use what I refer to as 'reverse actioning' as a way of planning scenes. In this process, I break a French scene down into a number of beats and I use actioning notation to decide what needs to happen in each beat. To illustrate, let's take a short piece of script from *The Railway Children*. This dialogue comes straight after the first song, 'Christmas is Here!', which is a fairly straightforward song that establishes the Ordinary World at a time of festivity. In E. Nesbit's original novel, this scene occurs at a birthday party, but we moved it to Christmas to allow us to more easily use the ensemble, Christmas being a celebration that everyone and anyone can celebrate. At the end of the song, Peter's new toy steam engine explodes. In planning the scene I wrote this (French scenes numbered on the right-hand side):

1. The engine explodes.                                        1
2. Peter *asks* Father what the problem is.
3. Father *promises* Jim to mend it.
4. A knock at the door.
5. Peter *begs* Father.
6. Ruth *enters*.                                              2
7. Ruth *tells* Father of two men wanting to see him.
8. Father exits.                                               3
9. Mother *questions* Ruth.
10. Ruth *requests* Mother to go to Father.
11. Mother exits.                                              4

---

\* If you are interested in this, you should read Marina Caldarone and Maggie Lloyd-Williams' book *Actions: The Actors' Thesaurus*. I also use it for the reverse actioning mentioned in this chapter.

12.  The children *interrogate* Ruth.

13.  Ruth *evades* the children.

14.  Ruth exits.                                                     5

As you can see, this is a very bald, simple description of the events of the scene and has nothing about character. It is numbered by beat and it is a combination of actioning notations (with a little extra information where needed) and entrances and exits (French scene changes). Reverse actioning is not as 'pure' as actioning used by actors, and I am much more free with the finer points of the system. You can see in most of the numbered beats above that I have had to define both the first and second person (the person speaking and the person they are speaking to). This is because I am only one person and I am writing for many characters. I am also quite happy to add a little extra information to keep the sense for myself, such as 'Ruth *requests* Mother to go to Father'. Let's be honest – no one else is going to see these notes, this is back-of-the-envelope stuff, and is in the garbage as soon as the scene is written, so I can be as free as I like.

The character objectives and actions worked out thus, it then became easier to write the actual dialogue for the scene, simply by adding the characters' voices and attitudes. The final scene reads like this:

*The toy train, which has been running around the
floor, suddenly explodes.*

PETER. Daddy, what's happened?

FATHER. I don't know.

PHYLLIS. It's broken.

PETER. Is it, Father?

FATHER. But I don't think it can be too bad. I'll fix it.

*There is a knock on the door.*

MOTHER. Who'd be knocking now?

PETER. When will you fix it?

RUTH *enters.*

RUTH. Excuse me, sir, there's two gentlemen to see you. I've shown them into the study.

FATHER. I'll fix it when I come back. Thank you, Ruth.

FATHER *exits.*

MOTHER. Who is it, Ruth?

RUTH. Ma'am, I think they want you to go in too.

MOTHER (*to all*). Now you all play nicely. I'll be back in a minute and then we'll have Christmas cake.

PHYLLIS. Hooray. I love cake. Mummy, you're a darling!

MOTHER *exits.*

ROBERTA. Who is it, Ruth?

PETER. I want Daddy to come back and mend my engine. It's new.

ROBERTA. What's going on?

RUTH. Ask me no questions and I'll tell you no lies.

PETER. Can you find out how long they are going to be?

RUTH *exits.*

Now, I am the first to admit that this scene is hardly Shakespeare, but it does set up a number of relationships very quickly and provides vital character traits that are maintained through the entire musical. Phyllis, for example, spends the whole show using the catchphrase 'You're a darling!' to anyone and everyone. It's not especially funny here, but by Act Two it is a charming character trait that gets a laugh. Ruth is established as no-nonsense and a little tough, Peter as needy and Roberta as businesslike and slightly more mature than the others. What is most important here is that you can see how the 'bald' beats of the reverse actioning have become living dialogue.

Writing a musical, I use exactly the same technique to generate both book scenes and lyrics, especially if the scene or song is full of incident.

I don't reverse action the entire synopsis at once; I would probably have a nervous breakdown if I did. The biggest unit I would reverse action is a scene. I would then write the dialogue for the scene and then move on to reverse action the next scene. Actors who work with actioning will also tell you that it is best done in small sections, which are worked into the text, and then to move forward.

---

### Reverse Actioning

Take a scene from your synopsis and break it down, firstly into French scenes, then into beats. Number the beats using reverse actioning to define exactly what is going to happen in each scene.

---

## What You Say and What You Don't: Dialogue and Behaviour

There are as many ways of writing dialogue as there are of making pastry. Everyone has their own way and, to be honest, your way is as good as anyone else's. As you write more and more you will find that it gets easier, less daunting and more fun. The American playwright Alfred Uhry says that he doesn't *write for* his characters, he *listens to* them. I understand what he means; there is simply nothing better than writing and realising that you know what the next line will be before you have finished typing the current one. It is like taking dictation from the gods. You can hear your characters talking to you. It took a certain amount of planning, thought and experience before I came anywhere near feeling that.

When I applied to Bristol Old Vic Theatre School to train as a director, I was interviewed by Chris Denys, a noted British director and writer, and at that time the Principal of the school. He told me there and then: 'I can't teach you to be a director. No one can. I can give you space to watch and help others do it. Usually, you will only learn how you *don't* want to do it. And I can give you space to direct and learn from doing it yourself. That's all I can do.' I feel the same way about writing dialogue.

No one can really teach you how to do it; they can only give you some guidelines and advice.

The best way to learn to write dialogue is to do so, and then get actors to read it. Get good actors, as experienced as you can find, who will give you honest feedback. Give them your text, get them to read it and understand it, and then ask them to improvise around it and get them to play with it. Listen to them. Most of all, ask them to be brutally honest with you.

I sometimes find writing dialogue difficult and I have developed a couple of techniques to help which I will share.

### Don't get it right, get it down

Remember that no one is going to see your work until you let them. You can rewrite before anyone sees it, and often it is in the process of writing that you will discover much about the characters and the work you have in hand. This is especially true in the early scenes, when you may not have a firm grip on the characters or situation. Beginnings can be notoriously difficult, but take a deep breath, dive in and get writing. You can always change it later.

### Where's the behaviour?

The great American playwright Terrence McNally, who wrote the books for *The Rink*, *Ragtime* and *The Full Monty*, mentored the writer of a new play I directed. He had one question that he returned to again and again: 'Where's the behaviour?' Behaviour is *how* characters do things – how they behave in certain situations, what this says about their character, and how this develops plot. In *Evita*, Eva Duarte walks into Juan Perón's apartment and packs the suitcase of Perón's Mistress, throwing her out. Little is said, but Eva shows the Mistress, and Perón, who is in control. In *Carousel*, Billy Bigelow, a character who is tragically inarticulate, stays out all night, hits his wife and his daughter, and dies attempting to commit a robbery, stabbing himself rather than being arrested. All of this is behaviour that illustrates character and furthers the plot, but involves a character saying very little. Characters are defined more by what they do than what they say.

## Don't write dialogue

This sounds crazy, but never use a line of a dialogue where you can do without it. There are many other ways of telling the story, especially in a musical. People can sing, they can dance, and they can do things. In *West Side Story*, think of all the ways in which the story is told *without* dialogue. The gangs fight, dance and sing. Think about the film *The Artist*; an entire full-length film made in 2011 that has (practically) no dialogue. Depending on the theatrical language of your piece, look carefully at whether you really need a scene to be spoken. Can the beats of the scene be told through song, dance or action?

### Silence is Golden

'A man is preparing to leave his wife when she returns home.' Take this scenario and write a scene that shows this information and how the situation develops through to a resolution – but use no dialogue. Everything must be shown through behaviour and action.

## Listen, listen, listen

Listen to the conversations going on around you. Operate like a real-life Henry Higgins and listen to the specific syntax of the conversations that you hear. I love to listen in on other people's conversations on the bus, on the train, anywhere you hear them. Look up interviews with people on YouTube and listen to their speech patterns. Be aware of all the character traits that feed into the way they speak.

Remember that certain formats of certain locations bring with them certain speech patterns. A priest in a church service will speak with certain speech patterns, as will lawyers in court, workers in an office, politicians being interviewed.

Certain relationships also carry different speech patterns: parents talking to their children (even those fully grown), people with their friends, couples. Status also has a bearing on speech patterns. Servants talking to employers might talk in one way, teachers to their pupils in another. Military personnel have a very codified set of speech patterns depending on their rank and role.

Different situations also bring different kinds of speech patterns: even though the characters are consistent. As an extreme example, think about the President of the United States. Here is a role with massive status, but in a variety of situations his speech patterns will change: giving a press conference, talking to another head of state, having a marital row, chairing a meeting of security staff, dealing with a crisis, stroking the White House cat, reading a child a bedtime story.

Every one of us changes the way we speak depending on who we are speaking to, because each of us behaves differently with different people.

Writers often 'clean up' the speech patterns of their characters, but remember that vocal tics can illuminate character, so long as they are not overused. Alecky Blythe and Adam Cork's musical docudrama *London Road* set a series of recorded interviews to music, including all the tics of real speech. The result was a fascinating example of the speech patterns of ordinary people suddenly talking about the extraordinary circumstances around them.

Listen, listen, listen.

---

### Different Speeches

Choose a well-known figure who is likely to have been interviewed in a number of situations. Politicians can be good, or entertainment stars who also are involved in political campaigns. Find two or three contrasting interviews and then transcribe them. Look carefully at the types of words, the tone and the speech rhythms of each one.

---

> ## Listen to Speech Patterns
>
> Record interviews with four or five different people who are important in your life. Choose people from contrasting parts of your life – a parent, a sibling, a friend, a work colleague or classmate. Ask them all the same questions but listen to the speech patterns in their answers.

## Period Dialogue: Modern People in Different Times

When writing for characters in a specific historical period, some (usually inexperienced) writers like to try and mimic a linguistic style they presume was used at the time. They sometimes feel this will be matched by a sense of 'period acting', which will have nothing to do with truth and lots to do with history. These writers forget one thing: everyone who has ever lived has lived in the most modern time there has been. We might think about the future, but we have no way of knowing what that will be. Chaucer thought himself a very modern man, as did Shakespeare, and I am pretty certain that even early man thought to himself, 'Yeah, I'm bang up to date!' Whenever I have written works set in historical periods, I have been careful to avoid any obvious 'modernisms' that will make the work date (dude!), but I have also been careful to avoid any obvious sense of 'historical writing', which, even with the best research, is going to be 90 per cent hokum.

If you are writing pastiche of another style, such as the B-movie style of *Little Shop of Horrors*, you might want to listen to and absorb some of the rhythms and specifics of the genre, but if it is a historical period you are going for, the avoidance of faux-historical or bang-up-to-date modern language will help create a timeless style that will not date.

## Comedy Scenes

If you are writing comedy then you will now be faced with writing comic dialogue. In each scene, you will be plotting the hideously painful journey of your Hero and tightening the screws on him. In some scenes, you might be rewarding him momentarily with some triumph (such as Seymour and Audrey getting together), but this will only be so that you can tighten the screws and your Hero can keep on being knocked back, until the final scene when he may truly triumph.

If you have structured the piece properly and you are raising the stakes in each scene, then you will find that the piece will be funny. Be wary of writing 'jokes'. They have a tendency to stick out like sore thumbs and destroy the audience's belief in your piece. They tend to reek of a writer trying too hard. When we did the first reading of *Twang!!*, I immediately knew that some 'jokes' I had included were simply unnecessary and were working against the show. The rewrites involved taking them out.

The laughs are generated by the characters in the situation, but there does need to be wit in the dialogue. There are a few techniques that can help you garner laughs:

*The rule of three:* Comedy lines often work in threes: the premise, the reinforcement of the premise, and the undermining of the premise. Take this short exchange from a British pantomime version of *Aladdin*, in which the villain Abanazar is trying to get Aladdin's mother, Widow Twankey, to help him:

ABANAZAR. But surely you recognise me?

TWANKEY. I *don't* recognise you. (*Offers her a bag of gold.*) Funny how your memory starts coming back.

It is simple, but the first line establishes the premise, the second reinforces it, and the third undermines it, creating comic effect.

*The unexpected response:* Sometimes the simply unexpected can create comic effect. This is like the rule of three, but it doesn't need the second step because the contrast between the first line and the response is strong enough to create the comedy. It usually requires the possibility of a misinterpretation of the premise. Stephen Fry interpolated one of the oldest music-hall (British vaudeville) gags into his revised script for *Me and My Girl*:

DUCHESS. Usually I buy myself a new hat if I'm down in the dumps.

SIR JOHN. So that's where you get them from.

*The comedy 'k':* Bear in mind that the 'k' is the funniest individual sound in the English language. Harder-sounding consonants are always funnier than the softer sounds of vowels, or the softer consonants, probably because they are more percussive, and 'k' beats the lot. One of the reasons why Twankey's line – 'Funny how your memory starts coming back' – is funny is because it ends on the explosive 'k'.

*Rhythm:* Comedy is all about rhythm and, luckily, if you are writing a musical, you are likely to have at least a sense of rhythm (if not, the composer in your team ought to have one, or you really are in trouble). Comic lines have their own rhythm that you simply can't ignore. Which is the funnier of these two lines?

'Funny how your memory starts coming back.'

Or:

'I must have had some kind of amnesia and I think I have recovered my memory.'

I hope you agree that the first line is funnier and it is not only that it is shorter. It has 'punch'. It has a rhythm that leaves you feeling like there is space for a laugh.

## Script Layout

How you lay out your script is an important consideration as to how it will be read, understood and, ultimately, performed. There are some basic rules that are considered to be industry standards and, if you want to appear as professional as possible, it is best to abide by these.

As far as script length is concerned, a non-musical play by a writer like Ibsen or Shaw uses roughly 10,000 to 12,000 words per hour of stage time. A musical generally uses roughly 8,000 to 10,000 words per hour, depending on the proportion of lyrics. These are very rough guides, and obviously the figures for a musical depend on the amount of simultaneous singing of different lines.

Here is a standard format for a manuscript, which is an excerpt from my adaptation of *The Wind in the Willows*, which I wrote with composer Richard John. In this excerpt, Mr Toad is escaping from prison, and this is the text preceding a long number called 'The Great Escape':

WIND IN THE WILLOWS                                    56.


                    TOAD
    And I shall miss you, my pretty miss.
                    (To Washerwoman)
    Thank you madam, for a fine outfit!

                                    The Daughter starts to tie up the
                                    Washerwoman.

                    DAUGHTER
    You're the very image of her. Go straight down
    the way you came up; but remember you're a
    widow woman, quite alone in the world, with a
    character to lose.

                    WASHERWOMAN
    A very good character. Very fine and demure.

            MUSIC NO. 11: THE GREAT ESCAPE

                    TOAD
    I'm sure. Goodbye, ladies!
                    (Sings)
    I WAS STUCK IN THE WAZOO,
    NOW IT'S PRISON, TODELOO,
    I'LL BE GONE, JUST YOU SEE,
    WHERE ON EARTH WILL I BE?
    I'LL BE GONE, I WILL FLEE,
    TALLY HO, MR TOAD, MR TOAD, MR TOAD, WILL BE FREE!

                                    By the time the music has ended
                                    Toad is out of prison and the
                                    walls of the prison have become a
                                    Railway Ticket Office.

                    TOAD
    Aha! What a piece of luck! A Railway.
                    (Moves to window - the ticket clerk is
                    there. He speaks as Toad, unaccustomed to
                    being dressed as a woman.)
    I'd like a first class ticket to that fine
    gentleman's residence, Toad Hall.

                    CLERK
    Toad Hall? Three shillings.

                    TOAD
    Ah! Oh!
                    (And he reaches down and realises that he
                    hasn't got any money and he is in a dress
                    - turns into a lady in front of our eyes,
                    but unlike the washerwoman he is frilly
                    and girly. The music becomes cod-opera.)
    I HAVE BEEN A SILLY GIRL,
    A VERY FRILLY, SILLY GIRL,
    FOR I HAVE COME FORTH FOR TO ROAM,
    BUT LEFT MY PURSE AT HOME

This script was created with Final Draft, an industry-standard scriptwriting software package that runs on Windows and Mac.

In this format, note how the character names are placed centrally above the dialogue or lyric, and the lyrics are in capital letters. Stage directions and action are tabulated to the right-hand side.

Bear in mind that the libretto is designed to be used as a script in the rehearsal room and as such, it is important to use a point-size that is big and clear enough for actors to read easily. This standard format, printed on US foolscap, or UK A4, in Courier point size 11, will give you approximately one page per minute. Most script or screenwriting software will format like this. Personally, I like Final Draft, which is also capable of running reports to give you handy information, like which characters have the most lines and which scenes a character appears in. This is a very good manuscript layout, although if the work is published, publishers generally have their own house style. You can see other acceptable formats by looking at the libretti for musicals that are already published.

Remember that lyrics take longer to sing than spoken text, so the more your characters sing, the less they can say. If you are writing a through-sung show, you need to pare your text back to the dramatic essentials.

## Beginning to Write

The book of a musical must be lean and to the point. Characters are developed more through the musical numbers than the scenes. Every line of dialogue needs to earn its place, and if you can do without it, then do.

If you are the bookwriter, the first draft of the book is the one that the songwriters will want to see. Where there are moments that you have all identified as potential songs, write as much as you think necessary or that your collaborators want you to. It might be that you write the entire sequence with monologues and dialogue, or it might be that you write very clear descriptions of everything that happens, in terms of plot, action and character development in the song.

There is no magic to it. Just plan each scene carefully and then begin to write...

**Write the Book**

Work through each scene in your synopsis in order. With each scene, reverse action the beats and then write the scene. Then move on to the next scene. Keep moving forward until you have reached the end of the synopsis and don't worry about rewrites at this stage. Get it down – don't get it right. There is endless time for rewrites later.

# 9
*Songs*

# *Songs*

The distinguishing feature of a musical is that songs play an integral relationship in the narrative. This means that the songs created need to be capable of forwarding plot, developing character, commentating on the action or otherwise functioning in the storytelling. This is not a book about the intricacies of songwriting and there are many good guides and extensive online resources on that subject.

Songs written as stand-alone pop songs are often not capable of this integration because, since the 1950s, pop songs have been written to be the background music of our lives, not to be listened to within certain situations. It is the very generality of the songs that makes them popular. If they were too specific, not enough of us would relate to them to make them hits. Of course, pop artists perform concerts, singing their songs live in a very focused situation, but, crucially, the people who go to pop concerts tend to know the songs already.

Pop songs are designed for lazy listening, so catchy musical hooks and generalised lyrics about common universal emotions are the order of the day. There is nothing wrong with lazy listening; it is perfect for cooking, doing your homework or driving, which require concentration in themselves. The best pop songs sound as if they are designed for precisely this sort of lazy listening, but are often musically and lyrically complex, even puzzling, so that if you do concentrate, you realise there is much more going on.

Watching a theatre piece is not an act of laziness, even if it is done by those tired after a long day's work. The theatre is a place of concentration, which takes the audience vicariously through a situation to a place of resolution and stability. The songs, then, have a different job to do; not to provide background music to the characters' lives, but to forward the story.

This is the reason why the jukebox musical is such a tricky form. Both Broadway and the West End have seen few real successes in the form (*Mamma Mia!* and *Jersey Boys* come to mind), but a heap of musical crashes have surprised the producers, shoehorning the songs of The Beach Boys, Rod Stewart, Blondie and Elvis into generally witless books. It is easy to see the attraction for the producer: if the audience go in humming the songs, they will come out humming the songs. The songs are less important to the drama and more important to the marketing. If that band can sell a million records, there are a million people out there who might buy a ticket. That's the thinking, anyway.

The best jukebox musicals are successful for three reasons, and I reckon you need at least two of them to score a hit:

1. The book is genuinely original, witty or inventive.
2. The songwriters of the band were writing more complex and interesting songs than the norm.
3. It is not possible to see the original band perform live.

This final reason is key to a producer's thinking. If the fans can see the originating band, why will they pay in sufficient numbers to see someone else perform the songs? The West End musical *Never Forget*, using the music of the boy band Take That, ran for six months, but the producers must have been cursing when, halfway through the creative process and once the pre-West End tour was booked, the band announced they were reforming. With there being no chance of ABBA, Queen or The Four Seasons performing live with their original line-ups, the producers of *Mamma Mia!*, *We Will Rock You* and *Jersey Boys* are on a much safer bet.

Although it has its detractors, *Mamma Mia!* is a uniquely successful example of the genre, both commercially and dramatically, as the book was fresh and witty at the time of opening and, importantly, ABBA's Benny and Björn had invented dramatic situations for their characters when writing their pop songs. Often in an ABBA song a character will reach a moment of decision or self-knowledge that is rare in a pop song. Similarly, Bob Gaudio and Bob Crewe's songs for The Four Seasons are of a similarly high order and are matched with some interesting storytelling in the book of *Jersey Boys*. The music of Queen has its own theatricality, which was built around the remarkable late Freddie Mercury, but I have to admit that the attraction of the long-running *We Will Rock You* has always evaded me. I saw it in late previews and found Ben Elton's book to be among the worst that has ever graced the stage – lazy, self-indulgent and witless – although the original London cast and band were phenomenally good. I am not alone in my dislike – it is one of those shows: nobody likes it but the public!

Songs in musical theatre should demand the same level of concentration as scenes. The success of the TV series *Glee* and *Smash* has shown that there is a substantial audience for the intelligent use of songs in dramatic situations. The show's producers have clearly been very careful to mix musical-theatre songs that require concentration with the most intelligent pop songs where the drama can recontextualise the lyric.

One of the great differences between pop and musical-theatre songs is that the pop song is designed to be listened to, lazily, many times. The musical-theatre song is designed to be heard once, in a dramatic situation, and must form an integral part of the action.

Of course, some songs from musicals have had significant chart success. Andrew Lloyd Webber has had number-one hits with 'Don't Cry for Me, Argentina', 'No Matter What' and 'Any Dream Will Do' and The Beatles covered 'Till There Was You' from *The Music Man* on their second album. However, in a world where the music industry is increasingly fractured, the chart hit is elusive for the musical-theatre writer.

Presuming you are creating new songs for your musical, you will be able to avoid the pitfalls of the jukebox musical and create songs that are designed to be heard in a theatrical setting, and that develop plot and story. These songs can be in any style you like; I am not advocating any particular musical or lyrical style.

## Which Comes First, Music or Lyrics?

It's up to you and your collaborators. There are no rules and different partnerships work in different ways. Richard Rodgers wrote the music *before* the lyrics when working with Lorenz Hart, and the music *after* the lyrics when working with Oscar Hammerstein. Kander and Ebb used to work together in the same room at the same time, whilst Andrew Lloyd Webber has generally written the music before the lyrics in his relationships with many lyricists.

In my working relationship with Richard John, I usually write a draft of the lyric, to which Richard sets music, sometimes altering my work with dummy lyrics of his own. He then plays me the song, and then I take the lyric away and clean it up, removing his dummy lyrics. Sometimes, when he first plays the song to me, I suggest musical changes – and we count ourselves lucky that we both work without ego getting in the way of the creative process. We listen to each other's work and invariably agree with the other's notes. We firmly believe that unless both of us are happy with the song, then it shouldn't have a place in the show. We have never had an argument about a song.

Sometimes Richard writes the music first. This will tend to be in specific situations; for example, if we are writing a song that has many musical parts working simultaneously, or if we decide that the music of the song needs to be particularly prominent (such as a soaring romantic ballad).

For us, we find that by writing the lyrics first, it is easier to develop the scene dramatically through the song, giving a clear arc to the storytelling before the music is composed.

## Song Form

All art has form and songs are no different. The form determines the sound and musical language of the song. In songwriting, different forms are referred to through a variety of terms, so you might hear talk of a spiritual, a doo-wop or a rock 'n' roll song, referring to the song's style. These forms are described through the use of alphabetical letters to indicate where music is repeated and where it is not. The simplest form of pop song is known as AABA, that means an A section (the first piece of music is always referred to as the A section) followed by a repeat of the A section, followed by a new piece of music called, not surprisingly, the B section, and followed once more by a repeat of the A section. You might think of it like this:

| | | |
|---|---|---|
| Chorus | A | *followed by* |
| Chorus | A | *followed by* |
| Bridge | B | *followed by* |
| Chorus | A | |

– and you can see the AABA form. Many songs, including 'Can't Help Lovin' Dat Man' and The Beatles' 'Revolution', use exactly this form.

The A section is often called the refrain or chorus, and the B section is known as the middle eight or bridge and this whole song form is sometimes called 32-bar form, giving each section eight bars.

This can be varied as an ABAB form, such as 'Fly Me to the Moon' and varied further to ABAC form, where the C section refers to a third piece of music, such as 'The Shadow of Your Smile' and 'Moon River'.

If the song uses a slightly altered version of an A or B section, this may then be known as an $A^1$ or a $B^1$. 'Old Man River' and 'The Way We Were' both have an $AA^1BA^2$ structure.

A new section on the end to finish the song may be known as a coda, such as the lines at the end of 'Over the Rainbow' that start 'If happy little bluebirds...'

The term 'verse' is a confusing one. Until the 1950s, a verse would often precede the song itself, setting the scene to contextualise the A section, and this would be known as a 'sectional verse'. These verses were sometimes quite long, such as in the song 'Meet Me in St Louis', which has a verse that explains how the singer had a lover who was called Louis and how she had left him for more adventure and how she would be in St Louis. These verses were often cut for recording and in concert, but if the song appeared in a musical comedy (and from the 1920s to the '40s practically all musicals were musical comedies) then the verse would often facilitate the song being included in the show. Noël Coward's 'If Love Were All' has a long verse, which makes perfect sense when performed in *Bitter Sweet*, but is usually cut in other contexts.

From the 1950s onwards, as rock 'n' roll was built around repeated choruses, the term 'verse' came to mean a repeated section between the A section. John Lennon and Paul McCartney pushed the development of pop song forms, experimenting with form and creating new kinds of pop songs that defied categorisation.

All songs outside the concert and opera repertoire (which has different forms) can be labelled in the A B C D... form. Different genres of songs have different forms, and there is nothing to say that you have to follow any pattern.

If you are writing pastiche songs, you will need to identify the song forms for the genre you are pastiching and stick pretty closely to it, or you will lose the form of the work – and therefore the effect of the pastiche. For instance, twelve-bar blues has an A section of twelve bars that is repeated. Take away the form and it is no longer twelve-bar blues.

Let's look briefly at the form of some songs:

| | |
|---|---|
| 'If I Were a Rich Man' (from *Fiddler on the Roof*) | A B B A B C B A Coda |
| 'Somewhere That's Green' (from *Little Shop of Horrors*) | Verse A A B A¹ |
| 'Bring Him Home' (from *Les Misérables*) | A A¹ B A A¹ |
| 'Send in the Clowns' (from *A Little Night Music*) | A A¹ B A² |
| 'The Winner Takes It All' (from *Mamma Mia!*) | A B A B B A B B A |

### Song Form

Analyse some songs that you like, identifying their A B C format. In particular, look at genres that you might be interested in writing in. For example, if you are thinking about writing punk (usually in an A A A A form), analyse some punk songs.

# Why Do Characters Sing?

There is a cliché that characters sing when the emotional pitch reaches a level at which speaking is no longer appropriate, and they dance when the emotional pitch reaches that at which singing is no longer appropriate. This is only true of some emotional situations, especially those pertaining to joy; it is exactly the way that 'June is Bustin' Out All Over' is motivated in *Carousel*.

The actual reasons why characters sing are most clearly defined by the theatrical language the writer is using. Your characters can sing only the most rapturous emotions, or the most mundane banalities, but as long as it is consistent with the theatrical language of the piece, then the audience will accept it.

Obviously, the higher proportion of songs in the show, the greater the danger of singing the mundane. One critic pointed out that in the through-sung *Aspects of Love* there were more drinks orders set to music than in any other musical. However, in *London Road*, it was the very banality of the lyrics (based on actual verbatim speech), contrasted with the hugely traumatic serial killings taking place, that gave the show its dramatic interest.

Characters sing for many reasons – and emotional pitch is the most common. However, do not treat emotional pitch as synonymous with romantic emotions. Characters are just as likely to sing because they are joyful, hurt or furious. In *Mack and Mabel*, the character of Mabel Normand does all three of these: she is bursting with pride and joy in 'Look What Happened to Mabel', hurt and desperate in 'Time Heals Everything' and furious in 'Wherever He Ain't'.

Characters may also sing because the music may reveal the subtext of the scene. In one of the best love songs, *Carousel's* 'If I Loved You', the emotional pitch is high, but the characters are inarticulate. The romantic, passionate music is at odds with a lyric about lost love and missed chances, but as the scene progresses, and Julie and Billy each sing the identical lyric, it is clear that they understand each other more deeply than words can express. When they wordlessly move towards each other and kiss as the music soars and the blossom falls, the audience is moved more within those first twenty minutes of *Carousel* than it is across the three hours of many other musicals.

When you are writing songs, you have the opportunity to let the audience experience two 'scripts' simultaneously, the musical and the lyrical. One of the best reasons to treat a scene musically is to create a tension between the two, just as Rodgers and Hammerstein do in 'If I Loved You'.

Characters might also sing as a commentary on the action, in the Brechtian technique of *Verfremdungseffekt*. This is often translated as 'alienation', but is more accurately described as a 'distancing' from the emotional journey of the characters, in order to force the audience to consider the issues at stake in the play. Brecht and Kurt Weill used this extensively in their musical-theatre works like *Die Dreigroschenoper* (translated as *The Threepenny Opera*) and *The Happy End*. It has become a surprisingly popular technique in commercial musicals, most notably *Cabaret* (which drew heavily on the Brecht/Weill legacy), but also in works like *Sweeney Todd*, in which Sondheim uses the chorus as a narrator, and to set the work within a wider social context.

The format of the scene can often facilitate musicalisation. A wedding scene is an obvious example, and we can find these in many musicals from *The Sound of Music* to *Me and My Girl*, but less obvious formats can also be 'shorthanded' for the audience, such as the court scene in *Chicago*.

> ### Why Characters Sing
>
> Work through the songs that you have already spotted in your musical and note why the characters are singing in each of them.

## Songs as Scenes

From the first draft of the book, you should now have a good idea where the songs are going to be placed, and their function.

With songs involving more than one character the challenge is to musicalise the scene whilst creating an effective song. I find reverse actioning especially useful here to map out the moments of the scene and the reversals.

Take, for example, the song 'Mushnik and Son' from *Little Shop of Horrors*. This is a good example of a simple scene set to music. Mushnik, the florist, scared that Seymour will take the plant away from the shop, invites the young man he has always mistreated, to be his son. If you listen to the song you can see how Howard Ashman has developed the scene, and we can imagine that if he had reverse actioned it, his plan might have looked something like this:

1.  Mushnik is scared of losing the plant.
2.  Mushnik has an idea.
3.  Mushnik invites Seymour to be adopted as his son.
4.  Seymour is surprised.
5.  Mushnik tempts Seymour.
6.  Seymour reminds Mushnik of their relationship.
7.  Mushnik dismisses Seymour's concerns.
8.  Mushnik prompts Seymour to agree.
9.  Mushnik threatens that he will hold his breath until Seymour agrees.
10. Seymour agrees.
11. Seymour and Mushnik celebrate.

Any scene that needs to be musicalised can be reverse actioned as a first step. For *The Railway Children*, we created a production number for the opening of Act Two in which the whole village celebrates the bravery of the children having saved a train from crashing. The owners of the railway award them pocket watches. The scene already had a format, that of a medal-giving, and we wanted this number to have a catchy chorus along the lines of great production numbers like 'June is Busting Out All Over', or 'Once a Year Day' from *The Pajama Game*. I hit on the hook of 'A Once in a Lifetime Day', and wrote a chorus that expressed the idea that whenever one might be feeling down, the memory of that day will cheer them. Having written the chorus, I then reverse actioned the scene, noting the form that I intended the song to take:

| | Action | Form |
|---|---|---|
| 1. | Perks (the Stationmaster) welcomes everybody. | A |
| 2. | Perks praises the children's bravery. | |
| 3. | Perks sings the chorus, teaching it to everyone. | B |
| 4. | Perks presents the children with their watches. | |
| 5. | Perks introduces the Engine Driver. | |
| 6. | The Engine Driver is shocked at being asked to speak. | Spoken |
| 7. | The Engine Driver begins to tell story. | C |
| 8. | The Engine Driver gets excited in his own tale. | |
| 9. | Perks and the Engine Driver share a chorus between them. | B |
| 10. | Roberta leads the children to the podium. | |
| 11. | Peter begins to thank, but falters. | D |
| 12. | Roberta helps Peter. | |
| 13. | Phyllis interrupts Roberta. | |
| 14. | Perks, the Engine Driver and the ensemble sing in celebration. | B |
| 15. | The celebration becomes a dance. | Dance Break |
| 16. | All sing and dance in celebration. | $B^1$ |

As you can see, as I reverse actioned it, I also gave it a form, even if the decisions about the verses and the extension to the chorus section to finish it (as a B¹) had not yet been made, and weren't until I really began to work on the lyric in earnest. There is little drama in this scene: it is not about a reversal or a conflict, it is about a celebration, but this reverse actioned sketch provided a very useful starting point for the song, which you can hear on the original cast album, or read in the published libretto.

## Songs as Moments of Character Development

Solos and some duets can also be about character development. 'I Wish' songs tend to be essentially about character exposition, letting the audience know what the character wants so that the desire can fire the plot. These do not need to develop a situation, but let the audience know about the character.

There are other songs that truly develop character and, often along with it, plot. The character begins to sing, and by the end of the song has realised something about how they feel, or what they must do. Sometimes it is a matter of reinforcement, such as My Fair Lady's 'Hymn to Him'. It might be a moment of growth or new confidence, such as Eliza's 'Just You Wait', which begins with gritted teeth, surliness, and develops into full-voiced rage.

The same show has a tremendous example of a song of realisation: 'I've Grown Accustomed to Her Face'. Higgins goes through the following emotions:

- Higgins loathes Eliza.
- Higgins recognises the role she has occupied in his life.
- Higgins ridicules Eliza's plan to marry Freddie.
- Higgins imagines Eliza's squalid life with Freddie (and without him).
- Higgins imagines Eliza deserted.
- Higgins relishes Eliza's misery.
- Higgins imagines Eliza crawling back to him.
- Higgins emphasises his own generous qualities.

- Higgins rejects Eliza's (imaginary) appeal for return.
- The music indicates a softening in Higgins's heart.
- Higgins misses Eliza.
- Higgins regrets their parting (indicated musically).

At the beginning of the number, Higgins is furious with Eliza; by the end he has realised how much he cares for her. It is a brilliant piece of musical-theatre writing. Whatever method Alan Jay Lerner used, it is quite possible to see that he might have written this lyric if he had started in this way.

When writing lyrics, the reverse actioning is an incredibly useful tool in establishing the character journey through a song. For example, the title song of *The Railway Children* used these actions:

1. The Old Gentleman notices the children.
2. The Old Gentleman befriends the children.
3. The Old Gentleman invites the children to dream.
4. Roberta informs the Old Gentleman of Szczepansky.
5. Roberta asks for help for Szczepansky.
6. The Old Gentleman is surprised by Roberta.
7. The Old Gentleman promises to help Szczepansky.
8. The Old Gentleman remembers the plight of the children's father.
9. The Old Gentleman promises to help the children.

This became the following lyric (with dialogue):

'THE RAILWAY CHILDREN'

*The* OLD GENTLEMAN *is reading a letter.*

OLD GENTLEMAN (*sung*).
　　Ev'ry single day I see them watching,
　　Ev'ry day they wave.
　　How can I ignore the children wishing,
　　Asking for my aid?

　　On a hill so green,
　　There you stand, my railway children,

How you cheer an old man's journey.
Small against the sky,
Make a wish, my railway children,
Waving in the blue,
Wishes do come true.

*The lights reveal* ROBERTA *on the hillside.*

ROBERTA (*spoken*).
To our dear Old Gentleman. Mother has taken in
this Russian man. We found him on the station.
His name is 'Shpansky'. She says he wrote a book
and people locked him up. He is looking for his
wife and child, who are in England somewhere. Is
it possible you could find out where they are?

OLD GENTLEMAN (*spoken, in rhythm*).
Now, this Russian chap
Is it *the* Szczepansky?
Wrote a book, then locked in prison
Now, he's turned up here.

(*Sung.*)
Yes, my little friends,
I'll try to help you,
And help Szczepansky too.

Watching from afar
Knowing of your father,
Knowing who you are,
Knowing your darker sorrow.

ROBERTA (*spoken*).
Signed Peter, Roberta and Phyllis.

ROBERTA *exits.*

OLD GENTLEMAN (*sung*).
On a hill so green,
There you stand, my railway children,
How you cheer an old man's journey.
Small against the sky,
Make a wish, my railway children,
Waving in the blue,

> Watch me wave to you,
> Make a wish and wave,
> Wishes do come true.

It might appear that reverse actioning is little more than writing a detailed plan for the song, and in many ways it is. By using transitive verbs wherever possible, you will define what the character is doing and to whom, so it becomes more useful than simply making a checklist. It may feel tricky and complex to begin with, but you will soon get the hang of it and your work will be more focused as a result.

Reverse actioning also helps to prevent the most common flaw in musical writing: that the play comes to a stop when the music starts. If your book scenes and your songs cover the same ground, then your show becomes repetitive and dull.

Notice how 'Mushnik and Son', 'I've Grown Accustomed to Her Face' and 'The Railway Children' all carry reversals within them. Seymour agrees to become Mushnik's son, Higgins changes from fury to affection, and the Old Gentleman goes from being passively amused to agreeing actively to help. These are songs that are dramatically effective.

---

**Scenes as Songs**

Take a short scene from a play, TV or film script. It should probably be between three and five minutes long. Establish what the scene is about, identifying any reversals. Reverse action it and then establish what you think the structure of a song based on it might be (verses, choruses, bridges and, possibly, dance breaks).

---

## The Hook

The essence of a song is known as 'the hook'. This might be a musical idea or a lyrical idea – the best of them are both – and it is an idea that stands out and is memorable. The hook may appear anywhere in the song, but the beginning or the end of the refrain is the most common place, and it may be repeated.

When the hook is both a musical and lyrical idea working simultaneously, it is often the title of the song, as in:

- 'People Will Say We're in Love' (from *Oklahoma!*).
- 'Suddenly Seymour' (from *Little Shop of Horrors*).
- 'This is the Moment' (from *Jekyll and Hyde*).
- 'Wouldn't It Be Loverly?' (at the end of the refrain, although the lyric also appears in the verse).
- 'Don't Cry for Me, Argentina' (at the beginning of the refrain).

In each of these cases above, the lyrical hook is the title and the musical hook is the musical setting of that phrase. Sometimes the hook is a lyrical idea that is set to different musical phrases throughout the song, such as 'On My Own' from *Les Misérables* where the phrase is set at the beginning of the verse and at the end of the song. A lyrical hook might be repeated many times in one song, as it is in the Burt Bacharach/Hal David 'I Say a Little Prayer', Carly Simon's 'You're So Vain', Queen's 'We Will Rock You' or Sondheim's 'Leave You'.

A musical hook might also be repeated many times, but with different lyrics at some repetitions, such as 'Love Changes Everything' or 'Mack the Knife'.

Not every song has a hook, and in musical theatre, especially in through-sung musicals, not all songs will have strong hooks. 'Pilate's Dream' in *Jesus Christ Superstar* and 'Dog Eats Dog' from *Les Misérables* do not have strong hooks, either lyrically or musically, but they are effective within the musical. They can provide a different listening experience to the songs with strong hooks, which is refreshing for an audience across an entire performance.

Hooks are often associated with pop songs, although Beethoven created one of the strongest musical hooks ever in his Fifth Symphony, the three G notes followed by the E flat. The extent to which you might use strong hooks in your musical will also depend (again) on the theatrical language of the piece, and your own musical and lyrical style.

Creating memorable hooks is an art in itself, but it mainly comes from exploring all the possibilities around the theme or the moment of the song. Sometimes one may be self-evident, popping into your head in a moment of pure inspiration. More likely, it will be the result of hours of perspiration. Remember that a hook is nothing more than a neat idea that captures the essence of the moment, and like all incredibly simple art, it is the simplicity that can make it fiendishly difficult.

I tend to use brainstorming techniques, simply throwing ideas out onto a piece of paper. For one number in *The Railway Children*, I wanted to capture the essence of a girl becoming a woman, having just experienced her first kiss. The scene was located in the English countryside at the end of summer, and the girl was not highly educated. When I began writing down emotional words and images, I kept returning to words that were about the spring, about emotions bursting forth like flowers in spring, or birds hatching from eggs. The contrast between the season of the scene (the end of summer) and the season of her emotions, (being the 'spring of her life') led me to the phrase 'I can't believe it's nearly autumn, when it feels like spring' – and the song was born.

Brainstorming is a simple technique of taking a piece of paper and allowing ideas to flow. Start with the central idea you are dealing with:

**Spring**

Then just add lines and boxes as they come to you:

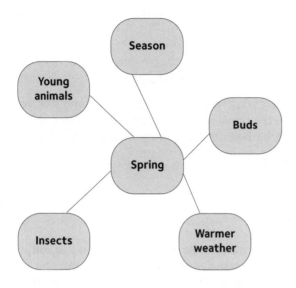

And others join on from those:

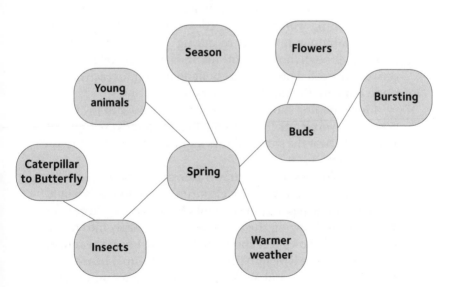

Just keep going on a big piece of paper, adding new boxes with new ideas as they generate themselves. Remember this about brainstorming: every nine ideas will be dead as rock – the tenth *could* rock!

---

**Brainstorm**

Taking the reverse-actioning process for a song that you created in the previous exercise, brainstorm some ideas for hooks, both musical and lyrical, that you might use for the song.

---

## Clean-Up

Whether you decide to write music or lyrics first, at some stage the composer and lyricist (presuming they are not one and the same) will find themselves in a room working on the song together.

It is at this point that both of you must be satisfied with the work. If you are not, you must voice these opinions now or never. Nothing will upset your co-writer like telling him his work is fabulous now and recanting later. I cannot stress strongly enough how important it is for the relationship between the collaborators to be built on respect for each other's work, but with the freedom to be honest.

I love the first moment of hearing music set to my lyrics. When the two elements come together it is always exciting, but as soon as I hear the song, I always know what I need to do with my own work.

In the old days of hand-drawn animation, there used to be a department responsible for 'clean-up'. The animators would create the drawings, but these would be traced into clear lines by 'clean-up', bringing the character more sharply into focus. That is exactly how I feel about the first time I hear the music: I can now put the lyric into the stage of 'clean-up'. I hear all the flaws in the lyric and make small, sometimes minuscule changes until I am finally happy with my own work. The composer does the same, and we normally do this in the same room at the same time. It is polishing the song until it is ready for a singer.

But now, let's go back a little and look at how to create that music and those lyrics...

# 10
## *Lyrical Matters*

# Lyrical Matters

For all the importance that the book has in making a successful musical, it is the songs that audiences remember and it is the lyrics that can make or break a show. Most theatre critics reserve most of their opprobrium for the lyrics in the event of a flop, and most praise in the event of a hit. One of the reasons for this is that all critics learn very early that lyrics quoted out of context, in isolation on a newspaper page, often read worse than they sound, and are therefore easily mocked and knocked. The lyrics must be able to carry drama, but must also be appropriate and polished: the rhymes must be perfect and the scansion correct, to help the audience understand the sense in the midst of the drama.

## Rhyme

Many people think lyric writing is largely a matter of rhyme, and for some lyric writers it is clearly a matter of rhyme before reason. Do you have to rhyme? No. So why bother going through the rigours of what Christopher Hampton, who wrote book and lyrics with Don Black for the musical version of *Sunset Boulevard*, likened to 'wrestling with elephants'?

One must be sure to rhyme *with* reason. If you are rhyming simply for the sake of rhyming, you are losing sense and character, and in a musical that will lessen the impact of the song. What the character is trying to say is more important than the rhyme; the trick is to find the perfect rhyme with the perfect sense.

Rhyme is used to guide the listener through the song, to enable them to make sense of the lyric even though they are hearing it to music and at speed. Musical-theatre songs, indeed any songs performed live, are heard 'in the moment' as part of the dramatic experience. You are asking the audience to understand a lot of information quickly and set to music. Rhyme helps to facilitate sense. The brain can process rhyme because it subconsciously expects to hear a similar sound to the one it has just heard. As a result, rhyme acts as a kind of guide for listeners.

Technically speaking, rhyme is the repetition of an identical vowel sound and all the consonantal and vowel sounds that follow it. Rhyme is not a matter of spelling, only the sounds matter.

Songs and poetry using rhyme have rhyme schemes, which describe the way in which rhyme is used. Confusingly, these are labelled with the same A B C descriptive shorthand that is used for parts of a song. A song may have an A A B A form, but an A A B B rhyme scheme within that form. So:

| | | |
|---|---|---|
| Chorus | A | *followed by* |
| Chorus | A | *followed by* |
| Bridge | B | *followed by* |
| Chorus | A | |

– and the choruses would each have an A A B B rhyme scheme, which might be something like:

| | |
|---|---|
| I see the beauty in your face, | A |
| Trapped inside your crystal case. | A |
| I'll never cast your love aside, | B |
| Although you're in formaldehyde. | B |

Note how unimportant the spelling of the words is to the rhyme.

Having decided on the form of 'A Once in a Lifetime Day' (which we saw in the previous chapter was A B C B D B (Dance Break) B¹), I then began to write the chorus and came up with this rhyme scheme:

| | |
|---|---|
| A once in a lifetime day, | A |
| A day to remember for ever, | B |
| Your once in a lifetime day, | A |
| A day you'll remember whenever | B |

| | |
|---|---|
| You're feeling blue, | C |
| Or down in the dumps, | D |
| Dropped in the stew, | C |
| Or riding the bumps, | D |
| When you think your life is a flop, | E |
| Think of the day when you were on top! | E |
| Think of your once in a lifetime day! | A |

As with song form, it is worth analysing rhyme schemes, especially if you are considering pastiche, or particular song forms, as they often have distinctive rhyme schemes. Blues, for example, tends to have an AAB scheme, where the first two lines are identical (called an identity).

---

### Analyse Rhyme Schemes

Analyse some rhyme schemes for songs that you like. Again, look at different styles of songs and the ways in which their rhyme schemes differ.

---

There are different types of rhyme that lyricists use to analyse and describe their work:

*Perfect rhymes* must use identical vowel sounds and different consonant sounds, and in English the five vowels of the alphabet can make twenty different sounds, depending on the consonants surrounding them. 'Park' and 'lark' rhyme, but 'pack' and 'park' never will, even though the only vowel in each word is an 'a', because the sound of the 'a' is altered by the 'ck' and 'rk' immediately following.

There are two elements that come into play in order to define types of rhyme:

- The accented vowel found in the two rhyming words, and all the following sounds. These must be the same.
- The different consonants preceding that vowel. These must be different.

*Single or masculine rhyme* is when the sound of only the last syllable is identical and stressed, e.g. 'bit' and 'pit', 'gripe' and 'hype'. 'Repaid' and 'afraid' is also a masculine rhyme, even though there are two syllables in each of the words, because the stress of the words is on the final syllable. Similarly, 'chairmanship' rhymes with 'horsewhip'.

*Double or feminine rhyme* is when the last two syllables are identical and the stress comes on the penultimate syllable, e.g. 'bitter' and 'sitter'. In English there are some large word groups that create feminine rhyme, including:

- Those that end in the sound 'shun': 'accommodation', 'Haitian', 'medication'.
- The various perfect (past) tenses formed by adding –ed: 'skated', 'abbreviated', 'vaccinated'.
- The various continuous tenses formed by adding –ing: 'fanning', 'planning'.

However, you must be careful that the vowel sounds preceding these sounds are identical or it is not a perfect rhyme: 'tanning' rhymes with 'scanning' but not with 'gaining' or 'going'.

*Triple rhyme* is when the last three syllables are identical and the stress is on the third syllable from the end, e.g. 'breeziness' and 'cheesiness', 'conventional' and 'intentional' or 'odious' and 'melodious'.

*Composite or mosaic rhymes* are those that are made up of more than one word, such as *'snobbery'* and *'rob her he'* or *'cacophony'* and *'off a knee'*.

*Internal rhyme* is where rhyme comes within a line, which normally already has a rhyme at the end. I used these extensively in a song for an overenthusiastic airport security guard who sings about the joys of air travel, 'Lock 'Em Away' from *Terminal Four Play*:

The child of four, the row behind, who likes to kick your *seat*
He really likes to *play*, I'll lock the kid *away*!

The slob in front who thinks reclining seats are such a
    *treat*
He's on his holi*day*, I'll lock him far *away*!

Rhymes that obey these rules are called *perfect rhymes*. Rhymes that are not perfect are (not surprisingly), known as *imperfect rhymes*, *false rhymes* or *near rhymes*:

*Paper rhymes* are words that look like they should rhyme, but do not, such as 'cough' and 'enough'.

*Identity* is when two words sound exactly alike, even though they are written differently, such as 'fair' and 'fare'.

*False rhymes* are often ignored by lazy listeners, but will always grate to someone listening carefully. Some very famous songs are stuffed full of false rhymes, which haven't harmed their commercial prospects, but there is always a jarring quality, like a spelling mistake in something you are reading. The song 'Fame' has two bad false rhymes. It rhymes 'hands' with 'am' (which is assonance not rhyme), and 'together' with 'forever' (note that the 'th' sound is different to the 'v').

*Regional or accent rhyme* is when two words rhyme only in certain accents. As a Londoner, 'castle' and 'hassle' don't rhyme, but to an American it is a perfectly good rhyme. 'Been' is one of these words – it is pronounced to rhyme with 'scene' in some accents, or to rhyme with 'sin' in others. Musical-theatre writers need to be very careful about their choices when they are writing for accents different to their own.

On the whole, imperfect rhyme is never as good as perfect rhyme and is always best avoided, except in very specific circumstances when it might be used for comic or similar effect. Listen to 'Popular' from *Wicked* and you will hear imperfect rhyme used for comedy. If your rhyme is imperfect just because you haven't thought of anything better, then you need to be more rigorous about your work.

Some songwriters denigrate the use of a rhyming dictionary to help with rhyming, but I have no problem at all with their use. Be very careful of the rhyming dictionary you use. If you are writing in British English, do not use an American rhyming dictionary and vice versa, and be aware that most rhyming dictionaries are based in a specific accent.

Beware of online rhyming dictionaries. Many of these are filled with some pretty broad definitions of rhyme and will give you imperfect rhymes. I have two smartphone apps for rhyming dictionaries and they have limited word choice and some very odd rhymes – but they have sometimes got me out of a jam when I have been in rehearsal! Like most technology, use it with care and intelligence and you will be fine. It is an assistant to your brain, not a replacement for it. If you can write a perfectly rhymed song without a rhyming dictionary, then do; your own inspiration will often give your work a more natural feel and will be brighter and more fun. But there is no shame in using one.

Luckily, English has a limited number of consonant sounds and so I have constructed a simple 'rhyme ready reckoner' you can copy on to a card or into a notebook to carry with you.

Firstly there are twenty-six simple consonant sounds:

| | | | | |
|---|---|---|---|---|
| **P** | Pit | | **Th** | Thin |
| **B** | Bit | | **Th** | Then |
| **T** | Tin | | **S** | Sap |
| **D** | Dinner | | **Z** | Zap |
| **K or C** | Cut | | **Sh** | She |
| **G** | Gut | | **S (zh)** | Measure |
| **Ch** | Cheap | | **Ch** | Loch, Chanukah |
| **J** | Jeep | | **H** | Ham |
| **M** | Map | | **Wh** | Whine, Where |
| **N** | Nap | | **W** | We |
| **Ng** | Bang | | **R** | Run |
| **F** | Fat | | **Y** | Yes |
| **V** | Vat | | **L** | Left |

Then there are roughly the same number of compound consonants (sounds made up of more than one consonant):

| | | | | |
|---|---|---|---|---|
| **Pl** | Plop | **Thw** | Thwart |
| **Pr** | Price | **Sn** | Snail |
| **Bl** | Black | **Sp** | Spell |
| **Br** | Broke | **St** | Stale |
| **Tr** | Tray | **Sw** | Swallow |
| **Tw** | Twin | **Sk** | Skin |
| **Dr** | Drive | **Sl** | Slay |
| **Kl** | Close | **Sm** | Smell |
| **Kr** | Crime | **Spr** | Spray |
| **Kw** | Quite | **Str** | Stray |
| **Gr** | Grow | **Spl** | Splutter |
| **Gl** | Glow | **Skr** | Scrap |
| **Fl** | Flee | **Skw** | Squire |
| **Fr** | Free | **Shr** | Shriek |
| **Thr** | Throw | | |

Be aware that these are for English only, and even these will vary according to accent. Foreign languages have some different consonant sounds, such as 'Vl' (as in 'Vladimir'), and whilst you might use some of these words in an English script, they are rare.

These are the commonly found vowel sounds in English, (when spoken in Received Pronunciation, as other accents will differ):

| Pit | Luck | Car | Day | Bear |
|-----|------|------|-----|------|
| Pet | Good | Door | Sky | Tour |
| Pat | All | Girl | Boy | Go |
| Pot | Meat | Too | Beer | Cow |

The sound of the 'a' in 'all' is an interesting one: it is known as the 'schwa', and can be created by any of the five vowels depending on the consonants around it. The BBC use this sentence to illustrate it: 'To s**u**rvive th**e** cold weath**er** you have t**o** make thor**ough** prep**a**rations.' All of the bold sounds are the 'schwa', which is the most-used sound in all of the English language.

To use this 'rhyme ready reckoner', simply combine the vowel sound of the word you want to rhyme with the different consonant sounds and see which of them make words. Let's use the vowel sound 'ay' as in 'day'. So for the simple consonants, you get:

| | | | | |
|-----|------|------|------|------|
| **P** | Pay | **Th** | (as in 'thin') Thay |
| **B** | Bay | **Th** | (as in 'then') Thay |
| **T** | Tay | **S** | Say |
| **D** | Day | **Z** | Zay |
| **K or C** | Kay | **Sh** | Shay |
| **G** | Gay | **S (zh)** | Zhay |
| **Ch** | Chay | **Ch** | Chay |
| **J** | Jay | **H** | Hay |
| **M** | May | **Wh** | Whay |
| **N** | Nay | **W** | Way |
| **Ng** | Bay | **R** | Ray |
| **F** | Fay | **Y** | Yay |
| **V** | Vay | **L** | Lay |

You can then do the same with the compound consonants and the vowels to create a full range of sounds, some of which will be actual words:

| | | | | |
|---|---|---|---|---|
| **Pl** | Play | | **Thw** | Thway |
| **Pr** | Pray | | **Sn** | Snay |
| **Bl** | Blay | | **Sp** | Spay |
| **Br** | Bray | | **St** | Stay |
| **Tr** | Tray | | **Sw** | Sway |
| **Tw** | Tway | | **Sk** | Skay |
| **Dr** | Dray | | **Sl** | Slay |
| **Kl** | Clay | | **Sm** | Smay |
| **Kr** | Cray | | **Spr** | Spray |
| **Kw** | Kway | | **Str** | Stray |
| **Gr** | Gray | | **Spl** | Splay |
| **Gl** | Glay | | **Skr** | Scray |
| **Fl** | Flay | | **Skw** | Skway |
| **Fr** | Fray | | **Shr** | Shray |
| **Thr** | Thray | | | |

Try not to rhyme the same final consonant of a compound consonant with a simple consonant; it will lessen the effect of the rhyme. So 'peek' and 'seek' is a better rhyme than 'peek' and 'speak' because the 'p' is the same sound in both. The same applies to rhyming compound consonants with other compound consonants: 'crow' and 'grow' is not as good as 'grow' and 'go'.

My 'rhyme ready reckoner' is good for masculine rhymes, but harder to use for feminine or more complex rhymes.

---

**Rhyme Ready Reckoner**

Take a simple syllable sound like 'at' or 'on'. Using the rhyme ready reckoner, combine your syllable with each of the consonant sounds. How many of them are useful words?

Now do the same with a two-syllable sound, where the stress comes on the first syllable, like 'itter' or 'other'. Again, how many words can you make?

---

## Other Types of Word Play

In addition to the many types of rhyme there are other examples of wordplay that can be of use, although they are rarer.

*Consonance* is the repetition of consonant sounds in a non-rhymed way, as in Shakespeare's expression 'stru*ts* and fre*ts*'. This is more often used in prose than song as it gives a naturally rhythmic feel.

*Assonance* is the repetition of vowel sounds in a non-rhymed way. One of the best examples was a Hoover advertisement from the 1950s:

'It beats... as it sweeps... as it cleans!'

Note how it doesn't actually rhyme, but feels like it does.

*Alliteration* is the close repetition of a consonant sound, on nearly every syllable such as 'fifty-five fingers'. The effect is often comic, but use it like a strong spice. Too much alliteration can distract the ear away from the sense of the lyric.

*Onomatopoeia* is a very long name for words that mimic natural sounds, like 'buzz' or 'tinkle'. These words can be very effective in songwriting because the sounds aid sense, and there is often a delightful playfulness for the listener.

## Consistency in Rhyme

As a lyricist writing a song, you will write a number of A sections, probably some B sections and maybe others. Most important is that the rhyme scheme in each A, B or C section is consistent. If you are using an ABABAB rhyme scheme in the first A section, you must use exactly the same ABABAB form in the second A section you write. This includes whether you have used masculine or feminine rhymes at the ends of the lines. If you do not, your composer will not be able to set it to the same music and the song will lose form. Look at these lines from 'All On Time', a hymn to the railway sung by a stationmaster and enthusiast. These are the first six lines of two A sections of the song. I actually wrote the A$^2$ section first, and then went back to the others.

A$^1$     All the folks who pass through
         Often shout 'How d'you do?'
         I am friends with the whole population,
         From ladies and lords,
         To the populous hordes,
         For the station's their link to the nation.

A$^2$     There is nowt to compare
         with the smell in the air
         Of an engine departing the station,
         Or of taking a ride
         In the wide countryside,
         For a right bloomin' mighty sensation.

You can see here that the rhyme scheme is AABCCB, and that the A and C lines have masculine rhyme and the B has feminine. The rhyme scheme is consistent, which meant that the composer could set it to exactly the same music and the song retained its form.

## Scansion

Rhyme isn't the only thing that needs to be consistent: the stresses of the language also need to be respected and kept consistent through sections of songs. English has stressed and unstressed syllables which can fall anywhere in the word, unlike Italian where it is nearly always the penultimate syllable that is stressed; that is why Italian is a much easier language to set musically than English.

This is not only an issue for words with more than two syllables, because when words are put into sentences or clauses they develop a series of stresses in the context of the sentence. The composer and lyricist must match the musical accents to the natural accents of the phrases. In songwriting, the relationship between the stresses of the words and the stresses of the rhythm is known as scansion. The next chapter features some comments about rhythm and musical stresses.

There are a number of ways of describing and notating the stressed and unstressed syllables, but the most common are these two:

| / | *Ictus* | Stressed syllable |
|---|---------|-------------------|
| ˘ | *Breve* | Unstressed syllable |

So a piece of text can be marked like this:

  ˘   /  ˘    /   ˘    / ˘  /  ˘   /

But *soft!* What *light* through *yonder* win*dow breaks*

Or this:

  ˘   /  ˘  /   ˘    /  ˘ /   ˘    /

The *rain* in *Spain* stays *main*ly *on* the *plain.*

Each stressed syllable is the end of a unit, or foot. A foot is a repeated stress pattern within a line, and although it doesn't have to end with a stressed syllable, this is the most common in English. We can mark each new foot like this (the dividing line is called a 'virgule'):

  ˘  / |˘  /  |˘   /  |˘ / |˘  /

The rain| in Spain |stays main |ly on |the plain

You have probably recognised by now that both of these lines are in iambic pentameter, which is the verse pattern in which Shakespeare's blank verse is written. Just to recap, an iamb is a foot made up of an unstressed followed by a stressed syllable. Pentameter means there are five feet in the line. There are many other types of feet, all of which have their own specific technical terms, but the iamb, trochee, dactyl and anapest are the most common feet in English.

| Symbol | Example (two feet of each) | Name |
|---|---|---|
| ˘ / | ˘ / \| ˘ / <br><br> But soft\|what light | Iamb |
| / ˘ | / ˘ \| / ˘ <br><br> Although \| I wake | Trochee |
| / ˘ ˘ | / ˘ ˘ \| / ˘ ˘ <br><br> called little \| Buttercup | Dactyl |
| ˘ ˘ / | ˘ ˘ / \| ˘ ˘ / <br><br> All the folks \| who pass through | Anapest |

There are also technical terms for the number of feet in the line, taken from the Latin numbers:

| One foot | Monometer |
|---|---|
| Two feet | Dimeter |
| Three feet | Trimeter |
| Four feet | Tetrameter |
| Five feet | Pentameter |
| Six feet | Hexameter |

For 'All On Time', I wanted to capture the rhythm of a train in the lyric, so I chose to use two unstressed beats, followed by one stressed in an anapestic foot to represent this. I wrote this much and then went back and analysed it like this:

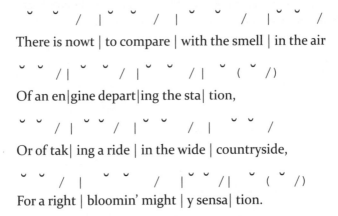

There is nowt | to compare | with the smell | in the air

Of an en|gine depart|ing the sta| tion,

Or of tak| ing a ride | in the wide | countryside,

For a right | bloomin' might | y sensa| tion.

The final unstressed syllable, being the unstressed part of the feminine rhyme, gives two silent beats in the foot at the end of the line. The fact that the two syllables are silent indicates that the line has ended and leads the composer into setting the syllable on a longer note. With that caveat, the lines are in anapestic tetrameter.

The number of feet in a line can be anything you like, but it must be consistent between verses. You do not necessarily need to worry about lines conforming to particular metres so long as there is consistency between sections – this is so that the lyrics can be set to the same music.

### Analysing Scansion

Mark the lyrics of some of your favourite songs with the ictus and breve symbols to show the stressed and unstressed syllables in each line. Bear in mind that sometimes a syllable's stress varies according to the syllables around it. Rap is particularly interesting in this exercise, as it tends to have good contrasts between the stressed and unstressed syllables – although sometimes stresses are altered to fit the scansion.

## Sounds That Sing and Sounds That Don't

Lyric writing is the art of finding the right word for the right note at the right time. In English, there are some sounds that sit better on notes than others. Of the consonants, 'm', 'n', 'l', 'r' are by far the best, and the hard plosive sounds of 'k', 'b', 'p', 'd', 't' are the least singable, especially when they sit at the end of the line. Oscar Hammerstein always maintained that the reason 'What's the Use of Wondrin'?' never found a status as a standard was that the song ended on the 'k' of 'talk', which cut the song off abruptly; perfect for *Carousel*, dreadful for the song's commercial prospects. Of the vowels: 'aw' (as in 'all'), 'o' ('show'), 'i' ('wine'), 'a' ('made'), 'ah' ('photograph') are the best.

Of course, you are not going to be able to write much if you limit your choices to these sounds, but if you are looking to discover why something isn't quite sounding right to the ear, it could well be that you have tricky consonants or vowels in the line.

Remember, too, that singers use the open sounds of the vowels to sing; the sound of 's' or 'd' will invariably be made right at the last moment of singing a line. So in this song from *The Railway Children* –

Nothing to fear, nothing to fear, my friend.

– the singer singing this phrase lets the open vowel sound of the 'fear' float into the air, and then will sing 'frie—nd', using the 'nd' to close the sound.

Beware of using double consonants that are the same or very similar. Unless treated very carefully by the singer, they can lead to all kinds of misinterpretations. One of the most famous is the line from *A Little Night Music*'s 'Send in the Clowns', that Sondheim specifically indicated needed to be separated: 'Don't you love farce?' It doesn't look problematic on the page, but in the mouth of the lazy singer becomes 'Don't you love arse?', which I don't think is what Mr Sondheim had in mind at all. Similarly, in the theme song from the film *Titanic*, 'My Heart Will Go On', there is the line 'I believe that the heart does go on', the 't' of 'heart' right next to the 'd' of 'does', combined with Celine Dion's rather bizarre vowel sounds, always makes it sound like 'I believe that the hot dogs go on'. I never realised it was a song about a barbecue.

## Inversions

My biggest bugbear is the inversion. This is where words are moved around their natural sentence order to create rhyme or to fit an existing scansion pattern. Take these two lines. The scansion and the rhyme scheme are correct, but it is nonsense:

> How sorry I am that you threw me out,
> My heart is a mess, now you I'm without.

No one would ever talk like this in English. The first line is fine, but the second line is an inversion. The sense is:

> How sorry I am that you threw me out,
> Now I'm without you my heart is a mess.

Of course, this doesn't rhyme or scan, but the trick of lyric writing is to able to make the rhyme, the scansion and the sense all come together in one perfect moment. If it doesn't sound like you could say it, you shouldn't write it.

## Filler

Sometimes lyricists need words to help the scansion, to fill out lines so that the stresses work. Words like 'baby', 'very' and 'just' are often used in this way, but should be avoided unless absolutely necessary. If you do need to use fillers, try and get them to carry their weight in some way. In the line:

Or of taking a ride in the wide countryside

I used a filler with the word 'wide'. What I wanted to write was:

Or of taking a ride in the countryside

but this did not scan. After considering many options, I chose the word 'wide' because it gave a feeling of the expansiveness of the countryside seen from a train, and because it gave an extra internal rhyme in the line. It was a good choice, but it is still filler – and if I could have done without it, I would have.

## Imagery and Poetic Language

Many songs use poetic imagery in their hooks and in their lyrics, like 'The Shadow of Your Smile' or 'The Windmills of Your Mind'. Imagery can be very powerful, but never forget that songs are written to be listened to, not studied like poetry. This is even more true of musical-theatre songs, which must principally be listened to in a dramatic situation through one theatrical sitting, where the listener cannot go back and listen again. Paul Simon is a songwriter I rate very highly, who has made imaginative use of imagery in his long career, but I remember seeing his short-lived Broadway musical *The Capeman* and being bored senseless. I believe that one of the major reasons the show failed was that the score was too poetic, and the audience's brains couldn't make sense of the songs in the short time frame that the drama allowed (coupled with the fact that the book was a mess). I have since listened to his album *Songs from 'The Capeman'*, and I enjoy hearing it in relaxed surroundings where I can fathom out some of the complexities. A musical is not written for the songs to be listened to many times, but to be experienced in the moment, even if many people enjoy listening to cast recordings.

## Character and Lyrics

Unlike pop songs, musical-theatre songs are specific to character and plot, and as such they must be appropriate to the setting and the theatrical language of the show. If you are writing a piece set in Victorian London or among New York street gangs, your characters need to speak and sing appropriately.

The theatrical language of the piece is also very important. Duncan Sheik and Steven Sater's musical version of *Spring Awakening* created a theatrical language where the nineteenth-century language of the book scenes was very closely based on Frank Wedekind's 1891 play, contrasted with a twenty-first-century language for the songs, to make the point that adolescence is hellish whenever you were born. Similarly, the writers of *Avenue Q* wrote often childlike music in the style of *Sesame Street*, but often matched it with adult lyrics, creating comedy in the incongruity.

The difference between the two shows is that the characters in *Spring Awakening* sing in a lyrical style of modern American pop, not in the same style that they speak the book scenes; and in *Avenue Q*, the characters sing in exactly the same style as they speak, with the same bad language and adult themes.

You need to make sure that the lyrical style you use is consistent with the language of the book, or that it can be made consistent. My advice in the earlier chapters to avoid faux-historical writing stands firmly when it comes to lyrics. I worked on a dreadful musical set in the 1500s (don't ask why!) in which the (novice) lyricist had written a heap of lyrics in the worst kind of faux-historical style, which was his idea of poetry. It was impossible to match his style in the few book scenes I wrote, without making the whole exercise even more ridiculous than it already was. I went for a more direct approach but there was always a terrible dislocation between the two styles. The show languishes in a filing cabinet somewhere in Western Australia, and the best thing that came out of the experience was that I met my writing partner Richard John.

Take a look at the character bugs you created for your characters and discuss with the bookwriter the linguistic style of the show. You should get a good idea of this from the scenes the bookwriter has written. Look at the factual information for the characters, such as location, education and status, to give you clues as to their appropriate language. Sondheim has talked at length about how Maria's lyrics in 'I Feel Pretty' (from *West Side Story*) are inappropriately sophisticated for an uneducated Puerto Rican girl. He later wrote: 'You know she would not have been unwelcome in Noël Coward's living room.' You wouldn't want to be making the same mistakes as Sondheim!

The song I mentioned earlier, 'All On Time', is a patter song for an uneducated stationmaster. A patter song is a song with a moderate-to-fast tempo in which each syllable corresponds to one note, giving an effect of lyrical dexterity. Isn't that too erudite for that character? Throughout the rest of the show he uses very simple language, but I wanted to capture his enthusiasm – this is a man who does nothing but talk about railways, they are his whole life. He'd much rather be down at the station than at home with his children, and so the number begins simply and quite slowly, but speeds up with each A section until he is gabbling away, having found an audience who want to hear about his passion. There is an earlier A section in the song, which takes us into it:

> In the white signal box,
> Where the signalman stops,
> All the lines are controlled with precision,
> So the one on the line
> Will arrive bang on time,
> Being sure to avoid a collision.

Now the B rhyme is a perfect feminine rhyme, but 'box' is an imperfect rhyme with 'stops', and 'line' is an imperfect rhyme with 'time'. These imperfect rhymes are used to emphasise Perks' lack of education. Slowly, he works himself up to a rhythm where he can say everything he has always wanted to about his beloved trains.

If you are writing the lyrics before the music is written then you will be starting with a blank piece of paper and it will your job to decide upon form. If the music is being written first then you will be fitting words to the music. Either way, you need to collaborate with your composer and discuss the kind of song you want for that moment.

## Writing Lyrics to Existing Music

In a 'music first' situation, two things help me write lyrics. One is to record the song so that I can play it back as I write, and the other is to get the composer to give me the sheet music. This allows me to see where the musical stresses sit, which helps when dealing with scansion. From the sheet music, you can write out the scansion pattern if you need to. For a song called 'Happy Ever After' we wrote for *Comrade Rockstar*, we had decided the music would be written first and Richard sent me this:

I was able to mark this up:

With this scansion exercise, I could see how many lines I would have (four):

I could also see that the first and third lines would have feminine rhymes the second and fourth would have masculine (if they were going to rhyme). If I thought of it in four lines, I could see that the first and third lines would both end with a ˘ ˘ / ˘ which would sing as 'da-da-dum-da' – this could be an effective rhyme.

I don't tend to use ictus and breve notation when it comes to actually writing. It is useful for analysing lyrics, but when creating I like to write above the notation rather than under it. I find a more immediate notation is to use an underline for an unstressed syllable and a double underline for a stressed. It is simpler and my brain understands it better, leaving me more space to think about the lyric. Here is my own underlining notation for the same piece of music:

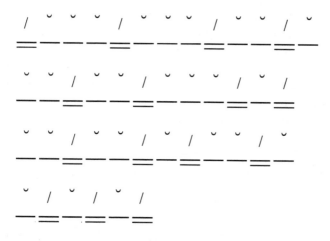

You can see that this is less technical, but it gives a good 'grid' upon which to write. I don't care that it is less technical – no one is going to see it but me. I could also see from the music that it was a slow song, and so the word choices did not need to work 'at speed'. The lyric it eventually had was:

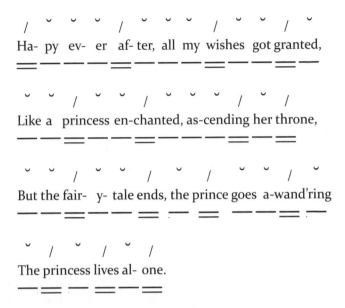

The rhyme scheme was not the one I envisaged at first. I rhymed 'granted' and 'enchanted' and then an internal rhyme in 'ascending' and 'ends'. The fact that there is internal rhyme, but not always rhyme at the ends of the lines, where it might be expected, is to indicate how the character's life is falling apart. Similarly, the 'throne' and 'alone' rhyme was indicated by the music and in such a way that not rhyming would have been very jarring to the ear.

With the music it looked like this:

Writing lyrics to existing music is clearly a more technical exercise than writing the lyric first.

## Writing Lyrics Before the Music

If you are writing the lyric before the music, obviously you have to decide on form. Sometimes this will come easily to you, by writing a verse that you are happy with, then noting the scansion and rhyme scheme and creating other sections to the same pattern.

If you are short of inspiration, you can always take an existing song or piece of music and write a lyric to it. I have used everything from film music to classical pieces to pop songs. *Never* tell the composer what music you have written to, because as soon as you do they will find it difficult to ignore it and they must be free to create from their own ideas.

You might think that you are restricting the composer by settling on a strict scansion pattern, but you will not. When I wrote 'All On Time' I was convinced that Richard would set it to a

$$\frac{6}{8}$$

or

$$\frac{12}{8}$$

rhythm, because I thought this was closest to the sound of the trains, but he heard it differently and set it to a

$$\frac{4}{4}$$

rhythm instead.

Whichever way you find you work best as a team, the process of helpful notes and suggestions to one another, and of 'cleaning up' your work is one that can begin once you have your draft of the song. If you are both honest and generous, together you can create something original, possibly remarkable.

### Writing a Lyric

Get hold of the sheet music for an instrumental piece that has a strong tune, and a song-like form; it might be something from a film score or ballet (Tchaikovsky is very good for this). Use a piano score, not an orchestral one, and identify about thirty-two bars of it that have a good hook. Analyse the scansion and then, choosing a situation, write a lyric for a character to fit this music.

# 11
# *Musical Matters*

# *Musical Matters*

Some of the greatest songwriters have not been highly skilled musicians. Irving Berlin wrote music and lyrics for nineteen Broadway musicals, eighteen Hollywood films and about 1,500 songs (including 'White Christmas' and 'God Bless America'), but wrote almost exclusively in F sharp, using a specially adapted piano that allowed him to transpose the songs to other keys. Lionel Bart, who wrote *Oliver!*, couldn't read or write music; the score was transcribed by Eric Rogers as Bart sang to his own guitar accompaniment.

Technological developments have revolutionised music over recent years, and it is now easier than ever for anyone to create their own music and to distribute it. Computer software such as Logic Pro and GarageBand mean that anyone can make music in their own home. Whilst this is undoubtedly a good thing, it is also true that a knowledge of the rudiments of music is very desirable, and, as with all the subjects in this book, the more you know, the more conscious you are of the choices available to you.

As I stated at the beginning of Chapter 9, this is not a book about the intricacies of songwriting, but I will touch on a few basics first and then discuss some of the issues of particular importance in writing a musical.

All music is made up of three components: melody, rhythm and harmony. These three elements are so entangled that their relationship is not unlike red, green and blue, the three colours of light, that combine together to make everything you can see.

## Melody

Humans can only sing one note at a time. As a result, the characters in your musical can only sing one note at a time. This means that as far as any song is concerned, the melody will be the most important element. The melody is made up of a series of intervals between the notes, and the rhythm that the notes have. The melody will include the hook of the song (the central musical idea), and this will be developed across musical phrases, building up to a structure for the song (as mentioned in Chapter 9).

How do you write a great melody? If I knew the answer to that I could make millions! What is clear is that a good melodic hook will take you far. Every writer has their own style of melodic writing, and musical-theatre composers often vary their melodic style according to the piece that they are writing. Sometimes these choices are very conscious, such as Sondheim's choice to use the Japanese pentatonic scale for many of the melodies in *Pacific Overtures*, and sometimes they are less conscious. Lionel Bart just drew on the inspiration of the East End pub songs that he grew up with for many of the songs in *Oliver!*

The melody is notated as a series of dots that follow each other. The difference in pitch between the notes is called an interval and, within any octave, there are twelve of these, each of these a semitone higher, which you can see (in the treble clef) below. These are each in relation to the first note, the middle C. You will see there are thirteen, not twelve, as there is the first option of keeping the note the same (which is known as 'unison').

There are names for each of these intervals, abbreviated above and relating to:

m2 = minor second

M2 = major second

m3 = minor third

M3 = major third

P4 = perfect fourth

TT = tritone (three whole tones, also known as augmented fourth)

P5 = perfect fifth

m6 = minor sixth

M6 = major sixth

m7 = minor seventh

M7 = major seventh

P8 = perfect eighth (an octave leap)

In the table over the page, you can find examples of intervals within songs, both rising and falling. The italicised syllables of the lyric are where the intervals occur.

| Interval | No. of Semitones | Rising | | Falling | |
|---|---|---|---|---|---|
| | | *Song Title* | *Lyric* | *Song Title* | *Lyric* |
| UNISON | 0 | 'Don't Cry for Me, Argentina' | *'Don't cry'* | - | - |
| MINOR SECOND | 1 | 'Windmills of Your Mind' | *'Like a cir-*cle' | 'Hernando's Hideaway' | *'I know* a dark secluded place' |
| MAJOR SECOND | 2 | 'People' | *'Peo-ple'* | 'The Way We Were' | *'Mem-'ries'* |
| MINOR THIRD | 3 | 'Mack the Knife' | *'Oh, the* shark' | 'Bewitched, Bothered and Bewildered' | *'I'm wild* again' |
| MAJOR THIRD | 4 | 'Kumbaya' | *'Kum-ba-ya'* | 'Swing Low, Sweet Chariot' | *'Swing low'* |
| PERFECT FOURTH | 5 | 'Away in a Manger' | *'A-way'* | 'Born Free' | *'Born free'* |
| AUGMENTED FOURTH (TRITONE) | 6 | 'Maria' | *'Ma-ri-a'* | | |
| PERFECT FIFTH | 7 | 'Twinkle, Twinkle, Little Star' | *'Twin-kle, twin-*kle' | 'Feelings' | *'Feelings'* |
| MINOR SIXTH | 8 | 'Love Story' | *'Where do I be-*gin' | 'Love Story' | *'Where do* I begin' |
| MAJOR SIXTH | 9 | 'My Bonnie Lies Over the Ocean' | *'My Bo-*nnie' | 'The Music of the Night' | *'Night-time'* |
| MINOR SEVENTH | 10 | 'Some-where' | *'There's a* place for us' | 'The Shadow of Your Smile' | 'The shadow of *your smile'* |
| MAJOR SEVENTH | 11 | 'Bali Hai' | *'Ba-li Ha'i'* (the *li* is an octave, the Ha'i the seventh) | 'Something Wonderful' | *'He will* not always say' |
| OCTAVE | 12 | 'Over the Rainbow' | *'Some-where'* | 'Spring Will Be a Little Late' | *'Spring will* be' |

As you can see, there is nothing in the box for the descending augmented fourth – that is because I simply couldn't find any songs with this interval. Maybe you can find one, or write one!

Every melody ever written is simply made up of these intervals placed one after each other. Sometimes writers play musical games: the 'Unlimited' theme from *Wicked* uses the first seven notes of the melody of 'Over the Rainbow' – it is Stephen Schwartz's musical joke.

Counterpoint is the weaving of simultaneous melodies over the same period of time. As a general rule, the human brain can process up to three melodies (with lyrics) at once. After that, it becomes difficult to distinguish them.

---

### Sounds and Words

At a piano, play different intervals, and really listen to the sounds. What words can you imagine fitting with these intervals?

---

## Rhythm

As melody moves through time, it does so to a rhythm. Whilst melody is about pitch, rhythm is about how long each individual note lasts. In music, each note is assigned a value against a regular beat, established at each performance of a piece. Music is transcribed using units called bars or measures, each of which is the same length and contains a fixed number of beats, usually three or four. The value of each beat is coded according to the unit of music desired. At the beginning of the music, a time signature gives the player the information. So:

– has four beats in a bar, that are crotchets (the code for a crotchet is four). Examples of songs in this time signature:

'Where is Love?' from *Oliver!*, 'Tomorrow' from *Annie*.

– has three beats in a bar that are crotchets. Examples: 'Something's Coming' from *West Side Story*, The Beatles' 'Norwegian Wood', 'Oh What a Beautiful Morning' from *Oklahoma!*

– has two beats in the bar that are minims (the code for a minim is two; it is twice as long as the crotchet).

With this time signature, you might presume that there are twelve beats in the bar, but here there are twelve quavers in the bar divided as four beats (giving a 'pulse'), and each of these is subdivided into three quavers, giving a pulsing to the four beats in the bar. Example: 'Memory' from *Cats*.

Time signatures that are divisible by two (such as 4/4 and 2/4 or 2/8) are known as 'simple times', and those that are not (such as 3/4) are known as 'compound time', but both have identifiable beats.

In any bar of music, the first beat of the bar is always accented and in 4/4 (or 'common time', as it is often known), the third beat is accented, but to a slightly lesser degree. And if these beats are subdivided into quavers or semiquavers, the notes 'on the beats' will be accented compared to the others. These accents, or 'stresses', are vital in songwriting.

If you create music electronically, using software on a computer, you will find that the bars are indicated, and the beats of the metronome are regular. Every bar must have exactly the same number of beats in it. The speed at which the beats (and therefore the bars) are played is called the tempo. It is, of course, possible to change time signature during a song, but this must be indicated by a new time signature being written in. Leonard Bernstein is famous for doing this in the score of *West Side Story*.

Classical music has many changes in tempo and it is the role of the conductor to control the tempo at any moment. In songs, the tempo tends to be constant, and, as a general rule, the quicker the song, the less the tempo will vary.

Rhythm is inherent to humans; it cannot be lost, yet even our closest genetic cousins, like chimpanzees, show no sense of rhythm at all. Howard Goodall, Leonard Bernstein and many others posit that rhythm is linked to a consciousness of the human heartbeat, and its role in how we do regular movements like walking. If you ask any human to clap in time, you will find that the clapping rhythm is linked to the heartbeat.

## Harmony

The melody is like a pencil sketch of a picture; the harmony is what gives it colour. In 'Mack the Knife', Kurt Weill created a simple, repetitive melody, but by subtly changing the chords under it, it never becomes boring.

Harmony is the use of simultaneous pitches, in combination. These are known as chords. Chords placed in an order through time are known as a chord progression. In popular music, the chords are generally labelled by their root note (normally the lowest note, but the one around which the chord is based), with other terms indicating the qualities or characteristics of the chord. Chords made up of three notes are called 'triads'.

As with melody, the important factor is the relative pitches between the notes. The following table lists the common intervals:

| Root | Major Third | Minor Third | Fifth |
|:---:|:---:|:---:|:---:|
| C | E | E♭ | G |
| D♭ | F | F♭ | A♭ |
| D | F♯ | F | A |
| E♭ | G | G♭ | B♭ |
| E | G♯ | G | B |
| F | A | A♭ | C |
| F♯ | A♯ | A | C♯ |
| G | B | B♭ | D |
| A♭ | C | C♭ | E♭ |
| A | C♯ | C | E |
| B♭ | D | D♭ | F |
| B | D♯ | D | F♯ |

By playing the root and the fifth together – and then varying between the major third and the minor third – you will hear a difference in feeling, between the bright open sounds of the major and the darker, more mysterious sounds of the minor.

As we discovered above, there are twelve notes in the scale (giving thirteen options), and any of these can be the root. So if C is the root, a corresponding fifth will be a G, whereas if G is the root, then the corresponding fifth will be a D. The great power of chords is that the relationships between the chords remains the same, regardless of the key, which means that any song can be sung in any key and the chords will remain the same, relative to each other.

By adding certain notes to the chord, you can create dissonance (a clash of sounds creating tension), or consonance (a pure sound with no tension). Generally in songs, dissonant chords resolve to consonant ones. This mixture of dissonance and consonance is what gives the music its character. The great Frank Zappa likened the relationship between the two to that of the good guys and the bad guys in a film. Without one, the other quickly becomes dull.

## Lead Sheets

The study of music, of melody, rhythm and harmony, is a life's work for many people, and it is entirely your choice how much you want to learn. Knowledge will make you aware of your choices and be more creative, but to write a musical you really need only to be able to notate a lead sheet – only the vocal line with the relevant chords.

Here's the beginning of a lead sheet as an example:

There are many software packages available to make creating and transcribing music easier. The most popular are Finale, Sibelius and Logic Pro. Finale and Sibelius are both music-notating software packages. Finale also has a songwriter package, which allows you to create songs and save them to MP3. Logic Pro is a package that effectively turns an Apple Mac into a virtual recording studio and allows you to create your own tracks. Apple also produces a low-cost app called

GarageBand, which is a more basic version of a virtual recording studio. Remember that, just as the invention of the typewriter did not create great novels, having a great virtual recording studio will not make you a great songwriter. Your own natural talent and inspiration will do that.

## Setting Words

All songwriters set words to music and in musical theatre it is important that the words can be understood by the audience in one listening, in the context of the play. There are two simple rules that will help this and make the words 'sing'. One is melodic and one is rhythmic.

The melodic rule is that you need to listen to the pitch of spoken words, and the patterns of the pitches within words, in order to set them effectively. Where words have only one syllable, or more than one syllable but the syllables stay largely on the same pitch, then you can set them pretty much as you like. Certain words of more than one syllable have a pitch pattern, which you need to be aware of when setting to music. The choices that you make in setting a word to music can vary the meaning or effect of the word.

Take, for instance, the word 'somewhere': in 'Over the Rainbow', the first word 'somewhere' is set on an octave leap (an interval of twelve semitones between the two notes), giving a strong yearning feeling, but emphasising the shape of the word. By setting 'somewhere' on these notes, Harold Arlen creates an unforgettable moment for the character because as soon as the audience hear Dorothy sing this, they understand her yearning. If you don't believe me, listen to the version sung by Judy Garland and then listen to the versions by Eva Cassidy or Israel 'IZ' Kamakawiwoʻole, which replace the octave leap with two identical notes (a 'unison'). The sense is still there, but the singer sounds much more ambivalent about wanting to travel over the rainbow. There is no soaring emotion; it is as if the singer has decided that the emotion of the octave leap is too potent for their easy-listening audience.

The word 'somewhere' also features in the song of the same name by Bernstein and Sondheim from *West Side Story*. Here, the setting is much closer to the spoken pitches of the sounds of the two syllables. The first time the word is sung, in the line, 'wait for us, somewhere', it is set on a downward melody, which conjures up the feeling of someone slipping away, as if the singer is unconvinced that the person to whom they are singing will be able to wait for them. When we reach the refrain, the setting on the upward melody gives a feeling of hopefulness.

The different choices made for the setting of the word 'somewhere' in the examples I have quoted give different emotions to the word, each carefully chosen by the songwriters. Each instance only works because the composers have listened to the natural melody of the word 'somewhere' and then decided how they want to adapt it to indicate meaning.

The second rule is similar but is about the rhythm of the words, and about where stresses fall within the words. Some of this has been covered in the section on scansion in the last chapter, but is vitally important when setting lyrics to music.

The setting of the words to the rhythm needs to respect the natural stresses of the words. Again, consider the word 'somewhere': the 'some' is stressed more than the 'where'. Both Bernstein and Arlen set the syllable 'some' on the stronger musical beat; if they did not, the word would sound odd. It would be stressed wrongly, and it would sound to the listener like a songwriting 'spelling mistake'; they can understand you but they will feel your error.

Scansion issues occur in many pop songs. Personally, I think Alicia Keys scans the words 'New York' wrongly in her big hit 'Empire State of Mind'. She made a very conscious decision to set the words 'New' and 'York' with the stress on 'York' not 'New', and this gives the song a very strange-sounding, but highly distinctive, hook. Whether you stress the 'New' or the 'York' partly depends on your accent. Alicia Keys not only stressed the word 'York', but the two words were set on a rising melody, further emphasising the second word. The song was spoofed on YouTube by a band who wrote their own version of the song about the less glamorous Welsh town of Newport. The interesting aspect was that in the word 'Newport', the stress is on the 'port' not the 'New', and so the scansion was correct. They had improved the scansion in the parody – and Alicia Keys' record company had the video removed from the internet!

Listen, in contrast, to John Kander and Fred Ebb's 'New York, New York', sung most famously by Frank Sinatra or Liza Minnelli. Here the 'New' is stressed and the 'York' is unstressed, with the 'York' often on a falling pitch during the song, and being set on a higher pitch when entering the bridge, where there is hope in the lyric. This song has become a standard.

---

**Setting Words**

Take a single two- or three-syllable word. Say it to yourself many times and try setting it to different musical phrases. How can you alter the meaning of the word by altering the musical setting?

---

## Vocal Ranges

Everybody's singing voice sits at their own pitch, and the notes that they are capable of singing are limited in most people to about two octaves. Most people's singing voices are roughly one of the following ranges:

Soprano        Mezzo Soprano        Alto

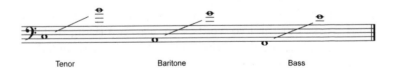

Tenor        Baritone        Bass

Ranges vary according to the person. Women also have two parts to their range, the lower register or chest voice, and the upper register or head voice. Between these two sits a range of a few notes called the 'passaggio', which is the weakest part of the voice and the hardest notes to sing. In some people the passaggio is just one or two notes and still a strong voice; in others it is a large range and the voice can be very weak in this area. The passaggio is an area of voice that can be greatly improved through vocal technique. The singer Yma Sumac* had a range of more than four octaves and could sing right down into the baritone range.

When writing a musical you need to be aware of the vocal demands on actors playing the role on a standard performance schedule of eight shows a week (six evenings and two matinees). Each role needs to sit comfortably within a range, or you will have great problems casting it, and you need to be aware of the 'tessitura' of each major role: this is the area of the range in which the role sits. For example, you might write a role well within a tenor range, but if it were all written in the upper notes of the range, then it would be said that the tessitura of the role is very high. If the role sits in the passagio then an actor is going to have problems singing it. Patti LuPone complains that her signature role of *Evita* had a tessitura that sat right on her passaggio, meaning that it took her a long time to master singing it. That role in particular, which is one of the largest in musical theatre, has always caused singers problems, and was the first role in which it became common for the actress to have an alternate performer, who played some performances every week, in order to relieve the vocal demands.

Do not think of vocal range as a restriction: it can be a great tool, and the different sounds within a range can be used by a composer to great effect. One of the cleverest aspects of *My Fair Lady* is that when Eliza is a flower girl, before she finds her ladylike voice, all her vocal writing ('Wouldn't It Be Loverly?', 'Just You Wait') is written for the actor's chest voice. Once she finds her voice, 'I Could Have Danced All Night' uses an arpeggio to take her up to her head voice and it finishes on top notes, indicating her femininity. The tessitura of the role then shifts significantly higher for the rest of the score.

---

\* It was a popular urban myth that Yma Sumac was actually a Brooklyn housewife called Amy Camus, her name spelled backwards. She was in fact Peruvian and her real name was Zoila Augusta Emperatriz Chávarri del Castillo.

## Songs and a Score

A musical score is not just a collection of songs, it is a road map through the emotional journey of the characters. One of the differences between writing musical theatre and writing pop songs is that there is a relationship between every song in the score and the others around it. The example of *My Fair Lady* above demonstrates how score writing can illuminate a character's journey, and score writing can also illuminate plot and theme. In *Sweeney Todd*, Sondheim uses the Beggar Woman's theme in the music for the scene in which Lucy is raped, letting an attentive audience suspect that Lucy and the Beggar Woman might be the same person.

In *The Railway Children*, there were two themes that became linked through the music: one was of fathers separated from their families, and one was of injustice. In the novel, the character of Szczepansky is a Russian dissident writer who comes to England to find his family who have fled there. At the same time, the children's father has been imprisoned on a false spying charge. Once Roberta discovers her father's fate, she helps Mother to campaign for his release, which is a key scene in the theme of her growing up. It was a moment of our own invention – in the novel she discovers the truth but remains passive. We created a campaigning anthem, 'One Voice', which I wrote as if it was one of Szczepansky's poems. The bridge was this:

When we came to write Szczepansky's 'Lullaby' for his missing children, which occurs earlier in the show, I wrote a text, which was translated by a Russian-speaking friend, and Richard set it to the music like this:

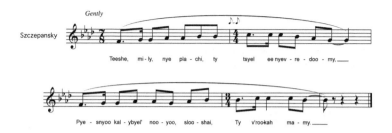

It is the same music, treated in two completely different ways, one as a thumping anthem of outrage, the other as a gentle lullaby, but they both link to the same character (Szczepansky as a campaigner and as a father) and the sense of the courage to take action whatever the personal consequences.

The attachment of a musical phrase to a specific character or theme is known as a leitmotif, and is most notably found in opera in the works of Richard Wagner, who threads leitmotifs throughout the score of the Ring Cycle. In musical theatre, they have become popular; a score that uses them notably is *Sweeney Todd*, in which most of the characters have a leitmotif. They can provide an excellent musical map for the audience, so that, for example, when Sweeney and Mrs Lovett are searching for Tobias in the bakehouse the orchestra plays his theme and we know what they are doing before they appear, or in the example of Lucy and the Beggar Woman above.

When does a reprise become a leitmotif? When it is used to signify more than one thing. So the repeating of the aristocrats' theme in *Evita* is a reprise because each time it appears it performs the same function, whereas the example of Lucy/Beggar Woman is a leitmotif because it is treated in different ways to mean different things.

You can play these musical games as much or as little as you like. Some scores are made up of songs that barely relate to each other, and others are much more musically sophisticated. Sondheim, a fan of board games and word puzzles, is a great master of this art. For *Merrily We Roll Along*, a musical where the plot moves backwards in time, he expertly constructed the score to work backwards, so that the usual musical relationships between numbers work in reverse; the reprises come before the numbers and fragments would be heard of songs that came later. In *Passion*, Fosca's music begins in minor keys and moves towards major keys as her relationship with Giorgio develops, whilst Clara's music moves from major to minor as hers disintegrates.

## Pastiche and Parody

Many musical scores include elements of musical pastiche or parody. Sondheim considers his ability to pastiche as one of his own greatest talents, and his score for *Follies* proves how adept he is at mimicking musical styles. Other shows have scores built entirely out of pastiche, including *Avenue Q*, which mimics the songs of *Sesame Street*, *Little Shop of Horrors*, which mimics early Motown; and *The Producers*, where the musical sound is entirely that of Broadway of the early 1960s, even though the show opened at the turn of the new millennium.

The difference between pastiche and parody is that parody implies a judgement of the original; the parody 'sends it up' whereas pastiche is non-judgemental mimicry. Musically they are often one and the same, although parody may be of a specific song, whereas pastiche tends to be of a genre.

You may find that pastiche comes easily to you. I know people who can hear songs and sit down and write something original that pastiches it straight away. Others have to study the music of the chosen genre carefully and immerse themselves in the sounds of the style. John Kander said that he listened to nothing but songs from Weimar Berlin before sitting down to write *Cabaret*.

## Underscore

Music under spoken scenes, or 'underscore', is another way in which the music can deepen the theatrical experience. You can use underscore to heighten emotions, like Rodgers and Hammerstein do in the spoken sections of the 'If I Loved You' sequence in *Carousel*, or you can indicate the real emotional subtext of a scene as Sondheim does in *Sweeney Todd* at various moments. This kind of underscore writing is like a film score, giving a clue to what is really going on between the characters.

Do not feel that you have to write all the underscore now, or that you need to time the dialogue to it. This is a job for later, when you begin to bring the whole show together, but if you have strong ideas, or if you want to create a piece of music linked to an element of the story that is not sung, write as much as you like now and leave as much as you like until later.

Remember that you don't want to underscore everything, and there is a useful effect in silence under scenes: an audience will be less distracted, and often more attentive, during dialogue scenes if there is no music under them.

## Dance Breaks and Ballets

Often songs in musicals, particularly in production numbers, have dance sequences, known as dance breaks. If a dance sequence tells a story of its own then it tends to be known as a ballet, such as the *Oklahoma!* 'Dream Ballet' or 'The Small House of Uncle Thomas' in *The King and I*. Ballets have fallen from favour since the 1960s, but most musicals still include dance music. This is usually written once the entire score has been completed and normally in collaboration with the choreographer of the original production. Some musicals have dance arrangers whose job it is to take the score and construct the dance music, and then arrange it within the confines of the orchestral line-up. Some well-known composers began their careers as Broadway dance arrangers, including John Kander, who was the dance arranger for Jule Styne and Stephen Sondheim's score for *Gypsy*.

Choreographers like to work with the composer or dance arranger to develop the dance music, because it allows them to formulate ideas for their work and to develop music that will facilitate the physical language of the show. It does mean that certain sections of the dance music may be forever tied to certain pieces of choreography. In one of my shows, the choreographer, Chris Hocking, included a clog dance which was historically and geographically correct for the piece. It is very specific music and foxes some choreographers who have staged subsequent productions.

Whilst you are writing the show, the most important thing is not to worry about dance and ballet music any more than you want to. Concentrate on writing the songs; the rest can, and often does, come later.

## Orchestration

Unless your musical is going to be performed with just a single piano or guitar, you will face the issue of orchestration, when the music will be arranged for the orchestral line-up available to the production. The line-up (the numbers and specific instruments that will play the orchestrated score), sometimes known as 'orchestral forces', will be decided in conversations between the composer and orchestrator, but will often be limited by economic factors, with the producer setting a budget for the orchestral salaries. Orchestration is a particular skill, related to, but separate from, composing, and it is rare for musical-theatre composers to orchestrate or arrange their own music. There is a difference between orchestration, dance arrangement and vocal arrangement: one person may be responsible for all three, different specialists may be brought in, or the composer may do all of this work himself.

Here's what each of the different arrangement terms mean:

*Orchestration* is the writing of the orchestral parts to be played in performance.

*Dance arrangement* is the writing of the dance music, which the dance arranger will usually orchestrate within the confines of the orchestral forces (i.e. the instruments agreed for the orchestra).

*Vocal arrangement* is the writing of the parts for the different voices in any choral part of the score. This is often done by the composer, but in certain circumstances a specialist vocal arranger may be employed, as in the case of the African musician Lebo M who gave a very specific sound to the score of *The Lion King*.

The classically trained composers Kurt Weill, Leonard Bernstein and George Gershwin orchestrated and arranged their own scores, but most Broadway composers work with orchestrators. Sometimes the composer works as part of a team of orchestrators, as Andrew Lloyd Webber often does.

The scale of the original production normally determines the orchestration. In New York, agreements with the Musicians' Union require that certain size orchestras are used depending on the size of the theatre. The increasing use of electronic instruments, and the constantly improving quality of these instruments, along with some composers writing music electronically, has created a challenging time for live musicians which will take many years to settle. However this develops, quality producers will always recognise that a score written for live musicians will always sound best played by live musicians. The economics of having live musicians means that when revivals are mounted it is often with new orchestrations, and these are invariably for smaller resources than the original. If revivals are conceived for a cast of actor-musicians, then the orchestrations are often very specifically tailored to a cast of performers and their musical skills. For the 1998 Broadway revival of *Cabaret*, in which the band are largely played by the actor-musician cabaret boys and girls, Michael Gibson created an orchestration which utilised a small 'core' group of musicians and then parts for a range of instruments that could be varied according to the casting. The ability to recast with a flexibility of musical parts was vital to the long-running success of the show.

Composing and orchestrating are two different skills and a good composer is not necessarily a good orchestrator. With modern technology it is tempting to think that, in order to show your score at its best, you should orchestrate it electronically using software. This is not necessary. When I was Artistic Director of the Global Search for New Musicals, I received over 120 demos of new musicals; orchestrations were more often a barrier to judging the work than an assistance.

Orchestrations can also *make* a score. I remember directing a production of *Oliver!* and being sadly surprised by how repetitive the songs were, until the band arrived and the brilliant musical arrangements lifted the whole score. Despite this, do not believe that musical arrangements are the answer to everything. At the heart of the orchestral sound is a character singing a song, and that song needs to be effective without the orchestrations. If the song works with a minimal piano or guitar accompaniment, it will always work.

The relationship between the composer and orchestrator is necessarily a close one, and the composer will have long discussions with the orchestrator. The composer must be prepared to discuss and share the influences on their score. Composers often choose the same orchestrator for many projects, building up a huge library of shared references that allows them to be specific about the sounds they both hear in the score.

George Stiles, the composer of *Honk!*, *Betty Blue Eyes* and the new material for the stage production of *Mary Poppins*, has a long professional relationship with orchestrator William David Brohn, and believes shared memory is vital:

> We've built a collaboration based on sharing lots of music, not just the show in question. The orchestrator needs to understand the drama and the passion that made you want to write a score. The more he understands where you come from, the more he's likely to make you happy and serve the drama.

Having been there himself, George gives this advice to composers who are experiencing having their work orchestrated for the first time:

> If you get the chance, get some of the orchestrations played by the band ahead of the production period, so that you have the chance to adapt, even change the line-up if something's not working. Most importantly, be open and be prepared to hear things you never imagined. Always listen at least twice to what the orchestrator has written before you suggest changes. It's sometimes just the shock of suddenly hearing other instruments play the music that can make you feel it's somehow 'foreign' for a while. And if you hear the band play without the voices, be very sure that the orchestration works around the voices, and not in the way of them.

## Compiling the Score

As you compose the score, and as the project develops, you will generate many pieces of music: songs, underscore, instrumental music. My advice is to assemble a single file (either on your computer or in hard-copy form) with the most up-to-date versions of each piece, in the order that they appear in the score. Keep your previous versions either at the back, or in a separate file. Personally, I would advise always keeping a printed hard-copy in a file. However well you back-up your computer, there is something comforting about knowing that you have a copy that can survive any computer meltdown.

Make sure that each page of the music is clearly labelled in a 'footer' at the bottom of the page, with the song title, the draft number and the creation date. Keeping an ordered, up-to-date copy of the score is vital as you move into workshops and production. Your musical is going to keep changing and it is easy to feel like you are drowning in a sea of paper, unable to find the piece you want. A single copy of the current score will make your work, and life, much easier in the coming months.

When you are revising a piece of music, in any way, keep a copy of the existing version electronically or on paper, and never destroy a version of a song, even if you think you will never want it.

Songs discarded from a score are known as 'trunk songs' because musicians used to keep a trunk of discarded songs. Now you are more likely to keep them electronically, but you may find a use for that material in another moment of the musical, or in a different show. You never know when you might use it. In 1980, Craig Lucas and Norman René approached Sondheim to create a revue out of songs he had discarded from his scores. The result was *Marry Me a Little*, which played off-Broadway and has had productions worldwide. Andrew Lloyd Webber wrote a piece of music when he was considering writing a musical version of *Sunset Boulevard* in the late 1970s. When it looked like *Sunset Boulevard* might never be produced onstage, he used the music in *Cats*. It became a song called 'Memory'.

# 12
# *Rewrites and Workshops*

# Rewrites and Workshops

After a frenzy of character bugs, reverse actioning, planning, writing scenes and songs, you will eventually have written something for every moment in the story. You will have the first draft of your musical.

There is a great temptation during the process to want to play your friends or family excerpts or to show them some of your work. Certainly they will want to hear some of it, and ultimately it is up to you whether you want to let them hear anything whilst you are still writing. Be careful, though, of getting blown off course. That terrible Australian musical set in the 1500s I worked on had a team that kept playing all their friends everything they wrote, and the result was that, as everybody made suggestions they incorporated them, whether they were good or not. They ended up with four hours of incoherent material. Remember that what you are writing is designed to be heard and seen in one sitting, when all the elements are in context. Some songs just don't work as well out of context. I like to keep the show out of sight until there is a first draft, even though this is not always possible.

As you write the first draft, you will be defining and refining the theatrical language of the piece, the storytelling and the tone. You may find that even before you have finished you begin to see faults with some of your work, but my advice is to carry on unless the change that you want to make has a direct effect on decisions you have yet to make. When you have completed a first draft, you and your collaborators can go back and discuss any changes.

The bookwriter and lyricist should work together to build the libretto. All the scenes and the lyrics need to be put together in one document. The characters who are singing need to be indicated at all times, and any dialogue that occurs within songs needs to be included. This may sound obvious, but I am constantly surprised by scripts I receive with the lyrics in a completely separate document, and the script containing only the titles where the songs will be placed. It all needs to be one document or it is impossible to assess how it all fits together. Similarly, the cues for the songs (the dialogue lines immediately preceding the music) must be written into the score and all the music put in order. If you have reprises, make sure you have copies of the music for each time the song is sung, with the relevant lyrics.

You and your collaborators should be the first people to consider the piece, and I suggest that you do this together in private. Get together in a room where you can sing the songs and read the script together, not skipping anything. Even if it is a commission for a theatre producer, do not invite them along, gather only the collaborators together. When you have finished doing this, put it in a drawer and lock the script and score away for at least a month (if that is possible). Straight away go with your collaborators and have a coffee, a drink or dinner and talk about the show. What do you like, what are you not sure about, what are the characters' journeys? Keep a note of your first impressions, and try to be as objective as possible. You have to look at the piece as if you are an audience seeing it for the first and only time. When you have finished talking, fix the date for when you can look at it again, and on that date arrange to get back together with your collaborators to talk about it. That is not to say that you cannot see your collaborators in this time, but don't look at the material. This time of reflection is important because it allows the chance to consider the bigger picture without being obscured by the detail. If you don't ensure that the big questions are answered satisfactorily now, it will soon be too late.

## Questions About Your Draft

With your collaborators, answer the following questions about your musical:

- Is the story clear?
- Is the plot clear?
- Are the characters' motivations clear?
- Are the characters' objectives clear?
- Is every scene necessary?
- In what way is every scene connected to theme?
- Does each song fulfil its function?
- Are all the aspects of the theatrical language clear?
- Are all the aspects of the theatrical language established early in the piece?
- What is this show about? (By that I don't mean, 'What do you intend this show to be about?' but 'What is it actually about now you have written it?' The smaller number of words you use for your answer, the better the focus of your piece.)

If any of your answers begin along the lines of 'Well, it's supposed to be that...' the answers are not clear enough and you need to look at what you have written.

At the end of the month, before you unlock the drawer and take the materials out, write yourself some notes about what you think about the show. Don't look at the answers you wrote earlier, but ask the questions above again and now see how you feel. Then arrange a meeting with your collaborators and take your answers to this next exercise with you.

## Rewrites

'Musical comedies aren't written, they are rewritten.' Sondheim's assessment of the process of writing a musical is entirely accurate. If you don't want to do rewrites, don't write a musical.

I wrote in an earlier chapter that musicals are like children. It is now that they begin to grow in their own ways and take on their own features. The writing of the first draft is a bit like the pregnancy, and now you are going to go through the growing up. The stage of rewrites is the stage of childhood. The show will become distinctive, take on its own style and become more individual. After all, isn't that what happens in childhood? Good parents don't scream, shout and throw tantrums; they nurture the child along the way, guiding and loving, sometimes disagreeing with each other and always trying to do best by the child.

Rewrites can be tough on the soul, but you will begin to discover what your musical needs at each moment. John Kander and Fred Ebb wrote over fifty songs for *Cabaret*, using sixteen in the original Broadway score. Certain editions of the cast album include Kander and Ebb singing some of the others as demos.

Stephen Sondheim and John Weidman wrote a musical that was conceived as a show called *Gold!*, had a production at the New York Theatre Workshop in 1999 called *Wise Guys*, was rewritten and opened in Chicago and Washington DC as *Bounce* in 2003, and finally had a further production in New York and London entitled *Road Show*. The title change is an indication of the writers changing the focus and emphasis of the work in its different rewrites and productions. Bookwriter Weidman said, 'Ideally the title is connected to what we hope the show is about.'

In recent years, a number of other original cast albums of classic musicals have been issued with bonus tracks of demos of songs that never made it into the final show. Whilst these are often of curiosity value, it is testament to the amount of rewriting that these musicals have had, that they have six or seven songs that are omitted from the final score.

The opening of your musical is likely to be one section that needs close scrutiny. Often it is not until the first draft is written that it becomes clear exactly what the first five or ten minutes need to be. You should have a good idea of what you need to teach the audience about the theatrical language, but have you created a song that is going to make the audience sit up and get excited? Jerry Bock and Sheldon Harnick's original opening for *Fiddler on the Roof* was a number called 'We Haven't Missed a Sabbath Yet', but director Jerome Robbins felt that it wasn't arresting enough; he kept asking what the show was about, and they finally wrote 'Tradition'.

Rewrite and rewrite, but make sure that you are always clarifying, illuminating and strengthening the moments. Every show is different, some need many rewrites, and some very few. With *The Wind in the Willows*, we pretty much went with the first draft and all of the songs were kept in their first versions, give or take the odd lyrical tweak; it was a very easy childhood and the show was a big success. It is possible to 'over-rewrite', gradually losing sight of what was good about the piece in the first place. Keep that list of the ten things you thought were great about the show and make sure you keep focused on those. Solve the greatest weaknesses, but never lose sight of the big picture.

## First Readthrough

When you are all happy with the piece in its draft form, it is time to move to the next stage. If the work is a commission and you have a producer on board, then now is the time to introduce him to the work. It is time for a readthrough.

Choose a very small number of people to attend this and make sure that they are people who will be honest with you and whose judgement you trust. Make it very clear to them that this is a first readthrough and that you want some feedback. At this stage I keep members of the theatre profession away from the readthrough, except for those very, very close collaborators who are friends first and colleagues second. The two exceptions to this are the commissioning producer and my agent, the first because he has paid for it and the second because he (or more usually she) will represent it to the world.

The exact decisions you make for your reading of your show will depend on the requirements of the piece. Aim for as small a cast as possible for this. If you have a story that revolves around two sopranos you might want to bring in two separate singers for the two roles; or if there is a lot of chorus work, you might want to bring in a small chorus to fill out the sound. Any of these can, and should, be you and your collaborators. At this stage, unless you are tone-deaf (in which case you are probably not writing a musical), you and your collaborators will deliver the material better than almost anyone else.

Depending on where you live and whom you know, getting good singers can be more or less of a challenge. If you don't know professional musical-theatre performers, most communities have amateur groups or local choirs. Wherever there are human beings there will be people interested in singing and you just need to seek them out. Wherever you live, whether it is in an isolated mountain village or right on Broadway, the value of networking cannot be overstated. Find singers and the people who can bring you singers, and very often they will be more than happy to help.

Personally, I make a point of always giving a small payment or gift to the people who help me out by singing or reading parts. For a workshop, if I am working with professionals, I always aim for Equity rates, but on a first readthrough this often isn't possible. I have paid people in money, chocolate and wine, but that token is always appreciated and they are always more likely to say 'yes' a second time if they feel valued.

A small cast and a small audience will be more use than anything bigger at this stage. These readthroughs normally take place around a piano, and don't worry if you need to read aloud the stage directions. Your audience will use their imaginations to fill in all the gaps – and their imaginations will always give them much more impressive pictures than the ones you can realise at this stage. Use the magic word 'Imagine' at the beginning of the readthrough and you will be away.

It is around this time that, unless you are a complete exhibitionist, you would probably feel more comfortable dancing in the nude for these people than reading your musical. That's okay. We all feel like that the first time we have an audience for our new show. You are saying to these people, 'Hey, we think this is good!' and then hoping that they feel the same. If you don't feel it is good, then you shouldn't be at the readthrough stage, you should still be rewriting.

When it's over, you need to talk to the audience, and also talk to any cast members you have who are not collaborators. And they will talk to you.

## Getting Notes

Theatre works through *notes*. Notes you give and notes you take. As a writer you will do both. A note is a point that someone raises with you. A director gives notes to his cast to improve performances, a choreographer gives notes to dancers, and a designer gives notes to a costume supervisor. Everyone gives notes differently and everyone takes them differently. One of the most common phrases you will hear in drama schools is 'Take the note.' This means, 'Don't argue back, don't try and justify your position, listen to the note, process it, and try and incorporate it into your performance.' You will see that notes generally come from people whose function is high-status in getting your musical on. Theatre is strong on hierarchy, of which more later.

As a writer, you will get notes from three groups of people. The first is people who will get your show on, such as the producer, director and other creative staff. These need to be listened to and carefully processed, because they will almost certainly be returned to at a later date.

The second is your cast. Listen carefully to them, as they are the people who are charged with delivering your work. If an actor raises a point, it will be because it bothers them, and if it bothers them now, it will bother others later. I had a rhyme in *The Railway Children* that had an unintentional double meaning, not rude, but just an odd image. Susannah Fellows, who played Mother in the original cast, raised it as an issue. After a day or two of struggling for a new rhyme, I did change it, and other members of the cast told me, 'I'm glad you have changed that line, it's been bothering me from the start.'

The third is the audience. With the audience for your readthrough, you will have hand-picked them and will want to hear what they have to say. That won't be the case later in the process. You will soon find that everyone is an editor. People will see you in the theatre foyer and tell you what you should have done, how their ideas would have made the show better. None of them were there when you sat down with your collaborators, a good idea and some blank paper.

The best way to take notes is to listen, smile sweetly, say 'Thank you' and think. If the note is coming from a cast member or a member of the production team, I always promise to go away and think about it. Even if I think it is a great note, and one that I want to incorporate, I still take the chance to go and think first. I also have a rule for notes at this stage of writing: if one person gives me a note, I listen and thank them; if two people independently give me the same note, I listen more; and if many people independently give me the same note, then I really take notice.

One final point: if, at any time, someone who is working on the show gives me a great note, or makes a really inspired suggestion and I put it into the show, I always make a point of crediting them with it to the rest of the team. Having been an assistant director and made suggestions to directors that have been incorporated, I can tell you that acknowledgement works wonders. One world-famous director always presents everyone else's ideas as his own, and the team always notice.

You also need to think about what *you* think about the piece. What did you think was most successful and what did you think was least successful? Did it get laughs where you expected? Were the songs the right tone for the scenes? Once you have had that conversation, there's a very strong chance that you will want to rewrite some of the show. Don't be afraid or disheartened at this stage; embrace the fact that you are making your work better. You may rewrite or lose moments, even songs, that you love, but that you now find do not work within the context of the show. Remember Samuel Johnson's words: 'Read over your compositions, and where ever you meet with a passage which you think is particularly fine, strike it out.'

## The Demo

It is around this time that you need to start to think about a demonstration recording or 'demo'. A demo is a recording that is only for demonstration purposes and is useful for giving people a taste of the show, and for allowing you and the creative team to work on it. It can also be useful for directors, choreographers, designers, etc., to get a feel for the show and for potential cast members when you come to casting.

Some writers like to record everything they write as they go, and this is always a good idea, if nothing more than a back-up. Stephen Sondheim apparently always records himself singing his songs when he is happy with them. Richard John and I always record everything, sometimes even before it is finished, so that we have a reference point. We do this on an Apple Mac with GarageBand, using a live piano. These recordings are never going to be released and are only for our use.

The best demos are the simplest. You can create one on a laptop recording studio or go into an actual studio to do it. It needs to:

- Feature the best-quality singers you can find.
- Use the best pianist you can find.
- Only have a piano or guitar track – it does not need to be fully orchestrated.
- Be sung by singers in the correct vocal register for each role.
- Be clear, accurate and well recorded.
- Include every song and reprise.
- Ignore dance music and underscore unless vital.
- Use only one voice for each vocal register.

Do not believe that a lack of orchestration will diminish it. If your score makes sense as a piano/vocal demo, anyone listening to it will fill in the gaps with their own imagination.

As with the readthrough, the exact casting decisions you make for the demo of your show will depend on the requirements of the piece. When you have completed recording, burn it to CD for easiest distribution, and make sure every CD is very clearly labelled. Control the distribution of your demo as much as you can. Give it to people who *need* it, not to people who *want* it; it is a private recording for demonstration purposes and you don't want it coming back to haunt you after you have a full-scale cast recording of a production.

## Workshops

After the first readthrough, you might decide to rewrite and possibly even have another readthrough of a newer version. At some point the word 'workshop' will be uttered. Workshops began in the 1970s when the economics of Broadway began to prohibit lengthy periods in out-of-town tryouts when the show could be rewritten and fine-tuned. Workshops have now become a key stage in the development of a new musical and it is rare for a major musical to reach the West End or Broadway without one.

The term 'workshop' is very loosely used. At one end of the scale, it might be a short period of just a few days in which small sections of the show are considered, or it may be very close to a full production which might have a public run, such as the workshop of *Rent*, which ran three weeks.

If you are considering a workshop, then it is important that you define the purpose for it. The reason for a workshop is that musicals only really come to life when performed by a cast for an audience, and this is the first time that the writers will truly have a chance to see what the show is like, and crucially how an audience responds to it.

Some workshops are presented to very small industry audiences whose response is sought, and advice is taken. This is usually to discover how the piece plays to an audience.

Workshops are sometimes presented in the hope of finding a producer for the show. This is very common in the UK, but I question the value of it. I know of very few musicals that have not already had producers attached, who have found them through workshops of this type. You are much better to contact producers individually and try to get them to have a meeting after you have sent them the demo, or been to play the score to them. You can destroy interest in a musical, rather than generate it, by holding a workshop which is more like an audition of the show for potential producers.

The workshop must be a tool for writers and creatives to try out ideas and to look at the show 'on its feet'. Invite an audience to focus the team, but do not expect a producer to run up to you with a chequebook straight after.

Workshops involve bringing together a small creative team and a cast to work on the show for a specific period, normally one to three weeks. This is usually done in a rehearsal-room situation and any final presentation is generally performed in the same way, with very simple hand props, little or no costume and a basic piano accompaniment.

Workshops require a creative team. Up until now, it is possible, indeed quite likely, that you have been working with your small team of collaborators with no one else involved, but now your circle of collaboration is about to get much wider.

## The Creative Team

Every theatrical presentation, whether a play, musical, concert or workshop, has a creative team. The size and structure of the team will vary from piece to piece, depending on the scale and the requirements. Also, sometimes individuals fulfil more than one function within the team; a director, like Susan Stroman, might also choreograph, a designer might design both set and costumes, or there might be separate designers for each. Now that your musical is at the workshop stage, it is worth knowing what everyone does, even if some of them won't be on board yet. Workshops tend to have very small creative teams and they are best kept to a minimum at this stage, but here's a list of who does what:

*The Producer* presents the show and he is the ultimate boss. On a day-to-day basis, the producer is responsible for the entire show, and for the commercial, administrative and legal matters. Some producers, such as Cameron Mackintosh, like to have considerable involvement in the artistic process, others take a more 'arm's-length' approach.

*The Director* is entrusted by the producer to realise the work onstage. Administrative staff work for the producer, but everything that goes on onstage is the responsibility of the director. The director is responsible for the staging of the piece, even though others will carry some of this out. A good director will have a vision for the piece, will know how to interpret it, will develop the tone of the work, and will be able to bring together all the disparate elements of the production into a cohesive whole.

*The Musical Director* is the head of the music department, and he is responsible for the musical quality of the work. The musical director will conduct or lead the orchestra on a daily basis. In recent years, with the advent of very long runs and musicals as global entities, the role of musical supervisor, who is above the musical director, has become more common. The musical supervisor has the same responsibilities as the musical director, but will not be at every performance.

*The Choreographer* is responsible for staging dances and specific movement. The role of the choreographer can vary according to the skills of the director and the requirements of the piece, but even a piece with very little obvious dance (like *Sweeney Todd*) will always have a choreographer, who may be credited with 'Musical Staging'.

*The Designer* is responsible for the visual look of anything physical onstage in the production. This role is often split into a set designer, who is responsible for the physical set, and a costume designer, who is responsible for everything that is worn by the cast.

*The Lighting Designer* is responsible for lighting the
show, and often for other small electrical pieces such
as smoke machines.

*The Sound Designer* is responsible for the sound of the
production, including recorded and live effects. For a
musical, the sound designer is responsible for how the
orchestra and vocals are balanced, and for ensuring
that the lyrics can be heard and understood as best as
possible.

There are other director and designer roles that occur if the
piece requires them, such as a fight director or a magic designer.
Each and every one of these creatives may have an assistant.
The hierarchy looks like this:

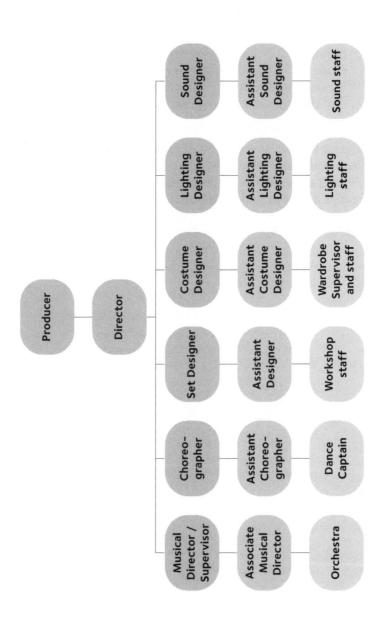

Once a musical moves into full production there will be other roles, but we will come to those later.

As a writer, you occupy a strange position in this structure. You are roughly at the same place in the structure as the director, but you are not part of the chain of command to actually get the show onstage. Remember that most of the time these people are used to working on productions without a writer in the room. There are some directors who subscribe to the idea that 'The only good writer is a dead writer'. These are people who usually work on plays by dead writers.

You should be aware that there are strict protocols in the theatre and that everyone works through the relevant chain of command. For example, the director would never give notes directly to the orchestra, he would give them to the musical director; and the musical director would not give notes about the dance to the dancers, he would give them to the choreographer.

Following these simple protocols can keep your relationships strong:

- Give all your notes to the director, in private, away from the cast and other creatives.
- Always support the director and creatives to the cast and each other (even if you have differences).
- Punctuality is important and expected in the theatre industry. For actors, lateness is a sackable offence. As a writer, if you are late, don't expect them to wait. They won't.
- During rehearsals, the director will lead the process. He will have final say on all business onstage. A good director will never let that final say seem autocratic.

## Getting the Workshop Produced

Obviously, the most important thing is *how* your workshop is going to be produced. If you have a producer on board already – well done! One of the most common questions I am asked by writers is 'How do I get a producer?', and there is no easy answer. As far as a workshop is concerned, there are alternatives to a commercial producer:

- Many theatres have new-writing initiatives, and some of these welcome new musicals, although these are more common in the USA than the UK. Within these initiatives they often have workshop programmes that may offer your musical a slot.

- Perfect Pitch (www.perfectpitchmusicals.com) is a not-for-profit company dedicated to the development of new British musicals and produce workshops and readings. They are always happy to receive unsolicited scripts and there is a lot more information on their website.

- Some drama schools have programmes where their students workshop new musicals. In the UK, the Royal Scottish Academy of Music and Drama and Central School of Speech and Drama both have these programmes, and schools such as ArtsEd often run them in holidays and use student casts or mixed casts of students and professionals. If you want to see your work on its feet, these can be a great opportunity, but you won't get the same kind of feedback from students as you will from professionals.

- You can produce the workshop yourselves. It sounds daunting, but it is really a case of booking a room and finding a director and a cast. It has the advantage of ensuring that you still have 100 per cent control over your work.

## Finding a Director and a Creative Team

Your producer may have a director he wants you to use, but if this isn't the case, then you will need to find one. If you have someone in mind then approach them. Be aware that the director needs to be someone you trust with your work. He can make or break your workshop. If he is not enthusiastic about it, then thank him for his time and be on your way.

Find the best director you can get. See musicals directed by people in your vicinity. If you are in a big city, see the work of emerging and vibrant directors who are making their mark. Get in touch with artistic directors of theatres in your area and ask their advice, contact anyone you know who may be useful. If someone has a play running at a theatre you can always write to them at that venue, and if they have a website, you can normally contact them through that. If you have an agent, then discuss this whole process with them and listen to their advice.

You will soon discover that theatre people are, on the whole, remarkably generous with their time. Everyone remembers when they were starting out and they will often recommend talented colleagues. I frequently get messages through my website, or through my agent, asking me to direct workshops and, if I'm not able to do the job, I will always try and pass it on to someone I think will do a good job.

As a writer your key relationship will be with the director. Relationships between writers and directors vary enormously. The director needs to have a vision for the piece, he needs to understand it and to be able to realise his vision. Excellent leadership skills are required for the role, and he must be able to bring out the best in people. As a writer, you should have approval over the producer's choice of director and before you grant this, you should have a meeting with the proposed director to see if you can work together. If a musical is like a child, then the director is like a teacher and he is going to influence and mould its childhood.

Directors invariably come with members of a creative team they know and trust. For a workshop, you will probably only need to add a choreographer and a musical director, and most directors will have close colleagues that they have worked with many times. Choosing his creative team is a key task for the director, as he will need to work closely with them through the process. When a director has already worked on a number of projects with another member of his creative team, they develop a kind of shorthand that can really facilitate speedy and quality work, both of which are vital.

Avoid getting involved as a creative yourself. Composers are especially prone to want to be the musical director, but the point of the workshop is to be able to sit back and assess the work. Although I have often directed workshops of my own writing, I have always gained more insight into the piece when someone else has directed, than when I have done it myself.

## Casting the Workshop

Casting the workshop is really the job of your director and the best ones will bring a collection of the best talent available. Casting is often a collaborative act, especially if money is tight. It does no harm to offer suggestions if there are people you think are perfect for the roles.

Try and cast the roles as if you were casting a full-scale production. If a character is heroic, cast someone who can play heroic; if a character is feisty, cast someone who can play feisty; most importantly, if a role is comic, cast someone who can play comedy. Talk to the director about who his choices are and make sure you are confident in them. Many a workshop has been ruined by bad casting choices. Cast the same number of actors as you would have in a production. This will allow you to see and hear the scale of your work.

Some casting may be dependent on whether you are paying your actors and exactly what commitment you are asking them to make. If you can pay them, then you may find it easier to cast them, but always make sure you give them something; after all, they are giving you their time, their experience and their talent.

## The Workshop Process

What actually happens in a workshop varies as much as the directors who run them, and the musical being worked on.

Some workshops are staged readings, in which the piece is read from the script, the songs learned and basic movements (staging and choreography) used. These are useful if the writers and creative team want to see how the storytelling arcs and the characters' journeys are working.

Other workshops focus on smaller sections of the work, and might involve looking in detail at certain sections or characters. Richard and I spent two wonderful days with students from Central School working on just ten minutes of a show, during which time we rewrote it three or four times.

The role of the writers will vary depending on the director and the piece. Sometimes rewrites will be requested, but avoid rushing anything. It is sometimes best to wait until after the workshop and then create something you really feel belongs.

If you want to make comments, give your notes to the director only – and do not do this in front of the cast or you will undermine his authority. Trust that he knows what he is doing, even if you don't like what you see. It is a very unedifying sight to see a director and a writer having a spat in front of the cast, and it will seriously damage everyone's creative relationships.


## The Workshop Presentation

Most workshops aim towards a presentation of some sort. This is important to focus the process, and to give it a sense of conclusion. Who you invite is up to you, but ensure that you have a friendly crowd who want your work to succeed. Let the cast bring guests. Invite friends and colleagues whose opinions you value, and be realistic about inviting producers. If it is a show for children or young people, make sure you have some of them in the audience.

During the presentation, sit as much in the middle of the audience as you can. It is tough to sit there, but listen to the audience around you. I always think a workshop presentation is like living through a car crash in slow motion; every line that doesn't land is like an arrow in your heart. You will learn a lot about your piece by seeing and hearing it with an audience.

When I rewrote the book of Lionel Bart's *Twang!!*, it was conceived as a comedy in the same mould as the British *Carry On* films. These films generated much of their comedy from double entendres, and they have a '50s attitude to sex. As soon as I saw the workshop with the audience, I knew that I hadn't quite hit the tone with it – my entendres were often single not double. When the show had crossed the boundaries of taste it was immediately apparent. I wanted to rush up onstage and cross out jokes I knew were coming before the cast got to them. But all this was fixed in the subsequent rewrites and the workshop had served its purpose.

## After the Workshop Presentation

After the workshop, talk to the audience and talk to the cast. If you can, then hold an after-presentation celebration, preferably in the pub! You'll need it and the cast will thank you for it.

I love actors and spend a lot of time with them, many of them are great friends, but never forget that they are trained to lie. An actor's life is entirely based upon convincingly telling untruths. They will often tell you what they think you want to hear, and they do it so well. Now you need them to be honest, because they have performed your piece in front of an audience. They know a lot about it, possibly more about certain aspects of it than you do. This isn't about what you *want* to hear, it is about what you *need* to hear. These are the people who said your lines and sang your songs and you need to hear the truth about what they think. I applaud Harrison Ford's honest comment to George Lucas during the filming of *Star Wars*: 'George, you can type this shit, but you sure as hell can't say it.'

Take all the notes away and process them. Make a list of what you think worked and what you think needs work. Talk to the creative team and talk to your collaborators.

I always make a point of filming or recording any workshop I am involved with. It is a useful record, but don't look at it for a while yet. Take time to decide what *you* think.

You might decide to do more rewrites; you might even decide to do another workshop. Two or three workshops are not uncommon, but keep a clear focus on the reasons for staging another workshop. What do you need to learn?

And eventually it is time to move to the next stage. Baby is growing up...

# 13
# *In Production*

# In Production

Adolescence is never an easy time and this is the period in your musical's life you are entering. You have done your workshops, your rewrites and you have a show that is ready to have its first full production. Theatre production is a very complex business. If you are interested in learning more about it I recommend James Seabright's *So You Want To Be A Theatre Producer?*

Finding a producer to present your musical is never going to be easy, especially if you are an unknown writer. The smallest musical is bigger than many plays. When I directed *I Do! I Do!*, a musical for two actors in its off-Broadway edition, using only two pianos for the band, I still had a musical director (MD) and a choreographer and the total wage bill was very similar to when, a year later, I directed a play with a cast of six.

Your musical might be a commission from a producer, and so you may already have a production lined up. If not, there are organisations that specialise in producing and developing new musicals. The most useful organisation for musical-theatre writers in the UK is Mercury Musical Developments (www.mercurymusicals.com), a writers' organisation that anyone can join, and which provides an invaluable mailing-list service, keeping writers up to date with opportunities. Mercury Musical Developments does not directly produce new musicals, but may be able to guide you about where to send it. They do have a professional reading service, where musical-theatre professionals will read your work and give you feedback on it, for a fee. From time to time, producers use Mercury Musical Developments to find writers for commissions; I was commissioned through them by the Estate of Lionel Bart to rewrite the book for *Twang!!*

In the USA, there are a number of theatres that specialise in developing new musicals and are happy to receive unsolicited works. I find the National Alliance for Musical Theatre (NAMT) website (www.namt.org) to be very useful. NAMT is an organisation for theatres and companies that produce musical theatre, and develop new works. There is also a membership list online, and from there you can check out the websites of the members and make a judgement on which companies your musical might be suitable for.

A commercial production is not the only way to get your work produced. Talk to the cast and members of the creative team who were involved in your workshop: they may have contacts or ideas for possible homes for your show.

Most writers who have large commercial productions playing started small with college, fringe or off-off-Broadway shows. Tim Rice and Andrew Lloyd Webber's first produced show, *Joseph and the Amazing Technicolor Dreamcoat*, was written for and produced by Colet Court School.

There are many ways to try and get your musical produced, or noticed, and I would advise you to try all of them:

- Send it to all the theatres you can find that produce new musicals. The show may be just their thing. However, theatres that do not produce new musicals are unlikely to present one from an unknown writer.

- Send it to drama schools that have new-writing programmes, especially if it has a large cast and lots of parts. Drama schools are always on the look-out for projects that can involve lots of students in featured roles.

- Get in contact with your local community or amateur theatre. This can be a great way to see your musical onstage.

- Get in contact with small-scale companies that might produce it in a modest way, maybe in a small theatre.

- Enter it for any competitions that it is eligible for. These can often lead to productions.

Try every possible avenue you can think of, and, if your musical gets turned down by a potential producer, ask them who they recommend you send it to. If you have to be tenacious there is a good chance it will be rewarded.

For a commercial producer, the rewards of a hit musical can be life-changing. In 2010, Bloomberg estimated that Cameron Mackintosh was worth around £635 million. Most producers are interested in the next big musical hit, and it just might be the one that has arrived from you.

However, do not underestimate the risk and the commitment of producing a new musical. A producer generally works on a new musical for at least two years before opening night. Added to that, a new musical will generally have to play to capacity business for a year to recoup the cost of putting it on. At the beginning of the twenty-first century, a large-scale West End or Broadway musical comes with a price tag of between £6 million and £10 million. That's a lot of time and money to risk.

A commercial producer is going to think very carefully before committing to a major production. To be honest, most producers are only going to commit to this kind of investment of time and money on tried-and-tested writers. It is one thing to raise £6 million on Andrew Lloyd Webber's name, but a different matter on Mr U.N. Known.

Some writers send their work to commercial producers through an agent. Agents can certainly be helpful, but getting one is a Catch-22 situation: few agents will represent unknown writers, and it is hard for unknown writers to get known without an agent. You are best to work hard to get your first work produced, rather than getting an agent – they can wait until later. Once you have a musical being produced, invite agents that you would like to represent you to come and see it.

## Writer's Contract

Bearing in mind Samuel Johnson's maxim that 'No man but a blockhead ever wrote, except for money', when you secure a production, you will sign a writer's contract with the producer that will outline the financial and legal arrangements for the production. You need to read this contract carefully as they all vary, and you need to be happy with what you are signing. Crucially, you need to ensure that you are providing a licence to *perform the work* and not *selling the copyright* to your work. The contract should also guarantee that you are credited with creating the work in all publicity and that you are remunerated.

Although the chances are that you will not be giving up your day job any time soon, you should have an understanding of standard industry practices. The standard way for writers to be paid is a percentage of the box-office takings, which are known as 'royalties' with an advance paid before the show goes into production. Royalties are always calculated from the total weekly box-office of the performances that week (called the 'gross box-office'), once any sales tax (such as VAT) and any commissions charged by credit-card companies have been deducted (this reduced taking is called the 'net box-office'). Writer's royalty rates are normally between 5% and 10% (usually 6%) *split* between all the writing partners; so 2% for the bookwriter, 2% for the composer and 2% for the lyricist.

| So, if the gross box-office is £100,000 for the performances played that week | Gross box-office | £100,000 |
|---|---|---|
| And sales tax is 20%, and credit-card commission is 5%, the net box-office is | ÷ 1.25 | £80,000 |
| If the royalty rate is 6% | X .06 | £4,800 |
| And if that is split between three writers (book, music and lyrics), that gives each of them: | ÷ 3 | £1,600 |

If one person is performing more than one function, such as a bookwriter-lyricist or a composer-lyricist, then they receive the combined sum for the two functions. For example, for *Sunday in the Park with George*, composer-lyricist Stephen Sondheim would receive the 2% for the composer plus the 2% for the lyricist, and bookwriter James Lapine would receive 2%.

Similarly, if more than one person is responsible for one element, then that 2% would be split between them. For example, for *The Sound of Music*, there are two bookwriters, Howard Lindsay and Russel Crouse, so the 2% would be split between them and the detail of that deal would be worked out between the two of them.

In the very commercial market of the West End and Broadway, royalties are sometimes calculated through something called a 'royalty pool', which, although it is still dependent on gross box-office, is linked to the amount of profit the production is making. Royalty pools can be complex, but writers can sometimes be better off in a 'pool' situation rather than a straight percentage royalty. If you are offered a contract with a royalty pool arrangement, you definitely need to consult an agent or lawyer.

A royalty advance is a payment made by the producer to the writers when the contract is signed, and it ensures that if the entire project falls apart and the show never reaches production, then there has been some payment. It is a sign of good faith from the producer, and you should never trust any producer who won't pay you one. It is an advance – a loan you have to pay back, not a gift – and will be earned back by the producer from your royalties before he pays you any more. If the producer paid you an advance of £1,000, and after the first week of performances the royalties are worth £5,000, he is only going to pay you £4,000 as he will recoup his advance. For the weeks after that he will pay you the full amount. If the advance is never cleared by your royalties (for example, if the show ends up not being produced), then you do not have to return the money to the producer; he has lost it!

If you have been lucky enough to be writing to a commission from a producer, you will have been given some money at the beginning of the project, and this may have been a fee or an advance. If it is a fee it is in addition to the royalties; if it is an advance it will need to be recouped by the producer before he pays you any more.

The contract *may* also guarantee you approvals over the director, some creative staff and lead casting. This means that you get to agree that someone else has made a good decision and approvals are not usually withheld unless you seriously object. Approval over the director is fairly standard, the others only come as you become more established and your negotiating position improves. Not granting approval on a director can break a project; if the producer has decided that he only wants to mount the show with a certain director, and you won't grant approval, then he may decide not to produce at all.

If your work is to be presented on Broadway, your contract should be what is called an 'approved production contract', which is a very comprehensive contract that covers most eventualities, and is the only contract a producer should operate under in a Broadway house. It is often used as a basis for productions in London and off-Broadway. Some aspects are negotiable, and my strong advice is to make sure that a lawyer or agent scrutinises any contract before you sign. Most big cities have good entertainment lawyers who are used to seeing contracts like this, and many agents will review and negotiate a single contract in return for the commission on that contract's earnings, even if they don't take you on as a client (this is called 'side-pocketing'). The advantage of using a lawyer is that you pay a single fee for the work regardless of how much the production earns; the advantage of using an agent is that you only pay a proportion of anything the show earns (10% or 12% is standard). For day-to-day contact and negotiation with the producer on issues such as approvals, it is best for the writing team to elect one of them as a representative and let him do the talking.

Once you have granted the approvals, the writer's contract will usually give the producer the right to stage the work as he wishes, and he will begin to work with the director and creative team towards rehearsals. How much you are involved is entirely up to you and the producer, but the key to producing a new musical is collaboration, and you may be asked to rewrite or edit the work or agree to changes the director proposes. Your contract on a new musical will give you the right to approve any changes to the writing and to undertake any rewrites required.

On a show that is established (i.e. has been produced once or many times) the contract will require that the show be performed as written without changes. Any changes will require your approval, and whether to grant them is entirely up to you – they are frequently denied.

## Casting and Pre-Production

You may have casting approval for the show, but even if you do not have formal approval it is quite common for writers to attend the final casting sessions on a new musical. If your show has a very substantial leading role (such as Tevye or Eva Perón) then you will obviously want to have some input into whoever is playing the role. It is time, though, to begin to take a back seat and enjoy the process of everyone else doing the work. Trust your creative team. When it comes to casting they will have auditioned many performers, especially if the production is in a big city, and they will have selected both the best, and the ones they most want to work with.

Casting a musical is a bit like putting a gang together. The director is the gang leader and he is going to decide who is in his gang. He will be looking to get together a *simpatico* group of people who he knows he can lead in the creative process.

Some writers are fascinated by auditions and some are bored rigid. Different directors have different methods, but with a musical, auditionees will generally be asked to either sing or dance first. Dance calls tend to be done in groups, one sex at a time, and singing calls are generally private. Except for the dance call, auditionees do not see each other audition. Any work on book scenes tends to be left until after the singing and dancing has been assessed. In professional auditions it is common to 'let people go' (i.e. reject them) during the dance call. It may seem harsh to dismiss people during the audition, but actors in London and New York might have five or six auditions a week, sometimes three in one day, whilst trying to juggle some other work, so if you are not going to use them, they would rather leave and get on with their lives.

There are 'recall' or 'callback' auditions where the actors will be asked to return, often having learned songs or scenes from the piece. Eventually there are the final recalls, which are the auditions you are most likely to be invited to. At these there will be two or more auditionees for each role (who will be seen separately) and once the decision has been made, the producer will make the offers of employment to the chosen actors' agents, who will negotiate on behalf of the actors.

## First Day of Rehearsals

A key date in the process of producing a musical is the first day of rehearsal. All the heads of departments (music, lighting, sound, design, etc.) come together with the cast, the director, the producer and administrative staff for the 'meet-and-greet'.

You will almost certainly be invited to this, and you may be even asked to say a few words about the show. You will soon notice that there are many more people involved than there were in the workshop, most of whom will be concerned with ensuring that the show runs smoothly once it is in performance.

*The General Manager* is responsible for the day-to-day running of the show and ensuring that the production happens. He is responsible for contracts and has ultimate responsibility for health and safety. He will employ a range of other administrative and financial staff, depending on the scale of the production.

*The Production Manager* is responsible for making sure all the technical aspects of the show arrive onstage on time and on budget. Along with the general manager, he is also responsible for ensuring that health and safety law and regulations are observed.

*The Company Manager* is the producer's representative in the theatre on a day-to-day basis. Depending on the nature of the production, his responsibilities vary, but he is generally in charge of everyone who is working on the show in the theatre. For example, if a member of the cast or technical crew is unable to work on any day, it is the company manager they will inform.

*The Stage Manager* (SM) is the person responsible for everything onstage during the performance.

*The Deputy Stage Manager* (DSM) is responsible for 'calling the show', the live coordination of the technical side of the performance as it happens, which run from a desk called the 'prompt desk', and 'called' through a system of headsets with microphones (commonly called 'cans').

*The Assistant Stage Managers* (ASMs) help run the
technical side of the performance.

There will also be staff members in each of the departments,
such as lighting and sound, members of the marketing
department, the press representative, associate and assistant
directors, assistant choreographers, assistant designers, etc. It
is quite common on a large-scale commercial production to
have more than a hundred people at the meet-and-greet, even
though the cast are unlikely to number more than thirty. You
probably won't have already met all the cast, and this will be
everyone's first chance to see them assembled together in one
room.

There's normally a series of introductions, and then a chat
about the show. Depending on the director, this may take
anything from five minutes upwards. Trevor Nunn is famous
for speaking for days! Some directors like to hold a readthrough, in which the cast reads the script. This is the norm for
the first day of rehearsals on a play, but directors vary in their
approach on a musical, as the musical content of the show has
not been learned at this point and so only the lyrics can be read.
Personally, I like the cast to learn all the songs in the first few
days, and then come together to read and sing the libretto.

## Rehearsals

After the first day of rehearsals, the company are off into the
process of getting the show on its feet. My advice to you is to go
away and do something else for a few days. Make sure you have
exchanged phone numbers with the company manager and
then go and spend some time with your family, your friends,
your day job – or write a new show.

Directors generally hate having the writer sitting behind
them, and you will probably soon grow bored. Directors have to
work with their cast to find their own way through the material,
and if they need you, they will quickly be in touch. They may
also make minor changes to the work whilst you are not there,
but should always inform you of these when you are next in. If
you have a problem, then negotiate with them; this is all about

collaboration. Don't sit at the back constantly throwing in 'helpful' suggestions. It is not uncommon for writers to get banned from rehearsals of their own shows! One (probably apocryphal) story was that the writer of a play kept interrupting director John Dexter in rehearsals until Dexter turned to him and said, 'If you don't shut up, I will direct your play like you wrote it!'

You will probably drop in to rehearsals once or twice a week to see how they are getting on. If you have any notes, obey the same rules as you did for the workshop; give them only to the director and always support the creative team publicly (including the cast).

Don't expect them to stop or do anything special when you are there, but it may be that the creative team want to ask you questions, or make suggestions to you. It may be that they are asking for rewrites, and you might find yourself in the classic situation of 'writing a new song by tomorrow morning'. This is less common in the age of workshops than it was when shows would open out of town to be fine-tuned, but it still happens.

Your precise involvement in rehearsals will depend on the piece and the creative team, but rehearsals lead towards an event called the 'producer's run'.

The producer's run is normally one of the last run-throughs in the rehearsal room. The cast will perform the show in rehearsal-room conditions, often without final costumes, with rehearsal props and with only basic scenery (which may or may not include pieces of the final set). Many of the people who attended the first day of rehearsals will return to see it, and it may well be the first time you have seen the cast perform the whole show.

You might want to thank the cast afterwards, but remember that any notes go only through the director. Sometimes actors think the writers can give them some special insight into the character, but remember that the director has been through a process with them. If an actor asks you a specific question, you will always be best to say to them, 'I think you should ask your director what he feels about that.' Sometimes the director may agree to you talking directly to the cast, but only do this after checking with the director first.

## Technical Rehearsals

It is a general rule in theatre that work onstage is undertaken in as short a time as possible. This is because for every night that the auditorium is empty, there is no income coming in, and there is expenditure going out. The chances are that the show has been rehearsing in a rehearsal room, and now comes the process of putting it onstage, with the sets, costumes, props and lights. This is a process that largely does not involve the writers, and whilst you may want to see what is going on, do your best not to get in anyone's way. It will often look like little is happening, but you can guarantee that somewhere someone is working hard to sort something out. The cast will be called for the technical rehearsal or 'tech', in which they will work through the show very slowly, taking anything from a day to a few weeks to get through the show once. This can be a frustrating/nervous/exhilarating/stressful/exhausting time for everyone and you are best advised to keep a low profile. Don't give the director (or anyone else) 'helpful' advice about how things might be done; you'll get pretty short shrift. During this time, the composer may be asked for music to cover the scene changes, which can only be timed when the set is in place and moving correctly. This may need to be done quickly, and will have to go straight to the orchestrator – although it is not uncommon for dress rehearsals to happen with some scene-change music being played on piano. Writers have different approaches to the tech. Some like to sit and watch; apparently Tim Rice prefers the cricket.

## Band Calls and the Sitzprobe

You will want to go to the orchestral rehearsals. These will probably be the first time you have heard the orchestrations played live and are always a special experience. Even more exciting is the sitzprobe, when the cast assemble with the orchestra for the first time and sing through the show. 'Sitzprobe' is German for 'sitting rehearsal', and involves the cast and orchestra rehearsing the songs without any other aspects of the production. It can take place onstage, or in another room in the theatre, and is generally one of everyone's favourite times in the process, because of the exhilaration of hearing the orchestration for the first time.

## Dress Rehearsals and Previews

When the tech is finished, it is time for the first dress rehearsal. This will be a full run-through in performance conditions, with full orchestra. You may get one, two or three of these before an audience is invited in and writers tend to attend all of them. It is your last chance to take a look at the production without an audience and give the director any notes you may have.

Previews are public performances that take place before the official opening night and are sold at reduced rates. The preview period might be anything from two or three performances to up to a month. Etched in the annals of Broadway is *Spider-Man: Turn Off the Dark*, which began previews on 28 November 2010, suspended all performances from 19 April 2011 to 12 May 2011, and finally held its press night on 14 June 2011, more than six months after it started previewing.

Previews will give you and the whole creative team the chance to assess how audiences respond. Be careful of rushing to judgement. Audiences change nightly, and a moment that plays to a fantastic response one night can be greeted with stony silence the next. Sometimes the audiences that are quietest during the performance can give the greatest ovation. Director Tommy Tune makes it a rule to never change anything until he has seen it with three audiences; the first two can be flukes.

If your musical is playing in a student, community or amateur production, you will probably not have the luxury of previews. You will go straight from dress rehearsal to opening night, and in many ways the notion of previews is academic. For most actors and creatives, once there is an audience, there is a performance and the time for rehearsal is over.

Sometimes musicals go through radical overhauls in previews, but this is generally the sign of a producer feeling the show is in trouble. More usually, it is a case of fine-tuning, for the cast to find how to land a certain line, how to ensure a laugh from the audience or phrase a song to get maximum effect.

Sometimes songs or scenes get altered or cut during previews, and you may be asked by the producer or director to make alterations, but at this stage you are likely to be asked to see the show and attend a meeting of the creatives.

In New York, and increasingly in London, it is common for critics to attend some of the final previews, and then to embargo their reviews until after opening night. This is for a number of reasons, primarily to stop the critics seeing the show at an opening night stuffed with friends and supporters, and also because, in an age of twenty-four-hour news and the internet, there is demand for a review the minute the press-night curtain has fallen. In the case of *Spider-Man* on Broadway, the critics got so irritated by the fact that they were being kept away whilst ordinary punters were being charged up to $140 a seat, that they broke the embargo and published their reviews.

The internet has also changed the nature of previews, as there are now many chat boards and forums where audiences discuss musicals before opening night, along with an increasing number of self-appointed online critics. Andrew Lloyd Webber's *Love Never Dies* was the first major musical to be particularly hit by bad 'word-of-internet' well before any of the press had seen the show, and before the show was finalised.

## Opening Night

After previews, it is time for your opening night. You will probably want to give cards, and possibly gifts, to the cast, creatives and crew, and it certainly never does any harm to say 'Thank you'.

You will probably be able to invite some guests to share the evening with you and hopefully it will be a huge success.

Dress up and step out.

Enjoy it, you've earned it.

When the performance is over, head to the first-night party.

Thank everyone you need to.

And celebrate!

# 14

# *The Lifetime After the Night Before*

# The Lifetime
# After the Night Before

That's it.

You have written your musical and it has been produced.

End of story.

Or is it?

Maybe it is only the beginning of a whole new adventure.

When you wake up the morning after the opening night, you will probably feel like you need a holiday, or at least a strong coffee. You have probably spent two years getting to today, and now you can think that your child has graduated and is going to make its own way in the world.


## Reviews

From any time after the opening-night curtain has fallen, you may be reviewed. This might be in the *New York Times*, the London *Times* or the *Tiny-Little-Village Times*. Whether the reviews are good or bad, remember that they are only one person's opinion and worth no more or less than that for being in print. What is true is that you remember the bad ones much more than the good. John Gielgud, when told of a series of outstanding rave reviews in all the national newspapers, is said to have replied, 'Yes, but the *Jewish Chronicle* hated me.'

The more reviews you get, the less they seem to mean or matter. I was always worried by them, until a play I directed got panned in the *New York Times*, in a review I found incredibly unfair to the playwright, and after that anything else seemed insignificant. Keep the good ones and use the bad ones to start a fire. You'll feel better for it.


## The Run

Your first run of performances might be a few nights or it might be years.

Runs of school, amateur and community productions tend to be less than ten performances. A small professional production is likely to be between three weeks and two months. In London, the press are reluctant to review any run of less than three weeks, unless there is a very good reason.

A West End production might open with a limited season, normally of thirteen weeks, and then might get extended if it is successful, but actors' contracts tend to run a year, and the producer can post the closing notice, stating when the run will end, three weeks before the final performance.

If it is an open-ended commercial run and your show is a hit, it could run a long time and the producer may end up having to recast it with a new group of actors. Writers are not usually involved in recasting in these situations, unless there are particular circumstances (for example if it were a one- or two-man show, or if the lead role is particularly difficult to cast).

If you have a hit in London or New York you may also have interest from producers in other countries who want to present your work. These are often mounted by your original producer (known as the 'originating producer') in collaboration with a local producer who is skilled at mounting musicals in that territory.

Just because a musical is a hit in the West End or on Broadway does not mean it will replicate that success on the other side of the Atlantic. *City of Angels*, *The Drowsy Chaperone* and *Spring Awakening* failed in their London transfers from Broadway, whilst *Salad Days*, *Buddy* and *Chess* bombed in New York despite long runs in London.

If a major overseas production is mounted and your originating producer is involved, then the chances are it will be a recreation of the original production, and you might be asked to approve the major casting. In these situations, you will continue to negotiate with the originating producer.

Sometimes translation agencies get in touch and want to translate your work and to facilitate productions in their own territories. The productions may be remounts of the original production or they may be local productions that have their own producers and creative teams. Your originating producer may be involved in these negotiations, and may take a share of any income, depending on your agreement with him.

Included in your contract with the originating producer will probably be a clause about residual rights. These are a proportion of the writer's royalties that get paid to the originating producer on future productions and other exploitation of the work. If a producer loses money on the original production, he can make some money back if the work is presented again, overseas, or licensed to amateur companies. It is recognition of the originating producer's faith in the work. An originating producer's involvement in these residual rights is usually limited to a fixed term, normally between five and ten years, which runs from the final performance he produced.

Sometimes, if a production is not doing as well as hoped, the writers may be asked to take a cut in royalties or a 'royalty waiver'. You may wonder why anyone would agree to the show playing without the writers getting paid, but there can be good reasons. For instance, if a musical has a good run and is attractive to the community (or 'stock') and amateur market for production, then there can be considerable money to be made, but the amateur companies tend not to want to do shows that are regarded as flops. Keeping the original production running might be a sensible option after all. Some musicals can establish very successful and lucrative national tours, like the American stage version of *9 to 5*, and again, the longer the run in London or New York, the better the prospects for the tour. Also, if you were nearing awards season and the producer thought there was a good chance of a prize for the show, this can significantly boost the future box-office. When these kinds of decisions are being made by producers, you need to consult with your collaborators and you need the advice of a good agent or lawyer.

Eventually you will come to the final performance. *Cats* was in London twenty-one years after its opening night and that record has since been superseded by *Les Misérables* and *The Phantom of the Opera*, but one day, maybe in the distant future, even *Les Mis* and *Phantom* will play their last performances in the West End. Final performances are always emotional events for writers, but never forget that every theatre performance is a unique meeting of cast and audience. Those exact people will never gather again to witness that single performance, the moments are unique and become history as soon as they happen. Every night is an opening night and a closing night.

## Original Cast Album

However long the initial run, whilst you have the original cast together, I advise you to try and make a cast recording of some kind if you possibly can. There are companies that specialise in cast recordings such as JAY Records, but they generally won't touch anything smaller than an off-Broadway run – and when they do they will take a very long hard look at the costs. As with all of the music industry, there is increasingly less money to be made.

If you have a commercial production, your originating producer will usually undertake the negotiations with the recording company, in a single deal, which will include the cast, writers, and rights to other items like the production's artwork.

If you cannot get a commercial recording, try to either get a studio and a producer and record it privately or record it live in performance. Your musical director should be able to find a producer for you if you don't know anyone, and your cast will generally be happy to record it so long as it is not for commercial use. If you can get the cast to agree to it, you might even be able to sell it through iTunes.

The reason for the recording is not vanity, but it is vital to have a good-quality demo for the future life of the project, and you are not likely to get a better quality recording than by using people who have rehearsed and performed the parts. During the production process you are very likely to have made changes and so your old demo will now be out of date, and this is the perfect opportunity to incorporate the new material.

## Making Sure You Get What is Owed to You

If you get a commercial cast recording, or if your songs are going to be recorded by a commercial company, you will need to join either the Mechanical-Copyright Protection Society (known as MCPS, UK residents) or the American Mechanical Rights Agency (known as AMRA, US residents). Other territories have their own societies, which you can find online. These organisations collect the royalties due on CDs and other recorded media and distribute it to the songwriters. There are standard rates for this, and most of them have reciprocal arrangements with their counterparts in other countries. Go online to find all the information about the one for where you live.

If the songs you have written for the musical are going to have a life in concerts, on the radio or other kinds of broadcasts, you will need to join the relevant Performing Rights Organisation (PRO) for your country. PROs deal with concert performances, radio and they also issue 'blanket' licences to organisations that play music in public settings, such as restaurants and bars. They then distribute this money to songwriters according to the popularity of each song. Songwriters usually join by paying a one-off fee and registering the song titles and writers online. The PRO makes its money by taking a small commission on all payments. In the UK, the PRO is the Performing Rights Society (PRS), and in the USA there are ASCAP, BMI and SESAC, of which songwriters only join one. Most countries signed to the Berne Copyright Convention have a PRO and they generally have reciprocal arrangements with PROs in other countries.

## Exploiting Your Musical

As you will have discovered by now, writing a musical is a lot of work.

Your first production may spur interest from other theatres or companies that want to perform the piece and you must be active in promoting it. Search around for companies that are like the one that produced it first. If that was an amateur group, then search online for other amateur companies that have performed the same kind of repertoire. If it was at a regional theatre, ask them about other regional theatres that might be interested. No arts organisation is an island; if one has already produced your show then there will be another company who might be interested.

If you have a musical that has been produced professionally, it might be worth contacting agents to see if any of them might be interested in representing it. Whilst you have that first production playing, invite them to see it. If they take it on, they will use their contacts and networks to try to secure further productions for you, in return for a percentage of the income you make.

You and your co-writers own a number of rights in the work, most notably the 'grand rights' and the 'small rights'. The grand rights are the rights for the musical as a whole and the small rights are the rights to the songs, scenes, dance music, etc. Each element of the show – book, music, lyrics – are generally treated equally in the grand rights, so any earnings are split equally between the three elements. The small rights generally reside with the creators of the specific element, so the composer and lyricist will own the songs 50 per cent each. My advice is to come to an understanding with your co-writers early on about any variations you might want to make to any of these. It is your right to define the terms between you, but sometimes defining the terms of your deal can make writing the musical look like a picnic!

Under the Berne Convention, the minimum copyright term is until fifty years after the death of the author. This means that there may be income from your work until fifty years after your death, and the term is seventy years after death in Europe and other countries who have voluntarily extended it. If you have works that are generating income for you, you should consider revising your will to take this into account. You will need a lawyer's advice for this.

One way of exploiting the musical that takes very little work on your part is to license it to a publisher like Samuel French, Josef Weinberger or Music Theatre International. You should invite them to see your show in its first production, and then, if they agree to include it in their catalogue, you will come to an agreement with them to license the grand rights to parties that want to perform it. Sometimes these agreements are only for stock (repertory) and amateur rights, and the rights for what are known as first-class productions (national tour, Broadway, West End) are reserved for your agent or lawyer to negotiate when there is a proposed production. With a commercial first run, the negotiations with the publishers will happen whilst the show is running but the piece will not be released for performances by other companies until the first production has ended. Rarely, with certain mega-hits, the rights have been released to amateurs before the end of the first run, but normally with very strict stipulations, such as the *Les Misérables Schools Edition*, which is only available to educational establishments and is an edited version of the show. Normally, the originating producer will also be involved in these negotiations (depending on his residual rights) and will take a share of the profit from this activity.

These publishers put details of your musical into their catalogues and handle the marketing to potential amateur or regional producers. When one is interested, they send them perusal materials, normally a libretto and demo recording (the original cast album if there is one). If the company wants to go ahead, the publisher takes a deposit and sends copies of the libretto, the vocal score and the orchestral parts, either for sale or on loan. The company agrees to pay a percentage of box-office from their performances, usually more like 13 per cent, rather than the professional 6–8 per cent, and they produce their version of the show, within the terms of the agreement they have with the publisher. These contracts always state that the company must perform the work *as written* and that any changes *must* have prior agreement. Any requested changes should be referred to you via the publisher, and it is very common to refuse them.

Once their production has ended, they send details of the box-office takings to the publisher, who calculates the royalty, collects the money and then sends you your share, having taken some commission off the top.

For the right titles, this can be a lucrative market, but bear this in mind: the reason to license your work to a publisher in this way is to minimise work and maximise income. What you lose is control. These productions will happen, and they will happen in the fashion that the production company sees fit. So long as they do not edit or add to your work, you will be pretty much powerless.

We licensed *The Railway Children* to Samuel French in 2007, and it began having performances about a year later. We had about forty productions in the first three years. Of those we have seen, they have varied enormously in ambition and quality. Bearing in mind the original production was in a professional regional theatre with a cast of West End actors, the first licensed production we saw had a cast of more than seventy, and with no one over fourteen years old onstage. It had its own charm, but was not like anything we had ever dreamed.

Licensing your work can make it available to a very large audience, and the non-professional companies watch each other's work closely, so your show can pick up momentum for many productions. At its best, it can give you moments like no other.

In early 2010, I was about to travel from my home in London to New Zealand to work on a new musical with some Kiwi writers, when I got an email from a community theatre company outside of Auckland telling me that they had just secured the rights from Samuel French's New Zealand agent to present the first production of *The Railway Children* in the Southern hemisphere. Less than a fortnight later I was standing in a theatre in Orewa, 11,000 miles from home, listening to a wonderful company singing:

A once in a lifetime day,
A day to remember forever,
Your once in a lifetime day...

And it truly was.

# Finally...

Musicals are like children. Some of them are tricky to parent, some of them are easy to love; sometimes they are incredibly painful and sometimes they bring you more joy and excitement than you had ever hoped.

That's the romantic view, but I think anyone who writes a musical has to be a bit of a romantic.

Someone once told me, 'You never finish a musical, you just stop working on it.' Sometimes, a few days after opening night, or after a final performance, I get a little depressed at the thought that I have stopped working on that musical, for now. Only days earlier it was demanding every ounce of my attention.

I guess it is the same as when children leave home: you know you are going to see them again, but you are no longer sure when, and they will no longer be in your everyday life, needing your help, making a mess. At some time in the future they may even need your full attention again, but not today.

For now, everything seems just a little too quiet, too still.

And in that silence, an idea starts to form...

# *Acknowledgements*

It's a very ancient saying,
But true and honest thought,
That if you become a teacher
By your pupils you'll be taught...

Oscar Hammerstein, 'Getting to Know You'
from *The King and I*

Firstly, I have to thank all my students at Goldsmiths College, University of London, the only university course in the UK in musical-theatre writing, and also Professor Robert Gordon at Goldsmiths for first asking me to teach the course, and thereby providing the kernel for this book.

Thanks to Simon Trewin, Neil Laidlaw, George Stiles, Daron Oram, Sue Westcott, Nellie F.M., Christine Donald, John Cohen and Anthea Woolford for their invaluable advice on different aspects of the process.

To Ralf Heine and David Pope for providing inspirational accommodation within which to finish the book. And to Paul Wendt, Ed Laxton and Rob Glenny for their unstinting support.

To all the actors who have worked with me on workshops and productions of new works, both my own and those by others I have been lucky enough to direct. Most notable of these are the original casts of *The Railway Children*, *The Wind in the Willows*, *Liberace Live from Heaven*, *BlueBirds*, *Terminal Four Play*, *Let Him Have Justice*. The workshop casts of *Comrade Rockstar* at ArtsEd, the Royal Scottish Academy of Music and Drama and Central School of Speech and Drama, and the workshop cast of *Twang!!* at ArtsEd deserve special thanks.

Thanks to my editor, Matt Applewhite at Nick Hern Books, for the rigour of his notes, for guiding me so expertly through the process of writing this book and for making it all fun.

I must also thank Chris Hocking, who has choreographed all the original productions of my work, always there with the perfect comments and the perfect steps.

Many thanks to Richard John for making the process of writing musicals as stimulating, friendly and fun as it can be, whilst always challenging me to produce my best work, and always responding positively when I make the same demands of him.

And mostly to Stephen Barlow, for everything he gives me.

# Bibliography

There are many books I have found useful in developing the craft of writing a musical. I have found these ones to be the most helpful:

Aristotle, *Poetics*, trans. Kenneth McLeish, Nick Hern Books, 1999

Alan Ayckbourn, *The Crafty Art of Playwriting*, Faber and Faber, 2009

Marina Caldarone and Maggie Lloyd-Williams, *Actions: The Actors' Thesaurus*, Nick Hern Books, 2004

Joseph Campbell, *The Hero with a Thousand Faces*, Fontana Press, 1993

Ted Chapin, *Everything Was Possible*, Knopf, 2003

Stephen Citron, *Song Writing*, Hodder & Stoughton, 1985

David Edgar, *How Plays Work*, Nick Hern Books, 2009

Lehmen Engel and Howard Kissel, *Words with Music*, Applause, 2006

Oscar Hammerstein, *Lyrics*, Hal Leonard Books, 1985

Jeffrey Hatcher, *The Art and Craft of Playwriting*, Story Press, 1996

Ken Mandelbaum, *Not Since Carrie*, St Martin's Press, 1991

Robert McKee, *Story*, Methuen, 1999

James Seabright, *So You Want To Be A Theatre Producer?*, Nick Hern Books, 2010

Stephen Sondheim, *Finishing the Hat*, Virgin Books, 2010

Stephen Sondheim, *Look, I Made a Hat*, Virgin Books, 2011

Mark Steyn, *Broadway Babies Say Goodnight*, Faber and Faber, 1997

Christopher Vogler, *The Writer's Journey*, Boxtree, 1996

John Vorhaus, *The Comic Toolbox*, Silman-James, 1994

# List of Topics

# List of Exercises

# *Index*

Names are included as references to real individuals, not characters based upon those individuals.